Contents

Introduction   ix

Blackstone's Police Q&As—Special Features   xi

Acknowledgements   xiii

1   The Policing Family   **1**

Study preparation   1
Questions   2
Answers   9

2   Complaints and Misconduct   **16**

Study preparation   16
Questions   16
Answers   22

3   Unsatisfactory Performance and Attendance   **27**

Study preparation   27
Questions   27
Answers   34

4   Human Rights   **40**

Study preparation   40
Questions   41
Answers   49

**5   Powers of Arrest (including Code G Codes of Practice)
     and Other Policing Powers**   **57**

Study preparation   57
Questions   57
Answers   66

Contents

6   Stop and Search   **74**

Study preparation   74
Questions   74
Answers   81

7   Entry, Search and Seizure   **87**

Study preparation   87
Questions   87
Answers   94

8   Harassment, Stalking, Hostility and Anti-social Behaviour   **100**

Study preparation   100
Questions   101
Answers   113

9   Offences Involving Communications   **126**

Study preparation   126
Questions   126
Answers   131

10 Terrorism and Associated Offences   **137**

Study preparation   137
Questions   137
Answers   144

11 Public Disorder   **152**

Study preparation   152
Questions   152
Answers   164

12 Sporting Events   **177**

Study preparation   177
Questions   177
Answers   183

13 Weapons   **189**

Study preparation   189
Questions   190
Answers   199

Blackstone's
Police Q&A

General Police Duties 2014

Twelfth edition

Huw Smart and John Watson

OXFORD
UNIVERSITY PRESS

OXFORD

UNIVERSITY PRESS

Great Clarendon Street, Oxford, OX2 6DP,
United Kingdom

Oxford University Press is a department of the University of Oxford.
It furthers the University's objective of excellence in research, scholarship,
and education by publishing worldwide. Oxford is a registered trade mark of
Oxford University Press in the UK and in certain other countries

British Library Cataloguing in Publication Data

Data available

ISBN 978–0–19–968209–6

Printed and bound in Great Britain by
CPI Group (UK) Ltd, Croydon, CR0 4YY

14	**Civil Disputes**	**210**
	Study preparation	210
	Questions	210
	Answers	216

15	**Offences Relating to Land and Premises**	**222**
	Study preparation	222
	Questions	222
	Answers	230

16	**Licensing and Offences Relating to Alcohol**	**238**
	Study preparation	238
	Questions	239
	Answers	255

17	**Offences and Powers Relating to Information**	**272**
	Study preparation	272
	Questions	272
	Answers	281

18	**Equality**	**290**
	Study preparation	290
	Questions	290
	Answers	298

Question Checklist		307

Introduction

Before you get into the detail of this book, there are two myths about multiple-choice questions (MCQs) that we need to get out of the way right at the start:

1. that they are easy to answer;
2. that they are easy to write.

Take one look at a professionally designed and properly developed exam paper such as those used by the Police Promotion Examinations Board or the National Board of Medical Examiners in the US and the first myth collapses straight away. Contrary to what some people believe, MCQs are not an easy solution for examiners and not a 'multiple-guess' soft option for examinees.

That is not to say that *all* MCQs are taxing, or even testing—in the psychometric sense. If MCQs are to have any real value at all, they need to be carefully designed and follow some agreed basic rules.

And this leads us to myth number 2.

It is widely assumed by many people and educational organisations that anyone with the knowledge of a subject can write MCQs. You need only look at how few MCQ writing courses are offered by training providers in the UK to see just how far this myth is believed. Similarly, you need only to have a go at a few badly designed MCQs to realise that it is a myth nonetheless. Writing bad MCQs is easy; writing good ones is no easier than answering them!

As with many things, the design of MCQs benefits considerably from time, training and experience. Many MCQ writers fall easily and often unwittingly into the trap of making their questions too hard, too easy or too obscure, or completely different from the type of question that you will eventually encounter in your own particular exam. Others seem to use the MCQ as a way to catch people out or to show how smart they, the authors, are (or think they are).

There are several purposes for which MCQs are very useful. The first is in producing a reliable, valid and fair test of knowledge and understanding across a wide range of subject matter. Another is an aid to study, preparation and revision for such examinations and tests. The differences in objective mean that there are slight differences in the rules that the MCQ writers follow. Whereas the design of fully validated MCQs to be used in high stakes examinations, which will effectively determine who passes and who fails, has very strict guidelines as to construction, content and style, less stringent rules apply to MCQs that are being used for teaching and revision. For that reason, there may be types of MCQ that are appropriate in the latter setting which would not be used in the former. However, in developing the MCQs for this book, the authors have tried to follow the fundamental rules of MCQ design but they would not claim to have replicated the level of psychometric rigour that is—and has to be—adopted by the type of examining bodies referred to previously.

These MCQs are designed to reinforce your knowledge and understanding, to highlight any gaps or weaknesses in that knowledge and understanding, and to help focus your revision of the relevant topics.

I hope that we have achieved that aim.

Good luck!

Blackstone's Police Q&As—Special Features

References to Blackstone's Police Manuals

Every answer is followed by a paragraph reference to Blackstone's Police Manuals. This means that once you have attempted a question and looked at an answer, the Manual can immediately be referred to for help and clarification.

Unique numbers for each question

Each question and answer has the same unique number. This should ensure that there is no confusion as to which question is linked to which answer. For example, Question 2.1 is linked to Answer 2.1.

Checklists

The checklists are designed to help you keep track of your progress when answering the multiple-choice questions. If you fill in the checklist after attempting a question, you will be able to check how many you got right on the first attempt and will know immediately which questions need to be revisited a second time. Please visit www.blackstonespolicemanuals.com and click through to the Blackstone's Police Q&As 2014 page. You will then find electronic versions of the checklists to download and print out. Email any queries or comments on the book to: police.uk@oup.com.

Acknowledgements

This book has been written as an accompaniment to Blackstone's Police Manuals, and will test the knowledge you have accrued through reading that series. It is of the essence that full study of the relevant chapters in each Police Manual is completed prior to attempting the Questions and Answers. As qualified police trainers we recognise that students tend to answer questions incorrectly either because they don't read the question properly, or because one of the 'distracters' has done its work. The distracter is one of the three incorrect answers in a multiple-choice question (MCQ), and is designed to distract you from the correct answer and in this way discriminate between candidates: the better-prepared candidate not being 'distracted'.

So particular attention should be paid to the *Answers* sections, and students should ask themselves 'Why did I get that question wrong?' and, just as importantly, 'Why did I get that question right?' Combining the information gained in the *Answers* section together with rereading the chapter in the Police Manuals should lead to greater understanding of the subject matter.

The authors wish to thank all the staff at Oxford University Press who have helped put this publication together. We would particularly like to dedicate these books to Alistair MacQueen who sadly passed away in 2008. It was his vision and support that got this project off the ground. Without his help neither Huw nor John would have been able to make these Q&As the success they are. We would also like to show appreciation to Fraser Sampson, consultant editor of Blackstone's Police Manuals, whose influence on these Q&As is appreciated.

Huw would like to thank Caroline for her constant love, support and understanding over the past year—and her ability to withstand the pressures of being the partner to a workaholic! Special thanks to Lawrence and Maddie—two perfect young adults. Last but not least, love and special affection to Haf and Nia, two beautiful young girls.

John would like to thank Sue, David, Catherine and Andrew for their continued support, and understanding that 'deadline' means 'deadline'.

1 | **The Policing Family**

STUDY PREPARATION

This chapter covers terms and conditions for regular police officers, under the Police Regulations 2003, as well as the similar conditions for the 'extended policing family' under the Police Reform Act 2002. This includes the introduction of powers to groups of people who are either directly employed by the police, or who work in close liaison with the police.

Under Pt 4 of the Act, the following people may be 'designated' by the relevant chief officer:

• police community support officers (PCSOs);
• investigating officers;
• detention officers;
• escort officers.

A further extension of the policing family comes in the form of accredited employees. Chief officers, in consultation with local authorities, may establish a Community Safety Accreditation Scheme (CSAS).

Further matters covered are the jurisdiction of non-police services and the powers given to special constables.

Attention is also given to 'whistle blowers' under the Public Interest Disclosure Act 1998.

QUESTIONS

Question 1.1

MANGLEY has recently been promoted to the rank of chief inspector. MANGLEY has a child under the age of 5 and is considering asking for flexible hours, to work part-time, due to family commitments.

Would the Police Regulations 2003 allow MANGLEY to work part-time as a chief inspector?

A Yes, any officer below the rank of superintendent may work part-time.

B No, only officers below the rank of inspector may work part-time.

C Yes, officers of any rank may work part-time.

D No, only officers of the rank of inspector or below may work part-time.

Question 1.2

Sergeant GUNNEY has been a part-time worker for two years. Due to a change in personal circumstances, Sergeant GUNNEY has submitted a report asking to return to full-time working within two weeks as a matter of urgency.

Would the Police Regulations 2003 allow Sergeant GUNNEY to return to full-time working within this time period?

A Yes, if it is considered reasonably practicable to do so.

B No, Sergeant GUNNEY should return to full-time working within two months.

C No, Sergeant GUNNEY should return to full-time working within four months.

D Yes, an officer can return to full-time duties at any time provided a request is made in writing.

Question 1.3

Special Constable PATTERSON is an officer with Northshire Constabulary. Special Constable PATTERSON's home force has a Football League Club in its own area and Special Constable PATTERSON works regularly with the police spotters team, identifying football hooligans. Special Constable PATTERSON has developed an expertise in this area and has been asked to attend away matches to assist regular police officers with preventing crowd trouble.

Would Special Constable PATTERSON enjoy the powers and privileges of a special constable, when working in other police areas?

A Yes, Special Constable PATTERSON would enjoy the powers and privileges of a special constable when working in any police area.

B No, Special Constable PATTERSON would only enjoy the powers and privileges of a special constable when working in an adjoining area, on mutual aid.

C Yes, but Special Constable PATTERSON would only enjoy the powers and privileges of a special constable when working in an adjoining area.

D No, Special Constable PATTERSON would only enjoy the powers and privileges of a special constable when working on mutual aid, but this may be in any police area.

Question 1.4

KYLE works for Eastshire Constabulary as a police community support officer (PCSO) and KNIGHT works as a detention officer in a custody office in the same force, but is contracted to work for the force by a private security company. Under Pt 4 of the Police Reform Act 2002, chief officers of police are given the authority to confer policing powers on non-police officers (such as KYLE and KNIGHT).

What flexibility, if any, does the chief officer of police of Eastshire Constabulary have when it comes to conferring policing powers on the individuals mentioned in the scenario?

A The chief officer is only required to confer such powers on KYLE, as a PCSO.

B The decision whether or not to confer any powers on either KYLE or KNIGHT rests with the chief officer, who has the flexibility to decide whether to grant such powers or not.

C The chief officer is only required to confer such powers on KNIGHT, as a contracted detention officer.

D The chief officer must confer some powers on both KYLE and KNIGHT, but has flexibility to choose which powers are appropriate.

Question 1.5

McCARTNEY and COLE have started work for Eastshire Constabulary on the same day. McCARTNEY is to work as a police community support officer (PCSO) and COLE is to work as an investigating officer.

Which of the following statements is correct, in relation to whether either McCARTNEY or COLE should be employed by Eastshire Constabulary, in order to perform their roles?

A Both McCARTNEY and COLE must be employed by Eastshire Constabulary before they can perform their roles.

B As an investigating officer, only COLE must be employed by Eastshire Constabulary.

C As a PCSO, only McCARTNEY must be employed by Eastshire Constabulary.

D Neither person needs to be employed by Eastshire Constabulary in order to perform their roles.

Question 1.6

JANEWAY is a self-employed security guard who works in an out-of-town shopping centre. A number of shops have formed a Business Crime Reduction Partnership and JANEWAY's wages are paid by the Partnership. The estate has been suffering anti-social behaviour by local youths and is considering whether JANEWAY could be 'accredited' with powers under a statutory Community Safety Accreditation Scheme to deal with the anti-social behaviour.

Would the Partnership be entitled to accredit JANEWAY in this way?

A Yes, provided JANEWAY enters into a contract with the Police and Crime Commissioner and the relevant local authority.

B No, a self-employed person cannot be accredited under this scheme.

C Yes, provided JANEWAY enters into a contract with the Police and Crime Commissioner.

D Yes, provided JANEWAY enters into a contract with the Police and Crime Commissioner and the Business Crime Reduction Partnership.

Question 1.7

FLETCHER is employed by Eastshire Constabulary as an investigating officer and has been 'designated' by the chief constable to perform this role. A complaint has been made that FLETCHER committed a serious assault on a suspect during an interview and the matter is being investigated by the Professional Standards Department. The officer in charge of the case is considering making a referral to the Independent Police Complaints Commission (IPCC).

Could the IPCC have jurisdiction over a complaint made against a designated employee, such as FLETCHER?

A No, because FLETCHER is not a police officer and is not covered by the Police (Conduct) Regulations 2012.

B Yes, but only if a joint allegation is made against a police officer and a designated employee.

C   Yes, but only because a criminal allegation has been made against FLETCHER.
D   Yes, regardless of whether the allegation is of a criminal nature, or whether a police officer was involved.

Question 1.8

Whilst on patrol in a local park, PCSO HILLIER spoke to BARTON, who was responsible for a dog which had fouled in a children's play area. PCSO HILLIER was designated to issue a fixed penalty notice for this offence. BARTON demanded to know what authority PCSO HILLIER had to issue such a notice.

Is PCSO HILLIER obliged to produce any documentary evidence of his authority, in these circumstances?

A   No, provided PCSO HILLIER was in uniform.
B   Yes, PCSO HILLIER must produce evidence of his designation as a PCSO.
C   Yes, PCSO HILLIER must produce details of all the standard and non-standard powers he has as a PCSO.
D   Yes, PCSO HILLIER must produce evidence of his designation as a PCSO and any non-standard powers he has.

Question 1.9

BECK is employed as a detention officer in a custody office on the same shift as Sergeant DELGADO. BECK is one of a number of people from a private security company contracted by the force to perform custody detention duties. Sergeant DELGADO has had to warn BECK several times of a failure to conduct visits and update custody records in a timely manner.

Which of the following statements is correct, in relation to whether Sergeant DELGADO can deal with BECK, either under the Police (Performance) Regulations 2012, or the Police (Conduct) Regulations 2012?

A   BECK may only be dealt with under the Performance Regulations in these circumstances.
B   BECK may only be dealt with under the Conduct Regulations in these circumstances.
C   Neither of the Regulations applies in these circumstances, but BECK may be dealt with under police staff Regulations relating to poor performance.
D   BECK is not an employee and may not be dealt with under any police officer or police staff Regulations in these circumstances.

Question 1.10

VAUGHAN has been appointed as an accredited employee who works on a large housing estate which has suffered significant anti-social behaviour problems. A Community Safety Accreditation Scheme (CSAS) has been agreed between the police, the local authority and VAUGHAN's employers, a housing association company. A complaint has been made about VAUGHAN's behaviour, alleging that she is aggressive towards residents.

Which organisation has responsibility for dealing with a complaint made about VAUGHAN's behaviour?

A Any of the three organisations could deal with the complaint.

B The complaint should be dealt with by the police.

C The complaint should be dealt with by VAUGHAN's employer.

D The complaint could be dealt with by the police or VAUGHAN's employer.

Question 1.11

WALTERS is an accredited employee who works closely with the Neighbourhood Policing Team in an out-of-town shopping centre. WALTERS is employed by one of the larger stores in the centre, as part of a CSAS agreed between the police, the local authority and WALTERS's employers. Sergeant POWELL has received a complaint from a store manager that WALTERS has regularly been seen socialising with people suspected of committing a number of shoplifting offences in the centre. Sergeant POWELL has submitted a report asking for WALTERS's accreditation to be withdrawn.

What process must take place before WALTERS's accreditation may be withdrawn in these circumstances?

A The chief officer of police may withdraw the accreditation, simply by issuing a written notice to WALTERS.

B A meeting must be held between the police and WALTERS's employers and a joint decision must be reached to withdraw the accreditation.

C A meeting must be held between the police and WALTERS's employers, but the final decision to withdraw the accreditation rests with the police.

D A meeting must be held between the police, WALTERS's employers and the local authority, but the final decision to withdraw the accreditation rests with the police.

Question 1.12

HANSEN is an accredited employee in her local policing area. ADEDEYO is considering making a civil claim as a result of an incident involving HANSEN. ADEDEYO claims that HANSEN unlawfully detained him while acting in her capacity as an accredited employee.

If ADEDEYO were to make a civil claim for unlawful detention, against whom should the claim be made?

A Either the police force, or HANSEN or HANSEN's employer.

B Both the police force and HANSEN.

C Both the police force and HANSEN's employer.

D The police force, HANSEN and HANSEN's employer.

Question 1.13

STEINBERG is one of a number of people from a private security company contracted to work as a detention officer in a custody office in the Eastshire Constabulary force area. STEINBERG is authorised, and has been trained, to take fingerprints from people in police detention. STEINBERG has been asked to take fingerprints from PARFITT by the custody officer; however, PARFITT is refusing to cooperate.

If necessary, would STEINBERG be entitled to use force to take PARFITT's fingerprints, in these circumstances?

A Yes, but STEINBERG must be accompanied by, and under the supervision of, a police officer.

B No, designated employees may only use force in order to enter premises to save life or limb, or to prevent serious damage to property.

C Yes, but STEINBERG must be given permission to do so by a police officer.

D Yes, STEINBERG has the power to use force without being given permission or being accompanied by a police officer in these circumstances.

Question 1.14

SAGNER works in the administration department of an international haulage company based in the United Kingdom. SAGNER has discovered that some of the drivers working for the company are engaged in people trafficking whilst driving on the continent. SAGNER has no evidence that any of the people are being trafficked into, or out of, the United Kingdom, but believes they engage in this activity between other European countries. SAGNER has considered reporting this to the company's management, but believes they may be aware of the activity and would turn a blind eye. SAGNER is considering disclosing this information to someone else.

Which of the following information is correct, in relation to 'protected disclosures', under the Public Interest Disclosure Act 1998?

A A 'protected disclosure' must be made to an employer, as the Act emphasises disclosures of an internal nature.

B A 'protected disclosure' must be made to an employer, or some other body nominated by the Secretary of State.

C This information would not amount to a 'protected disclosure', because it relates to possible criminal activity outside the United Kingdom.

D A 'protected disclosure' should be made to an employer, or some other body nominated by the Secretary of State, but in some cases may be made to another person.

Question 1.15

Constable JOHNSTON was Constable BRIAR's tutor; they were on patrol when Constable JOHNSTON arrested MILES, who was suspected of committing a burglary. When they returned to the station, Constable JOHNSTON persuaded Constable BRIAR to claim credit for the arrest, because it would look good in her probationary report. Both officers submitted statements identifying Constable BRIAR as the arresting officer. MILES was later charged with the offence and bailed to appear in court a week later. The day following the arrest, Constable BRIAR had second thoughts about her statement and was considering reporting the matter to the Professional Standards Department.

If Constable BRIAR were to disclose this information to the Professional Standards Department, would this amount to a 'protected disclosure' under the Public Interest Disclosure Act 1998?

A No, a miscarriage of justice has not yet occurred; therefore, the Act does not apply.

B Yes, because Constable BRIAR is making a disclosure about a serious criminal offence.

C Yes, provided the behaviour amounts to more than a mere disciplinary offence; Police Conduct matters are not covered by the Act.

D Yes, the Act applies to any wrongdoing by another individual.

ANSWERS

Answer 1.1

Answer **C** — Regulation 5 of the Police Regulations 2003 allows a chief constable, after consultation with local representatives of the staff associations, to appoint an officer to perform part-time service *in any rank*. Answers A, B and D are therefore incorrect.

General Police Duties, para. 4.1.3

Answer 1.2

Answer **A** — The Police Regulations 2003 set out the required notice period for part-time workers who wish to return to full-time duties. Part-time officers may give notice in writing of their intention to be reappointed as a full-time member and will be appointed within

- two months of the date the notice is received by the force, where there is a suitable vacancy; or
- when four months have elapsed since the day the notice was received; or
- from an earlier date if reasonably practicable.

The Police (Amendment No. 4) Regulations 2012 extended these timescales in response to proposals contained in the Winsor Review (from one month to two months and three months to four months). Therefore, the normal time period for officers returning to full-time duties would be two months; if there is no suitable vacancy, this may be extended to four months. However, the force may allow such a change in duties from an earlier date if it is considered reasonably practicable to do so. Answers B, C and D are therefore incorrect.

General Police Duties, para. 4.1.3

Answer 1.3

Answer **A** — The terms under which special constables may be appointed and deployed are set out in s. 30 of the Police Act 1996. Previously, special constables would only have powers and privileges in their own areas or adjoining police areas, unless they were used in mutual aid schemes, when they would enjoy the powers of a special constable in the area in which they were providing mutual aid.

However, the Police and Justice Act 2006 introduced significant amendments: para. 21 of sch. 2 allows special constables to use their constabulary powers in forces throughout England and Wales, regardless of the duties they are performing. Answers B, C and D are therefore incorrect.

General Police Duties, para. 4.1.8

Answer 1.4

Answer **B** — Under Pt 4 of the Police Reform Act 2002, chief officers of police are given the authority to confer policing powers on non-police officers, such as police community support officers, investigating officers, detention officers and escort officers. Part 4 allows the relevant chief officer to confer certain powers on different groups of people by designating or accrediting them.

The chief officer does *not have* to confer any powers on any such groups and he or she can decide to confer only a reduced number of powers or to place further limitations on those powers: the Act simply gives the chief officer the freedom and flexibility to do so. Answers A, C and D are therefore incorrect.

General Police Duties, para. 4.1.9

Answer 1.5

Answer **A** — Some roles created under the Police Reform Act 2002 (such as police community support officers and investigating officers) can *only* be carried out by police employees; if you do not work directly for the police, you cannot have these powers or perform these roles. In other roles (detention officers and escort officers), the person does not necessarily have to be employed by the police.

Answers B, C and D are therefore incorrect.

General Police Duties, para. 4.1.10

Answer 1.6

Answer **B** — The Police Reform Act 2002 allows people to be 'accredited' with powers that can only come from their accreditation under a statutory Community Safety Accreditation Scheme. If the person is not employed by the force, then their employer must have a contract with the relevant Police and Crime Commissioner. These people will have their powers contained in a 'designation' from the relevant chief officer. Since the contract must be with the Police and Crime Commissioner (and not one of the other organisations mentioned), answers A and D are incorrect.

However, in order to perform *any* of the roles and exercise *any* of the powers under Pt 4 of the Act, an individual must be employed by somebody because it is through the person's employer that the chief officer or the relevant Police and Crime Commissioner can exercise a degree of control over those auxiliary staff who are not directly employed by the police. Therefore, the legislation will not allow a person who is unemployed or self-employed to have the powers or to carry out any of the relevant functions. Answers A, C and D are incorrect for this reason also.

General Police Duties, para. 4.1.10

Answer 1.7

Answer **D** — Where designated staff are employees of the relevant force, the chief officer is responsible for dealing with reports of misconduct and complaints against them in the normal way.

The Independent Police Complaints Commission (IPCC) *also* has jurisdiction over any allegations or complaints made against designated staff who are employees of the relevant force. Answer A is therefore incorrect.

This is regardless of whether the allegation is of a criminal nature, or refers purely to a misconduct matter, and there is no requirement for the allegation to be made jointly against a police officer. Answers B and C are therefore incorrect.

General Police Duties, para. 4.1.12

Answer 1.8

Answer **D** — Under s. 42 of the Police Reform Act 2002, PCSOs, when exercising powers or duties, must produce on demand evidence of their designation as a community support officer and of any non-standard power which they exercise that has been conferred on them by their chief officer under s. 38. Answer A is incorrect as evidence must be produced. Answer B is incorrect as the evidence must include any non-standard powers the PCSO has.

PCSOs will not have to carry with them details of *all* the standard powers which have been conferred upon them by an order under s. 38A. The requirement to produce evidence of a designation could be satisfied by production of the designation itself, but could also be satisfied by something less, such as some form of document or card. Answer C is therefore incorrect.

General Police Duties, para. 4.1.13

Answer 1.9

Answer **D** — Under s. 39 of the Police Reform Act 2002, a chief officer of police may enter into a contract with a private company for the provision of services relating to the detention or escorting of people in custody. This allows the chief officer to designate employees of the contractor as either detention officers or escort officers or both.

Although their employee status is the source of control over these employees' activities and performance, the first thing to note is that they are *not* employed by the police force. These contracted-out personnel cannot be given the powers of PCSOs and investigating officers as they are not police employees, but they are given the same powers as police officers to conduct certain functions, such as searching and fingerprinting and photographing.

Because they are neither police officers, nor members of police staff, designated employees are not covered by the Police (Performance) Regulations 2012, the Police (Conduct) Regulations 2012 or any other performance regulations relating to police staff employees. Answers A, B and C are therefore incorrect.

Although s. 39 of the Act allows the Secretary of State to make regulations regarding the handling of complaints and misconduct issues arising out of the functions of designated employees, the practical answer to this question is that the police force involved may withdraw BECK's designation by giving the employee notice and asking for his or her services to be withdrawn (s. 42(3)). This power of revocation or amendment is absolute and there is no requirement for any misconduct or poor performance on the part of the employee.

General Police Duties, paras 4.1.14, 4.1.17

Answer 1.10

Answer **C** — Under s. 40(9) of the Police Reform Act 2002, it will be the duty of a chief officer of police who establishes and maintains a CSAS to ensure that the employers of the persons on whom powers are conferred by the grant of accreditations under s. 41 have established and maintain satisfactory arrangements for handling complaints relating to the carrying out by those persons of the functions for the purposes of which the powers are conferred.

Therefore, the chief officer of police has responsibility to ensure that VAUGHAN's *employers* have satisfactory arrangements for handling complaints. This implies that the employers actually have responsibility for dealing with the complaint.

Answers A, B and D are therefore incorrect.

General Police Duties, para. 4.1.16

Answer 1.11

Answer **A** — Section 42(3) allows an accredited employee's designation or accreditation to be withdrawn at any time by a chief officer of police.

There is no requirement to consult with the local authority, or the person's employer; therefore, answers B, C and D are incorrect.

General Police Duties, para. 4.1.17

Answer 1.12

Answer **D** — Under s. 42 of the Police Reform Act 2002, any liability for civil wrongs arising out of conduct in the course of an employee's accreditation or designation will be apportioned jointly between the police force, the employer and the individual (therefore answers B and C are incorrect). Answer A is incorrect, as the claim should be made against all three.

General Police Duties, para. 4.1.17

Answer 1.13

Answer **D** — Under s. 38(8) of the Police Reform Act 2002, a designated employee is able to exercise the same powers as a constable to use reasonable force, if a constable were entitled to use force in the circumstances. Section 38(9) of the Act allows designated employees to use force to enter premises only if they are in the company and under the supervision of a constable, or to save life or limb or to prevent serious damage to property.

However, the restriction mentioned in s. 38(9) does not also apply to the use of force by a designated employee who is required to exercise this power in other circumstances. Section 117 of the Police and Criminal Evidence Act 1984 would allow a constable to take fingerprints by force in these circumstances; therefore a detention officer would have the same authority.

Answers A, B and C are therefore incorrect.

General Police Duties, para. 4.1.18

Answer 1.14

Answer **D** — The Public Interest Disclosure Act 1998 refers to 'protected disclosures', which are generally disclosures made in accordance with the Act of information which, in the reasonable belief of the maker, generally tend to show criminal conduct, or environmental or health and safety breaches.

Because the Act is intended to protect disclosures of an internal nature, the person would normally be expected to report information to an employer. However, in some areas of employment, the Secretary of State has made regulations prescribing those people and bodies to whom some disclosures *can* be made where appropriate (e.g. the Independent Police Complaints Commission (IPCC) or the Inland Revenue, the Charity Commissioners and the Health and Safety Executive).

The Act does not state that it is mandatory to make disclosures to an employer or a body nominated by the Secretary of State; in fact disclosures may be made to other persons, if

- the employee reasonably believes that he/she will be subjected to a detriment by the employer if the disclosure is made; or
- there is no relevant or prescribed person and the employee reasonably believes that it is likely that evidence relating to the failure will be concealed or destroyed if a disclosure is made; or
- the employee has previously made a disclosure of substantially the same information to the employer or prescribed person.

Answers A and B are therefore incorrect.

Finally, it is immaterial that the relevant behaviour reported occurs or would occur outside the United Kingdom. Answer C is therefore incorrect.

General Police Duties, paras 4.1.19, 4.1.20

Answer 1.15

Answer **C** — The Public Interest Disclosure Act 1998 refers to 'protected disclosures', which are generally disclosures made in accordance with the Act of information which, in the reasonable belief of the maker, tend to show one or more of the following:

- a criminal offence has been committed, is being committed or is likely to be committed;
- a person has failed, is failing or is likely to fail to comply with any legal obligation to which he is subject;
- a miscarriage of justice has occurred, is occurring or is likely to occur;
- the health or safety of any individual has been, is being or is likely to be endangered;
- the environment has been, is being or is likely to be damaged;

- information tending to show any matter falling within any one of the preceding paragraphs has been, is being or is likely to be deliberately concealed.

'Protected disclosures' are not specifically restricted to serious criminal offences (answer B is incorrect).

On the other hand, the Act does not generally apply to 'any wrongdoing by an individual' (and does not generally cover disciplinary offences, unless the behaviour would point to one of the matters listed). Answer D is therefore incorrect.

Finally, the behaviour of the officers *may* amount to an act of perjury, especially if their statements are submitted as evidence in court. Disclosures under the Act are covered where a criminal offence *has been committed, is being committed or is likely to be committed* or where a *miscarriage of justice has occurred, is occurring or is likely to occur*. Therefore, although a criminal offence may not yet have been committed, a disclosure in these circumstances would still be covered (answer A is therefore incorrect).

General Police Duties, para. 4.1.20

2 | Complaints and Misconduct

STUDY PREPARATION

Although the concept of police misconduct may seem an unpalatable subject at the start of your course of study, the maintenance of proper professional standards is paramount to all police officers, supervisors and managers—and the communities they serve.

The Police (Conduct) Regulations 2012 set out the procedures for dealing with cases of misconduct or gross misconduct. The conduct procedures are supported by the Standards of Professional Behaviour—which provide the yardstick by which the conduct of police officers is to be judged.

The chapter guides you through the misconduct procedures, including the effect on individual officers and line managers, and misconduct meetings, tribunals, appeals and suspension from duties.

The Independent Police Complaints Commission (IPCC) has an oversight role in complaints against police officers, whether by supervising, managing or independently investigating a matter.

QUESTIONS

Question 2.1

Assistant Chief Constable MOREL was on suspension from duty, having been accused of a criminal offence under s. 2 of the Computer Misuse Act 1990. The officer was being investigated for accessing and using confidential information from a police computer system. Whilst on suspension, Assistant Chief Constable MOREL gave an interview to a national newspaper, claiming to be innocent and that he was being harassed by the force investigating the incident.

Could Assistant Chief Constable MOREL have breached the Standards of Professional Behaviour, under the Police (Conduct) Regulations 2012 (Discreditable Conduct), by giving the interview to the press?

A No, the Regulations only apply to police officers up to and including the rank of Chief Superintendent.

B Yes, the Regulations apply to all police officers, up to and including the rank of Assistant Chief Constable.

C No, the Regulations do not apply to police officers who are suspended, regardless of their rank.

D Yes, the Regulations apply to all police officers, whether they are suspended or not.

Question 2.2

Constable GOULDING is in police detention for providing a positive breath test, having been involved in a fail to stop road traffic collision whilst off duty. The officer in the case intends interviewing Constable GOULDING, who is represented by the duty solicitor.

Is Constable GOULDING also entitled to have a police 'friend' present at the interview, in these circumstances?

A No, a police 'friend' may not be present at an interview in connection with a criminal offence which was committed off duty.

B Yes, Constable GOULDING would be entitled to have a police 'friend' present at the interview, as well as the solicitor.

C No, a police 'friend' may not be present at an interview in connection with a criminal offence.

D No, a police 'friend' may not be present at an interview in connection with a criminal offence, committed whilst off duty, when the offence is not connected to the person's role as a police officer.

Question 2.3

Constable KEMP has been charged with causing the death of a pedestrian by dangerous driving—the officer was pursuing a stolen vehicle at the time of the incident and was not trained to do so. The Independent Police Complaints Commission (IPCC) has decided to independently investigate the incident. Constable KEMP's force (the appropriate authority) is considering whether or not the officer should be suspended from duty.

Which of the following statements is correct, as to the role the IPPC should play in the decision as to whether Constable KEMP should be suspended?

A If the IPCC is independently investigating a matter, it has decision-making powers as to whether police officers should be suspended.

B If it is independently investigating a matter, the appropriate authority should consult with the IPCC, but the decision rests with the force.

C If it is supervising, managing or independently investigating a matter, the appropriate authority should consult with the IPCC, but the decision rests with the force.

D If the IPCC is supervising, managing or independently investigating a matter, it has decision-making powers as to whether police officers should be suspended.

Question 2.4

Detective Inspector SAUNDERS works in the Professional Standards Department and has been appointed to investigate a complaint that a police officer has accessed information from a force computer system without authority. The inspector has narrowed the list of 'suspects' to two officers: Constable BREEN and Constable WONG. Detective Inspector SAUNDERS does not believe that the information accessed has been passed on to another person and after conducting a severity assessment, considers it will be appropriate to deal with the matter by management action. However, the inspector wishes to speak to both officers in the first instance, to eliminate one of them from the inquiry.

Would Detective Inspector SAUNDERS be required to serve Constables BREEN and WONG with written notification of an investigation at this stage?

A Yes, Detective Inspector SAUNDERS must give written notification to *both* officers, unless one of them can be eliminated from the inquiry before questioning.

B No, because Detective Inspector SAUNDERS has decided the matter can be dealt with by management action.

C Yes, because Detective Inspector SAUNDERS has decided the matter can be dealt with by management action.

D No, Detective Inspector SAUNDERS must give written notification to the officer who has *not* been eliminated from the inquiry, following initial questioning.

Question 2.5

Constable JACOBS is facing a criminal investigation, having been accused of assaulting a prisoner and causing injuries amounting to grievous bodily harm. Detective

Inspector AHMED of the Professional Standards Department (PSD) is leading the misconduct investigation and has been consulting with the Crown Prosecution Service (CPS) about interviewing Constable JACOBS for the criminal matter and the misconduct allegation and how the PSD should proceed.

What advice should the CPS give Detective Inspector AHMED in respect of interviewing Constable JACOBS in these circumstances?

A Two separate interviews must take place; it must be made clear to Constable JACOBS at the start whether the interview is taking place in respect of the criminal or misconduct allegations.

B Constable JACOBS must not be interviewed for the misconduct matter while the criminal investigation is in progress; anything the officer says in a misconduct interview (while not under caution) will be inadmissible in court.

C Detective Inspector AHMED may conduct two separate interviews; however, responses given in the criminal interview could be used in the misconduct investigation and a separate misconduct interview may not be required.

D Constable JACOBS must not be interviewed twice as this would be oppressive; the officer must be interviewed for the criminal matter only and the responses may be used in any subsequent misconduct hearing.

Question 2.6

Constable ANDERTON has been asked to attend a misconduct meeting, following a complaint by a member of the public about the officer's conduct. The officer's supervisor, Sergeant SAID, has been discussing the meeting with Inspector MANSFIELD, who is considering chairing it.

Which of the following statements is correct, in relation to who should be in charge of the meeting with Constable ANDERTON?

A The meeting must be heard by Sergeant SAID, as the officer's supervisor.

B The meeting must be heard by a sergeant, but it does not have to be Constable ANDERTON's supervisor.

C The meeting must be heard either by Constable ANDERTON's first or second line manager (Sergeant SAID or Inspector MANSFIELD).

D The meeting may be heard by a person of any rank, provided he or she is at least one rank above Constable ANDERTON.

Question 2.7

Constable GILLING has been given a final written warning, as a result of a finding at a misconduct hearing.

What should Constable GILLING be told in respect of how long the warning will remain 'live'?

A Any further misconduct in the next 12 months may result in dismissal, without exception.

B Any further misconduct in the next 12 months may result in dismissal; in exceptional circumstances, this may be extended for a further 12 months.

C Any further misconduct in the next 18 months may result in dismissal, without exception.

D Any further misconduct in the next 18 months may result in dismissal; in exceptional circumstances, this may be extended for a further 18 months.

Question 2.8

Constable DAWSON is attending a misconduct meeting, having been accused of being abusive towards the complainant, FROST, during a routine road traffic check. FROST has been asked by the officer conducting the meeting to attend to give evidence of Constable DAWSON's behaviour.

Which of the following statements is correct in respect of FROST's attendance at the meeting?

A FROST must leave the meeting immediately after giving evidence.

B Because this is a misconduct meeting and not a hearing, FROST may remain for the entire proceedings.

C FROST must leave the meeting once the officer conducting it has made a finding.

D FROST may remain at the meeting after giving evidence, but must leave after any character reference/mitigation is given, before the outcome is decided.

Question 2.9

Constable FARRELL has been found guilty of theft and has been sentenced by the court to six months' imprisonment. Constable FARRELL has appealed against the conviction and sentence and has informed the police service of this fact.

Are the circumstances sufficient for the appropriate authority to certify that this is a 'special case' and fast track the misconduct procedures against Constable FARRELL?

A No, they should wait for the outcome of Constable FARRELL's appeal before making this decision.

B Yes, if there is sufficient documentary evidence available to prove the case, and it is in the public interest to dismiss Constable FARRELL.

C Yes, they can proceed with the procedure simply because Constable FARRELL has been convicted of a criminal offence.

D Yes, if there is sufficient oral evidence available to prove the case, and it is in the public interest to dismiss Constable FARRELL.

Question 2.10

Assistant Chief Constable WALL has attended a misconduct meeting with the Deputy Chief Constable. ACC WALL was given a written warning at the meeting and is now seeking legal advice about making an appeal against the finding to a Police Appeals Tribunal.

Is ACC WALL entitled to make such an appeal in these circumstances?

A No, the Police Appeals Tribunal does not hear appeals against the findings or outcomes of a misconduct meeting.

B Yes, an appeal may be made to a Police Appeals Tribunal against any misconduct finding.

C Yes, an appeal may be made by an Assistant Chief Constable against the finding or outcome of a misconduct meeting.

D No, the Police Appeals Tribunal only hears appeals against the findings or outcomes of a special case hearing for gross misconduct.

ANSWERS

Answer 2.1

Answer **D** — The Police (Conduct) Regulations 2012 are supported by a code of ethics—the Standards of Professional Behaviour. The Standards apply to police officers of *all* ranks from chief constable to constable (including special constables). Answers A and B are therefore incorrect. (If you answered A to this question, you may have been confused by the Police (Performance) Regulations 2012, which only apply to police officers (including special constables) up to and including the rank of chief superintendent.)

The Standards of Professional Behaviour do apply to police officers who are subject to suspension; therefore answer C is incorrect.

General Police Duties, para. 4.2.2

Answer 2.2

Answer **D** — A police officer has a right to be accompanied by a police 'friend' at all stages of any misconduct proceedings (under the Police (Conduct) Regulations 2012). This includes interviews, misconduct meetings and hearings.

A police officer is also entitled, in certain circumstances, to be accompanied by a police 'friend' at an interview in connection with a criminal offence. Therefore, answer C is incorrect.

However, the circumstances in which a police officer is entitled to be accompanied by a police 'friend' at an interview in connection with a criminal offence are very narrow. If the officer is arrested or interviewed in connection with a criminal offence committed whilst off duty *that has no connection with his or her role as a serving police officer*, then the police 'friend' has no right to attend the criminal interview of that police officer. Answers A and B are incorrect for this reason.

General Police Duties, para. 4.2.3

Answer 2.3

Answer **C** — In cases where the IPCC is supervising, managing or independently investigating a matter, the appropriate authority will consult with the IPCC before making a decision whether to suspend or not. Answer B is incorrect, as this requirement applies whether the IPCC is supervising, managing or independently investigating a matter.

However, whatever the role the IPCC plays in the investigation, it is the appropriate authority's decision whether to suspend a police officer or not. Answers A and D are therefore incorrect.

Note that the appropriate authority must also consult the IPCC before making the decision to allow a police officer to resume his or her duties following suspension (unless the suspension ends because there will be no misconduct or special case proceedings or because these have concluded) in cases where the IPCC are supervising, managing or independently investigating a case involving that police officer.

General Police Duties, para. 4.2.5.1

Answer 2.4

Answer **B** — The initial assessment when an allegation of misconduct is made is conducted by the appropriate authority, and the purpose of the initial assessment is to

- ensure a timely response to an allegation or an issue relating to conduct;
- identify the police officer subject to the allegation and to eliminate those not involved;
- ensure that the most appropriate procedures are used.

If it is not possible to make an immediate assessment, a process of fact finding should be conducted but only to the extent that it is necessary to determine which procedure should be used. It is perfectly acceptable to ask questions to seek to establish which police officers may have been involved in a particular incident and therefore to eliminate those police officers who are not involved.

Where an appropriate manager decides at the severity assessment that management action is the most appropriate and proportionate way to deal with an issue of misconduct, *there will be no requirement to conduct a formal investigation and therefore no requirement to give a written notice to the police officer concerned in accordance with the provisions in the Conduct Regulations*. Since written notification is not required in these circumstances, answers A, C and D are incorrect.

Where at a later stage, either following the investigation or on withdrawal of the case (under reg. 20 of the Police (Conduct) Regulations 2012 or reg. 7 of the Police (Complaints and Misconduct) (Amendment) Regulations 2012), an appropriate manager decides to take management action, written notice of this will be given to the police officer as soon as possible. Management action is not to be confused with management advice. Management advice is a disciplinary outcome that can only be imposed following a misconduct meeting or hearing.

General Police Duties, para. 4.2.5.2

Answer 2.5

Answer **C** — Where a police officer is alleged to have committed a criminal offence a normal criminal investigation will take place, with the police officer being cautioned in accordance with the PACE Code of Practice. Where the matter to be investigated involves both criminal and misconduct allegations, it should be made clear to the police officer concerned at the start of the interview whether he/she is being interviewed in respect of the criminal or misconduct allegations.

Evidence gathering may be achieved by conducting two separate interviews; however, this is not mandatory. Depending on how the PSD decide to proceed, if two interviews are conducted, the responses given in respect of the criminal interview could be used in the misconduct investigation and therefore a separate misconduct interview may not be required. Answers A and D are therefore incorrect.

Care should be taken when conducting a misconduct interview where the police officer is also the subject of a criminal investigation in respect of the same behaviour, as anything said by the police officer concerned in the misconduct interview when not under caution and used in the criminal investigation could be subject to an inadmissibility ruling by the court at any subsequent trial. However, this does not mean that the officer *must not* be interviewed for the misconduct matter while the criminal investigation is in progress—it will be a matter for the investigating officer and the CPS to decide on the best approach. Answer B is therefore incorrect.

General Police Duties, para. 4.2.5.5

Answer 2.6

Answer **D** — Under the Police (Conduct) Regulations 2012, a misconduct meeting for non-senior officers (police officers up to and including the rank of chief superintendent and all special constables), will be heard by a police officer (or other member of a police force) of *at least* one rank above the police officer concerned. Since the officer hearing the case may be of a higher rank than the officer's immediate line manager, answer B is incorrect.

Whilst it might be good practice for the meeting to be heard by the officer's own line manager, it is not mandatory, and answers A and C are therefore incorrect.

Note that a police staff member can be appointed who, in the opinion of the appropriate authority, is a grade above that of the police officer concerned, but not if the case substantially involves operational policing matters.

Finally, in the case of a special constable, the member of the police force must be a sergeant or above, or a senior human resources professional.

General Police Duties, para. 4.2.6.3

Answer 2.7

Answer **D** — When issued with a final written warning, the police officer will be told the reason for the warning, that any future misconduct may result in dismissal, that he or she has a right to appeal and the name of the person to whom the appeal should be sent, and that the final written warning will be put on their personal file and remain live for *18 months* from the date the warning is given. Therefore, answers A and B are incorrect.

Only in exceptional circumstances will further misconduct (that justifies more than management advice) not result in dismissal. In exceptional circumstances, the final written warning may be extended for a further 18 months on one occasion only. Answer C is therefore incorrect.

General Police Duties, para. 4.2.6.10

Answer 2.8

Answer **C** — A complainant and any person accompanying the complainant will be permitted to remain in the meeting/hearing up to and including any finding by the persons conducting the meeting/hearing, after having given evidence (if appropriate). Answers A and B are therefore incorrect.

However, the complainant and any person accompanying the complainant will *not* be permitted to remain in the meeting/hearing while character references or mitigation are being given or the decision of the panel as to the outcome is being given. Answer D is incorrect, as the person must leave *before* the character reference or mitigation is given (which will also be before the outcome is given).

Note that the appropriate authority will have a duty to inform the complainant of the outcome of any misconduct meeting/hearing whether the complainant attends or not.

General Police Duties, para. 4.2.6.13

Answer 2.9

Answer **B** — The operation of the fast track misconduct procedures, referred to as 'special cases', are set out in Pt 5 of the Conduct Regulations. The special case procedures can only be used if the appropriate authority certifies the case as a special case, having determined that the 'special conditions' are satisfied or if the IPCC has given a direction under para. 20H(7) of sch. 3 to the Police Reform Act 2002.

The 'special conditions' are that there is sufficient evidence, in the form of written statements or other documents, *without the need for further evidence*, whether written or oral, to establish on the balance of probabilities, that the conduct of the police officer concerned constitutes gross misconduct, and it is in the public interest for the police officer concerned to cease to be a police officer without delay. Answer D is incorrect, as the hearing may proceed without oral evidence—in fact, the only oral evidence given at such a hearing will be from the police officer concerned (and the hearing may be heard in the officer's absence if necessary).

There is no requirement to wait for the outcome of the officer's appeal. The panel will merely need to decide, on the balance of probabilities, if it is in the public interest to dismiss the officer. Answer A is therefore incorrect.

A person's conviction for a criminal offence will not automatically provide sufficient grounds for the appropriate authority to certify that this is a 'special case' and fast track misconduct procedures. However, such evidence would certainly be relevant. Answer C is therefore incorrect.

General Police Duties, para. 4.2.8

Answer 2.10

Answer **C** — A police officer has a right of appeal to a Police Appeals Tribunal against any disciplinary finding and/or disciplinary outcome imposed at a misconduct hearing or special case hearing held under the Conduct Regulations. Senior police officers (Assistant Chief Constables and above), in addition, have the right to appeal to a Police Appeals Tribunal against any disciplinary finding and/or outcome imposed at a misconduct meeting. Since a Police Appeals Tribunal *may* hear an appeal in relation to a finding at a misconduct meeting, answer A is incorrect.

However, since this right is restricted to senior police officers, answer B is incorrect.

Answer D is incorrect because appeals can be made against findings in misconduct hearings *or* special case hearings (or meetings in the case of an ACC).

General Police Duties, para. 4.2.9

3 | Unsatisfactory Performance and Attendance

STUDY PREPARATION

The previous chapter dealt with the Police (Conduct) Regulations 2012. In this chapter, we examine the Police (Performance) Regulations 2012.

These Regulations cover both performance and absence management, and the chapter guides you through the procedures for dealing with both aspects of the regulations.

The catalyst for changing these Regulations, initially in 2008, was the Taylor Review. The review recommended simplifying processes, with the emphasis on *improving* poor performance and attendance, instead of punishing individuals. As a line manager, you will find that the aspects of misconduct and performance are closely related.

The final part of this chapter deals with the offences that can be committed by people in public offices, including police officers, who abuse their powers.

QUESTIONS

Question 3.1

Constable DALE has been asked to attend a second stage unsatisfactory performance (UPP) meeting, for continued poor performance. Constable DALE is disputing the evidence of poor performance and has expressed a wish to be legally represented at the meeting.

Is Constable DALE entitled to legal representation at this meeting?

A Yes, police officers are entitled to legal representation at all stages of the misconduct and performance procedures.

B No, legal representation is restricted to misconduct meetings and hearings.

C No, but the officer will be entitled to legal representation if the matter progresses to the third stage.

D No, in relation to performance, legal representation is restricted to cases of gross incompetence, at the third stage.

Question 3.2

Sergeant GANT has arranged a first stage meeting with Constable RUSH to discuss the officer's poor attendance record. Sergeant GANT intends issuing the officer with an improvement notice, seeking an improvement in the officer's attendance at work. Sergeant GANT is newly promoted and wishes to seek advice on how to conduct the meeting and the possible outcomes.

Which of the following statements is correct, in relation to the advice Sergeant GANT may seek?

A Sergeant GANT may ask a Human Resources (HR) professional to be present, or a police officer with relevant experience, who is independent of the line management chain.

B Sergeant GANT may seek advice from an HR professional, or a police officer with relevant experience, before the meeting, but they may not be present.

C Because the meeting is to do with attendance and not performance, Sergeant GANT must have an HR professional present.

D Sergeant GANT may ask an HR professional to be present, or a police officer who is part of the line management chain, provided the officer is not the second line manager.

Question 3.3

Inspector GREEGAN was due to hold a second stage unsatisfactory performance (UPP) meeting with Constable O'NEIL, regarding the continued submission of poor paperwork. An hour before the meeting, Inspector GREEGAN read a report from Constable O'NEIL's line manager outlining the officer's poor timekeeping. Constable O'NEIL had been warned several times recently for arriving at work late. A request was made that in the report by the line manager Inspector GREEGAN discuss the additional matter at the second stage meeting, alongside the original unsatisfactory performance matters.

Which of the following statements is correct, in relation to the request made by Constable O'NEIL's line manager?

A The planned meeting should continue and a separate first stage meeting should be arranged to discuss the additional matter. Unconnected UPP matters must always be dealt with separately.

B Due to the timing of the line manager's report, Inspector GREEGAN may adjourn the planned meeting and arrange a second stage meeting at a later date to discuss both matters.

C Inspector GREEGAN may discuss both matters at the planned meeting, because new information has come to light about Constable O'NEIL's performance during the specified period.

D The planned meeting should continue and a separate first stage meeting should be arranged to discuss the additional matter. Both matters may be consolidated if Constable O'NEIL reaches stage three of the procedures.

Question 3.4

Constable RICE has attended a second stage meeting, having failed to meet an action plan relating to poor attendance. Constable RICE has been given a written improvement notice and the second line manager has decided that the officer should be given a six-month action plan to improve attendance. Constable RICE has now approached a Police Federation Representative to inquire whether there are grounds to appeal against the length of the period specified for improvement.

Which of the following statements is correct, according to the Police (Performance) Regulations 2012?

A An appeal may be made against the length of the period specified for improvement if it is unreasonable.

B An appeal may only be made if there was a breach of the procedures set out in the Regulations or some other unfairness relating to the meeting.

C An appeal may only be made against the actual finding that an officer's performance or attendance was unsatisfactory.

D An appeal may only be made against the length of the period specified for improvement if the matter relates to poor performance and not poor attendance.

Question 3.5

COLLINS is the senior Special Constable in Eastshire Constabulary and has been asked to attend a third stage unsatisfactory performance (UPP) meeting in relation to Special Constable WATKINS, regarding the continued submission of poor work.

In relation to COLLINS's presence at the meeting, which of the following statements is correct?

A COLLINS will be a member of the panel and will have a role in determining whether or not Special Constable WATKINS's performance is unsatisfactory.

B COLLINS must attend the meeting to advise the panel, but will not have a role in determining whether or not Special Constable WATKINS's performance is unsatisfactory.

C COLLINS must attend to advise the panel beforehand, but must not be present at the meeting with Special Constable WATKINS.

D COLLINS must attend the meeting to advise the panel, and will have a role later in determining whether or not Special Constable WATKINS's performance is unsatisfactory.

Question 3.6

Sergeant AITKEN is being dealt with for poor performance and was issued with a final written improvement notice at a third stage unsatisfactory performance (UPP) meeting three months ago. Sergeant AITKEN has been given notice to attend before a panel at another third stage unsatisfactory performance (UPP) meeting, due to continued concern over the officer's performance. Sergeant AITKEN has met with a Police Federation representative to discuss the possible outcomes of the meeting.

What options are available to the panel to deal with Sergeant AITKEN, under the Police (Performance) Regulations 2012 (dealing with UPP)?

A The panel may redeploy, reduce in rank or dismiss Sergeant AITKEN; however, they may extend the officer's final written improvement notice if this is the appropriate course of action.

B The panel must, at this stage, extend Sergeant AITKEN's final written improvement notice, before it considers any other punitive action against the officer.

C The panel may redeploy, reduce in rank or dismiss Sergeant AITKEN; however, the panel may not extend the officer's final written improvement notice at this stage.

D The panel may redeploy or reduce Sergeant AITKEN in rank; they may not dismiss the officer unless they extend the final written improvement notice and performance continues to be unsatisfactory.

Question 3.7

Constable PARKER has been on sick leave for 11 months having suffered a broken leg playing football. The officer has had two operations and is still unfit to return to work. Constable PARKER is currently at the second stage of the unsatisfactory performance (UPP) procedures and has failed an action plan which required him to return to work. Consideration is being given to serving Constable PARKER with a notice to attend a stage three meeting; however, the officer's Police Federation representative has stated that he is unfit for duty, which renders him unable to attend a meeting, quoting the provisions of reg. 33 of the Police Regulations 2003 (sick leave).

What impact does Constable PARKER's injury have on the panel being able to require him to attend the meeting?

A The Regulations do not apply; Constable PARKER may be unfit for duty, but he must attend the meeting.

B The Regulations will apply; when a constable is unfit for duty, he or she will also be unfit to attend a meeting.

C When an officer is incapacitated, the meeting must be deferred until he or she is sufficiently improved to attend.

D The Regulations do not apply; the meeting may be held at a location convenient to Constable PARKER, or if necessary, in the officer's absence.

Question 3.8

JESSOP has recently joined Eastshire Constabulary as a constable. Before joining, JESSOP was an active member of the Conservative Party, attending regular political fundraisers and meetings with other members.

In relation to sch. 1 to the Police Regulations 2003 (SI 2003/527) (restrictions on the private lives of officers), what would JESSOP's position now be, as a member of this party?

A Constable JESSOP would have to give up membership of this party, but could still attend political meetings.

B Constable JESSOP may remain a member of this party, but could not attend political fundraisers and meetings.

C Constable JESSOP would have to give up membership of this party and could not attend political meetings: all political parties are proscribed by the Secretary of State for police officers.

D Constable JESSOP could still attend political meetings and remain a member of this party, provided it does not become proscribed by the Secretary of State.

Question 3.9

Constable PURSEY creates a false piece of intelligence as a joke relating to a male believed to be in possession of a firearm. As a result, a member of the public is stopped and challenged by police officers with firearms. The member of the public is not happy and wishes to take action against the police for misconduct in a public office.

Which of the following is correct?

A The officer's actions amount to a tort (civil wrong) only and action in the High Court should be commenced.

B The officer's actions amount to a criminal offence only and criminal proceedings should be started.

C The officer's actions amount to a tort (civil wrong) and a criminal offence and both criminal and civil proceedings can be started.

D The officer's actions amount to a tort (civil wrong) and a criminal offence; however, only civil *or* criminal proceedings can be started, not both.

Question 3.10

The police had attended several calls during the week relating to a domestic disagreement between FRENCH and HOLLOWAY. On each occasion, the incidents had been classified as 'verbal arguments' and no action was taken. Both FRENCH and HOLLOWAY were usually very drunk. One evening, Constable NAPIER was contacted by the control room and told that FRENCH had telephoned to say that HOLLOWAY had threatened to kill him and asked for the police to attend urgently. Constable NAPIER refused to attend the call on the grounds that previous calls to the address had been a waste of the police's time. Approximately an hour later, the police received a call that HOLLOWAY had actually killed FRENCH.

Could Constable NAPIER be guilty of the common law offence of misconduct in public office, in these circumstances?

A No, this offence cannot be committed because of a failure to do something; it relates to the actions a person actually took.

B Yes, but only if it can be shown Constable NAPIER was aware of the duty to take particular action, and failed to do so.

C Yes, if it can be shown Constable NAPIER was aware of the duty to take particular action, and failed to do so, or was reckless as to the existence of the duty.

D No, this could not amount to a criminal offence; however, Constable NAPIER could be guilty of gross incompetence or misconduct.

Question 3.11

FARR is aware that special constables are entitled to free travel on the local buses. FARR makes a false warrant card with the term 'Special Constable' on it and a picture of himself. Every day he travels on the bus and produces this card to obtain free rides. He never states he is a special constable; he merely shows the bus driver his card.

Has FARR committed an offence of impersonating a police officer contrary to s. 90(1) of the Police Act 1996?

A No, as he did not say he was a special constable.

B No, as the legislation does not apply to impersonating special constables.

C Yes, provided his intention was to deceive.

D Yes, provided his intention was to obtain an advantage.

ANSWERS

Answer 3.1

Answer **D** — In relation to unsatisfactory performance (UPP), a police officer may seek legal advice at any time. However, legal representation for UPP matters is confined to third stage meetings where the procedure has been initiated at that stage. In other words, the officer is accused of gross incompetence and has bypassed the normal step-by-step process and has been fast tracked to a hearing. Answer A is therefore incorrect. This also means that if the officer arrives at level three having passed through the other stages, he or she is not entitled to legal representation at the level three meeting. Answer C is therefore incorrect.

Answer B is incorrect, because a police officer *can* have legal representation in relation to performance matters, albeit in limited circumstances.

General Police Duties, para. 4.3.2

Answer 3.2

Answer **A** — The formal procedures to deal with unsatisfactory performance and attendance are set out in the Police (Performance) Regulations 2012 and are referred to as 'UPPs'. There are potentially three stages to the UPP process, each of which involves a different meeting composition and possible outcomes. However, the process is the same whether the officer is being asked to account for their poor performance or their attendance. Answer C is therefore incorrect.

A line manager may ask an HR professional or police officer (who should have experience of UPPs) to attend a UPP meeting to advise him or her on the proceedings at the first stage meeting. Answer B is therefore incorrect. The line manager may also seek such advice before the meeting and answer C is also incorrect in this respect, because attendance at the meeting is optional and not mandatory.

If the experienced police officer is to attend the meeting, he or she must be independent of the line management chain (and not part of it at any level). Answer D is therefore incorrect.

General Police Duties, para. 4.3.8

Answer 3.3

Answer **B** — Generally, a police officer can only move to a later stage of the UPPs in relation to unsatisfactory performance or attendance that is similar to, or connected with, the performance or attendance referred to in any previous written improvement notice. Where failings relate to different forms of unsatisfactory performance or attendance it will be necessary to commence each UPP at the first stage (unless the failing constitutes gross incompetence). If more than one UPP is commenced, then, given that the procedures will relate to different failings and will have been identified at different times, the finding and outcome of each should be without prejudice to the others.

However, there may be circumstances where procedures have been initiated for a particular failing and an additional failing comes to light prior to the first or second stage meeting. In such circumstances it is possible to consolidate the two issues at the planned meeting provided that there is sufficient time prior to the meeting to comply with the notification requirements. Answer A is therefore incorrect.

If there is insufficient time to comply with the notification requirements (as was the case in this scenario), either the meeting should be rearranged to a date which allows the requirements to be met or a separate first stage meeting should be held in relation to the additional matter.

Therefore, Inspector GREEGAN would have the option to adjourn the second stage meeting to discuss both matters at the same meeting, but should not discuss the additional matter at the planned meeting. There would be no requirement to wait until the officer reaches stage three of the UPPs to consolidate the unsatisfactory performance matters. Answers C and D are therefore incorrect.

General Police Duties, para. 4.3.8.2

Answer 3.4

Answer **A** — According to the Police (Performance) Regulations 2012, a police officer has a right of appeal against the finding and the terms of the improvement notice imposed at stage two of the UPPs and against the decision to require him/her to attend the meeting. Any appeal should be made in writing and must clearly set out the grounds and evidence for the appeal.

One ground for an appeal is that there was a breach of the procedures set out in the Regulations or some other unfairness which could have materially affected the finding of unsatisfactory performance or attendance or the terms of the written improvement notice. Amongst the other grounds are that the finding of unsatisfactory performance or attendance is unreasonable, or any of the terms of the improvement notice are unreasonable. This would include an appeal against the length of the period specified for improvement. Answers B and C are therefore incorrect.

An appeal may be made against the length of the period specified for improvement if the matter relates to poor performance *or* poor attendance. Answer D is therefore incorrect.

General Police Duties, para. 4.3.10.3

Answer 3.5

Answer **B** — In cases where the police officer is a special constable, the force will appoint a member of the special constabulary of sufficient seniority and experience to attend the meeting to advise the panel (this is for the purpose of fairness). Since this person will be present at the meeting, answer C is incorrect.

However, the special constable adviser will not form part of the panel (answer A is incorrect), nor will he or she have a role in determining whether or not the officer's performance or attendance is unsatisfactory. Answer D is therefore incorrect.

General Police Duties, para. 4.3.11.3

Answer 3.6

Answer **A** — If, at the end of the validity period of the final improvement notice, the panel considers that sufficient improvement to the police officer's performance or attendance has not been made or maintained during this period, the panel chair will inform the police officer of the panel's assessment. Any such notification to the police officer must also include notification that he/she is required to attend a further third stage meeting.

A police officer attending such a meeting *may* be given an extension to a final improvement notice, but this is the only occasion at this stage that the officer may be given another chance. Answer C is therefore incorrect.

However, this is not mandatory and the panel may also decide to redeploy, reduce in rank or dismiss the officer (answer B is therefore incorrect).

Answer D is incorrect because the panel may decide to adopt *any* of the options mentioned; the decision to dismiss the officer is not dependent on him/her having been redeployed or reduced in rank, or having previously been the subject of an extended final written improvement notice.

General Police Duties, para. 4.3.11.8

Answer 3.7

Answer **D** — Attendance at any stage meeting is not subject to the same considerations as reporting for duty and the provisions of reg. 33 (sick leave) of the Police Regulations 2003 do not apply. In other words, an officer may not claim that because he/she is unfit for duty, he or she is also unable to attend a meeting—of course, it will depend on the individual's illness, but a broken leg is a physical injury and should not prohibit the person from discussing a return to work plan. Answer B is therefore incorrect.

If the police officer is incapacitated, the meeting *may* be deferred until he/she is sufficiently improved to attend. Every effort should be made to make it *possible* for the police officer to attend; however, this is not mandatory and a meeting will not be deferred indefinitely because the police officer is unable to attend. Answer C is therefore incorrect.

Whilst the 2003 Regulations may not apply, advice and guidance suggest that the chair of the meeting should make efforts to help the officer to engage in the meeting, which could include holding the meeting at a location convenient to him/her. It will be the officer's force's duty to find a way to communicate with him/her and forcing the officer to attend a meeting will play into their hands, when it may be possible to communicate with them in some other way, such as using video, telephone or other conferencing technology. Answer A is therefore incorrect.

General Police Duties, para. 4.3.12

Answer 3.8

Answer **B** — Schedule 1 provides that a member of a police force

- shall at all times abstain from any activity which is likely to interfere with the impartial discharge of his/her duties or which is likely to give rise to the impression amongst members of the public that it may so interfere;
- shall in particular—
  (a) not take any active part in politics;
  (b) not belong to any organisation specified or described in a determination of the Secretary of State.

For this purpose, the Secretary of State has determined that no member of the police force may be a member of the British National Party (BNP), Combat 18 or the National Front. Since these are the only proscribed organisations at this time, answer C is incorrect.

The wording of sch. 1 does not actually prohibit police officers from being members of other political parties and answer A is incorrect.

However, police officers *are* prohibited from taking an active part in politics. This means that Constable JESSOP could be a member of this political party, but *could not* attend political meetings and fundraisers. Answers A and D are incorrect for this reason.

General Police Duties, para. 4.3.16.1

Answer 3.9

Answer **C** — Misconduct in a public office is defined by common law as follows:

> It is a misdemeanour at common law for the holder of a public office to do anything that amounts to a malfeasance or a 'culpable' misfeasance.

(*R* v *Wyatt* (1705) 1 Salk 380)

This common law offence is both a tort and a criminal offence, which could give rise to litigation in both the criminal and civil courts. Answers A, B and D are therefore incorrect.

Misfeasance can cover many misdemeanours committed by police officers, from deliberately mistreating prisoners to improper use of the National Intelligence Model.

General Police Duties, para. 4.3.17.1

Answer 3.10

Answer **C** — It is a misdemeanour at common law for the holder of a public office to do anything that amounts to a malfeasance or a 'culpable' misfeasance (*R* v *Wyatt* (1705) 1 Salk 380). The conduct can be separated into occasions of *mal*feasance and *mis*feasance. The first requires some degree of wrongful motive or intention on the part of the officer while the second is more likely to apply where there has been some form of wilful neglect of duty: both are notoriously difficult to prove, but either could constitute an offence. Answers A and D are therefore incorrect.

A death in police custody has led to a clarification as to the nature of the criminal common law offence of misconduct in public office (see *Attorney General's Reference (No. 3 of 2003)* [2004] EWCA Crim 868). The elements of the offence were summarised by the Court of Appeal (Criminal Division) as follows:

A public officer acting as such [who]:
- wilfully neglects to perform his duty and/or wilfully misconducts himself,
- to such a degree as to amount to an abuse of the public's trust in the office holder,
- without reasonable excuse or justification [may be guilty of the criminal offence.]

Since the offence requires 'an awareness of the duty to act or a subjective recklessness as to the existence of the duty', answer B is incorrect.

General Police Duties, para. 4.3.17.1

Answer 3.11

Answer **C** — Impersonating a police officer is defined in the Police Act 1996. Section 90(1) states:

Any person who with intent to deceive impersonates a member of a police force or special constable, or makes any statement or does any act calculated falsely to suggest that he is such a member or constable shall be guilty of an offence.

As can be seen from the definition, the legislation applies to special constables, and therefore answer B is incorrect. The offence includes not only statements but also acts that suggest the person is a special constable. Such acts would include producing a false warrant card, and therefore answer A is incorrect. This is a crime of 'specific' intent and intention to deceive must be proved, not just an intention to gain an advantage, and therefore answer D is incorrect.

General Police Duties, para. 4.3.17.2

4 | Human Rights

STUDY PREPARATION

It is generally accepted that the introduction of the Human Rights Act 1998 (which incorporated the European Convention on Human Rights into our domestic law) had the largest effect on the use of police powers since the Police and Criminal Evidence Act 1984.

Many of the questions contained in this chapter are based on decisions made in the European Court of Human Rights. Under s. 2 of the Human Rights Act 1998, domestic courts and tribunals are under an obligation to take such decisions into account. However, it is important to remember that the Convention, as a 'living instrument', is constantly evolving.

When looking at the Convention rights in detail, it is also important to recognise the difference between an *absolute* right under the Convention (such as the right to freedom from torture under Art. 3), and a *qualified* or *restricted* right (such as Art. 5, the right to liberty). Probably, the most important consideration is to recognise how the 1998 Act sets out to *balance* the rights of the individual against the needs of a democratic society.

The 'three tests' must be learned, namely 'prescribed by law', 'legitimate objective' and 'proportionality', as well as who will be a 'victim' and who may be in breach of the Act. Lastly, there are several Articles contained in the Convention which directly affect the police, such as the right to life, freedom from torture, right to liberty and security, right to a fair trial and right to respect for private and family life. Other Articles, such as right of freedom of expression and freedom of assembly, also have a significant effect on everyday policing.

Human rights law does not exist in isolation. Therefore, although it is specifically addressed in this chapter, every aspect of the law contained in this book should be viewed with the 1998 Act in mind.

QUESTIONS

Question 4.1

McARTHUR works as a detention officer contracted by a private security company to work for Eastshire Police in a custody office. It has been alleged that whilst on duty, McARTHUR has sexually assaulted several drunken female detainees in their cells. During the investigation, it was discovered that there had been a failure in the vetting process by the private security company and that McARTHUR had previous convictions for rape. One of McARTHUR's victims is considering taking a case to the European Court of Human Rights (ECHR), alleging a breach of Art. 3 of the Convention (prohibition of torture).

Which of the following statements is correct relating to a 'public authority', as defined in s. 6 of the Human Rights Act 1998?

A McARTHUR would be a public authority under s. 6, alongside Eastshire Police; as a private contractor, the security company would not.

B Either Eastshire Police or the private security company would be a public authority under s. 6; as an individual, McARTHUR could not be a public authority.

C By acting as an individual, only McARTHUR would be a public authority under s. 6.

D Either Eastshire Police, the private security company or McARTHUR would be a public authority under s. 6.

Question 4.2

A demonstration at the site of a new out-of-town shopping centre had been authorised under of ss. 12 and 14 of the Public Order Act 1986; however, the police had received intelligence that passengers on a coach attending the demonstration intended causing disorder at the site. They responded by stopping the coach and escorting it to the other side of the city. The demonstration organiser, QUINN, was not on the coach and was intending to meet the demonstrators at the site later on. Instead, QUINN met the coach on the other side of the city and was told by the senior police officer that if the coach tried to return to the site now or in the future, the occupants would be arrested for a breach of the peace. Most of the occupants of the coach voted to call it a day and went home. QUINN has sought legal advice in order to challenge police action under Arts 10 and 11 of the European Convention on Human Rights (ECHR).

In relation to whether QUINN may use the ECHR to challenge the actions of the police, which statement is correct?

A QUINN should be advised that the pressure group should pursue a case under the ECHR on behalf of the coach passengers, as this would have more effect.

B QUINN was not directly affected by the police actions and may not pursue a case under the ECHR; an individual who was on the coach would need to do so.

C Although not directly affected by the police actions, QUINN was at risk of being so affected and may pursue a case under the ECHR.

D Neither QUINN nor the coach passengers may pursue a case under the ECHR at this stage; however, they would be able to do so if they returned to the site and the police carried out their threat to arrest people.

Question 4.3

FRIAR appeared in Crown Court, having been charged with supplying Class A drugs. The court heard that FRIAR had been the subject of a directed surveillance operation by plain clothes police officers. During the hearing, it was revealed that the officers had omitted to obtain the correct authorisation under the Regulation of Investigatory Powers Act 2000 and the judge ordered the case to be dismissed. FRIAR intends bringing proceedings against the police for infringing Art. 8 of the European Convention on Human Rights (the right to private and family life).

Section 7(5)(a) of the Human Rights Act 1998 provides a limited time period during which a victim must bring proceedings against a public authority. In FRIAR's case, when did that time period begin?

A When the infringement of FRIAR's human rights actually took place.

B When FRIAR realised an infringement of human rights had taken place.

C When the court dismissed the case.

D When FRIAR notifies the court of an intention to institute proceedings under this section.

Question 4.4

Constable ANDERSON is an authorised firearms officer who was responsible for the fatal shooting of a suspect whilst on duty and was called to give evidence in the Coroner's Court. Constable ANDERSON applied to give evidence anonymously on the grounds that she was a member of the local community and if her identity were revealed, it would represent a risk of serious harm to herself and her family. The court rejected the application by the officer.

Would there be any restriction on Constable ANDERSON bringing proceedings against the Coroner's Court (a public authority) for infringing Art. 2 of the European Convention on Human Rights (the right to life) in these circumstances?

A Yes, Constable ANDERSON was acting in the execution of her duty, which makes this an employment matter.

B No, this is not an employment matter and Constable ANDERSON may bring proceedings.

C No, there are no restrictions on police officers relying on the Convention rights.

D No, the only restriction on police officers relying on the Convention rights is in relation to recruitment proceedings.

Question 4.5

LAWTON was the father of an 8-year-old boy who was murdered by his neighbour, PEARSON, a convicted sex offender. Prior to the murder, LAWTON had made several complaints to the police that PEARSON had been seen pestering his child. Following PEARSON's conviction, LAWTON brought an action against the police under Art. 2 of the European Convention on Human Rights, alleging that the police had failed to prevent his son's death.

What must LAWTON prove to the court in order to convince it that the police failed to prevent the death of his son?

A Nothing—the police have an absolute obligation to protect life under Art. 2.

B That the police actually foresaw the risk to life, and that they failed to act upon it.

C That the police failed to see a risk to life which would have been obvious to a reasonable person.

D That the police did not do all that was expected of them to avoid a real and imme- diate risk to life.

Question 4.6

CONNELLY has sought legal advice about taking a case to the European Court of Human Rights (ECHR). He is alleging that his rights under Art. 3 of the Convention (prohibition of torture) were breached while he was in police detention, having been arrested under the Terrorism Act 2000. CONNELLY will state that while he was being interviewed, a police officer kneed him in the groin, causing a ruptured testicle. The matter has been investigated by the Independent Police Complaints Commission

(IPCC) in the UK, which has determined that the officer acted in self-defence following violent conduct from CONNELLY. CONNELLY disagrees with that determination and wishes to take the matter to the ECHR.

Which of the following statements is correct, in relation to CONNELLY's potential claim?

A Article 3 is not concerned with isolated physical assaults as they may be charged under primary legislation; this is not a case that will be heard in the ECHR.

B This is unlikely to amount to inhuman or degrading treatment or punishment; the ECHR has accepted that self-defence may provide an exception to a breach of Art. 3.

C This may amount to torture under s. 134 of the Criminal Justice Act 1988, but the statutory defence of 'lawful authority, justification or excuse' under that Act overrules the prohibition contained in Art. 3.

D This is definitely torture under Art. 3; there can be no derogation from an individual's absolute right to freedom from torture or to inhuman or degrading treatment or punishment.

Question 4.7

ZILICH is suspected of entering the country illegally and is wanted for murder in Kosovo. ZILICH has been held in a detention centre for over three years while the immigration authorities attempt to organise extradition procedures. ZILICH is fighting the extradition procedure by using Art. 5 of the European Convention on Human Rights (right to liberty and security), citing that his detention is unjust and oppressive because of the three-year delay.

What obligation, if any, do the authorities have to demonstrate that ZILICH's detention is not unjust and oppressive?

A They need only show that the detention was necessary—there is no requirement to justify the delay in ZILICH's extradition.

B There is no requirement to show either that the detention was necessary, or to justify the delay in ZILICH's extradition.

C They must show that the detention was necessary and that the delay in ZILICH's extradition was justified, otherwise the detention may be unlawful.

D ZILICH has been 'detained' for deportation; this does not constitute an 'arrest' and therefore Art. 5 does not apply.

Question 4.8

FOX was arrested for an offence under s. 4 of the Road Traffic Act 1988 (unfit to drive through drink or drugs). FOX was taken to a police station where subsequent blood tests proved negative. FOX is now considering bringing a case of unlawful arrest against the police, under Art. 5 of the European Convention on Human Rights (the right to liberty and security). The basis of FOX's case is that the arresting officer had formed a suspicion that she was drunk based on evidence provided by a member of the public. FOX claims that this suspicion was not 'reasonable' and, consequently, the arrest was unlawful.

In considering FOX's case, how should the court assess the officer's 'reasonable suspicion' that an arrest was necessary?

A Whether the officer was satisfied that the information received about FOX prior to the arrest amounted to a 'reasonable suspicion' that she was drunk.

B Whether an ordinary person would be satisfied that the information received about FOX prior to the arrest amounted to a 'reasonable suspicion' that she was drunk.

C Whether an objective observer would be satisfied that the information received about FOX prior to the arrest amounted to a 'reasonable suspicion' that she was drunk.

D Whether the witness in the case had formed a 'reasonable suspicion' that she was drunk.

Question 4.9

MENDEZ, a Premiership football player, is being taken to civil court by his estranged wife, who is seeking a non-molestation order due to alleged harassment committed by MENDEZ against her and their children. Following legal advice, MENDEZ intends asking the court for the hearing to be held in private. MENDEZ believes that any publicity generated by the case may prejudice the outcome, because of his celebrity status.

Which of the following statements is correct, in respect of whether the hearing should be held in public or private?

A The case may be held in private, if it is adjudged that the publicity would prejudice the interests of justice.

B The case may not be held in private; this facility is only available in criminal courts.

C The case may be held in private, but only if it is being heard in front of a jury.
D The case may be held in private, but only if it is adjudged that the interests of a juvenile need to be protected.

Question 4.10

MORTON is a well-known public figure and is taking legal advice about bringing a case against the police, under Art. 8 of the European Convention on Human Rights (respect for private and family life). The circumstances were that MORTON reported to the police her suspicion that someone was trying to hack into her emails. MORTON alleges that the police failed to act and as a result, the hacker subsequently managed to download several photographs of her with no clothes on, from emails sent by a friend. The photographs were displayed on the Internet and MORTON claims this was potentially ruinous to her career.

Which of the following statements is correct, in relation to MORTON's potential claim?

A The aim of Art. 8 is to protect a person's life from interference by 'public authorities': it therefore does not apply in these circumstances.
B The State has a positive obligation to prevent others from interfering with an individual's right to private and family life; therefore, Art. 8 may apply in these circumstances.
C The State has a positive obligation to prevent others from interfering with an individual's right to private and family life, but this does not extend to a person's correspondence; therefore, Art. 8 would not apply in these circumstances.
D The State has a positive obligation to prevent others from interfering with an individual's right to private and family life, but this duty only extends to maintaining public safety; therefore, Art. 8 would not apply in these circumstances.

Question 4.11

CLAYTON is appearing in the Crown Court, having been charged with an offence of stirring up racial hatred under s. 18 of the Public Order Act 1986. He had displayed a picture in his shop window, indicating that he would not serve refugees. He is pleading not guilty, claiming that his human rights have been interfered with, as he is entitled to express his opinions freely.

Would CLAYTON be able to use Art. 10 of the European Convention on Human Rights (freedom of expression) as a defence in these circumstances?

A No, as his actions are probably not proportionate to the crime committed.
B Yes, every person has a right to express themselves freely.
C No, but he could use Art. 9 (freedom of thought) as a defence.
D Yes, provided he held a genuine belief that his rights had been interfered with.

Question 4.12

The Westford anti-hunt lobby arranged a demonstration outside a farm where a fox hunt was being organised. The organisers of the hunt arranged for marshals to be present and the local police were also in attendance. Demonstrators protested peacefully in the road nearby but, on the instructions of the hunt organisers, the marshals attempted to move the protestors away from the scene. The demonstrators felt intimidated by the marshals, but the police did nothing.

In these circumstances, do the police officers at the scene appear to have infringed Art. 11 of the European Convention on Human Rights (freedom of assembly and association)?

A No, as they have not interfered with the rights of the protestors or the members of the hunt.
B Yes, they should have stopped the protest; it breached the rights of the hunters and the farm owner.
C Yes, they had a duty to prevent the unlawful interference with the rights of the protestors by the marshals.
D No, they would have a duty to act only if public order offences were imminent.

Question 4.13

HAWKINS and GREER are in a same-sex relationship and have sought legal advice about in incident that occurred recently. HAWKINS works for a local authority and has been selected to attend a team-building weekend at premises owned by the local authority, aimed at developing junior managers in the organisation. Staff were told that they could take partners along for the weekend and that double rooms were available for couples. When they arrived, HAWKINS and GREER were told that double rooms were only available for married couples. They are considering taking legal action against HAWKINS's employers on the grounds that they had been indirectly discriminated against due to their sexual orientation (i.e. they were unable to fulfil the criteria of being a 'married couple' as defined by the policy). They have asked their legal adviser whether or not the policy amounted to a breach of Art. 14 of the European Convention on Human Rights (prohibition of discrimination).

Which of the following statements is correct, in respect of HAWKINS and GREER's inquiry?

A The behaviour may amount to discrimination; however, Art. 14 does not extend to cases of indirect discrimination.

B The behaviour may amount to discrimination; however, Art. 14 does not extend to cases involving discrimination based on a person's sexual orientation.

C The behaviour may amount to discrimination; however, while Art. 14 *does* extend to cases of indirect discrimination, this is only applicable to a person's race, colour, language or religion.

D The behaviour may amount to discrimination and Art. 14 extends to all cases of discrimination, whether direct or indirect.

Question 4.14

PUGACH returned from working abroad to find that people were squatting in his flat. PUGACH obtained documentation from the court proving that he was a protected intending occupier, but used all his money doing so. PUGACH contacted the police, asking for assistance to remove the trespassers, but was told this was a civil matter and the police would not get involved. PUGACH tried several times over a six-month period, explaining that he had no money to go to court, but the police did not help. PUGACH eventually contacted a solicitor, who advised him that the police may have breached his human rights and that he should sue them.

Given that PUGACH was a protected intending occupier and the police *could* have used their powers under s. 7 of the Criminal Law Act 1977 to deal with the squatters, could they be in breach of Protocol 1, Art. 1 to the European Convention on Human Rights (right to enjoy possessions), in these circumstances?

A No, the police did not take possession of PUGACH's property at any time.

B Yes, the police could be liable in these circumstances.

C No, 'possessions' do not include land or premises for the purposes of this Protocol.

D No, the police cannot be held liable for a matter which is civil and not criminal.

ANSWERS

Answer 4.1

Answer **D** — Section 6(3) of the Human Rights Act 1998 states that a 'public authority' includes—

(a) a court or tribunal, and
(b) any person certain of whose functions are functions of a public nature, but does not include either House of Parliament or a person exercising functions in connection with proceedings in Parliament.

Therefore, not only are police organisations public authorities, but so are individual police officers—whether they are regular officers or special constables—and others who are employed by the police to exercise policing powers. McARTHUR *could* be a public authority under s. 6 and answer B is therefore incorrect.

There are two groups of 'public authorities'—those who are named or who are concerned solely with discharging functions of a public nature ('pure' public authorities such as the courts or the police) and those who have some public functions ('quasi-public' authorities such as security companies running prisons, prisoner escort services and government contractors). The private security company in this question would fall within the second category and by its failure to conduct an effective vetting process on McARTHUR, it would almost certainly bear some liability for failing to protect the prisoners. Answer A is therefore incorrect.

Eastshire Police would equally be responsible for what went on in its police cells and would have to explain how a member of staff was able to sexually assault drunken prisoners. It would certainly be a public authority under s. 6 and therefore answer C is incorrect.

General Police Duties, para. 4.4.3.5

Answer 4.2

Answer **C** — Under s. 7(1) of the Human Rights Act 1998, a person who claims that a public authority has acted (or proposed to act) in a way that is incompatible with his or her human rights (s. 6(1)) may bring proceedings against the authority in the appropriate court or tribunal.

In order to rely on s. 7, however, a person must first be a 'victim', and must show that he or she is either directly affected or at risk of being directly affected. Section 7 will not enable public interest groups to institute proceedings, only individuals. Therefore, answer A is incorrect.

Answer C is correct (and answer B is incorrect) because QUINN was an individual who was at risk of being directly affected (i.e. by attending the site, QUINN faced being arrested). This was confirmed in *Dudgeon v United Kingdom* (1983) 5 EHRR 573, where the petitioner was able to challenge the law proscribing consensual homosexual activity even though he had not been prosecuted under the legislation himself.

The circumstances in this question are similar to those in *R (On the application of Laporte) v Chief Constable of Gloucestershire* [2006] UKHL 55. In *Laporte* a lawful assembly had been arranged under the provisions of ss. 12 and 14 of the Public Order Act 1986 in connection with protests against the war in Iraq. As the result of a stop and search order made under s. 60 of the Criminal Justice and Public Order Act 1994, the police stopped a number of coaches en route to the lawful assembly at Fairford US Air Force base, and then escorted them back to London. Intelligence had been received that the passengers would cause disorder at the base. The Court of Appeal held that the police actions were reasonable to apprehend a breach of the peace. However, the House of Lords ruled that the police had acted unlawfully because a breach of the peace was not imminent when the coaches were stopped. This action interfered with the passengers' rights under Arts 10 (freedom of expression) and 11 (freedom of assembly and association) of the European Convention on Human Rights and therefore answer D is incorrect.

General Police Duties, paras 4.4.3.6, 4.11.2.2

Answer 4.3

Answer **A** — Section 7(5)(a) of the Human Rights Act 1998 states that proceedings under s. 7(1)(a) must generally be brought before the end of one year beginning with *the date on which the act complained of took place*, or such longer period as the court or tribunal considers equitable having regard to all the circumstances. Answers B, C and D are therefore incorrect.

General Police Duties, para. 4.4.3.6

Answer 4.4

Answer **B** — There are restrictions on police officers relying on the Convention rights in the context of recruitment *and* disciplinary procedures. Answers C and D are therefore incorrect.

The European Court of Justice regards police officers in Member States as being government servants and as such they cannot generally rely on their Convention rights against the employer (see *Pellegrin* v *France* (2001) 31 EHRR 26). Since the officer was not seeking to bring proceedings in an employment context, answer A is incorrect.

There are certain circumstances where police officers *may* be able to rely on their Convention rights, for example in *R (On the application of A and B)* v *HM Coroner for Inner South District of Greater London* [2004] EWCA Civ 1439, where the coroner refused to allow police officers to give evidence anonymously in a fatal shooting case. The Divisional Court held the risk of serious harm to the officers and their families was sufficient to engage Art. 2, and the coroner ought to have protected their anonymity.

General Police Duties, paras 4.4.3.6, 4.4.5

Answer 4.5

Answer **D** — The circumstances are similar to those in the case of *Osman* v *United Kingdom* (2000) 29 EHRR 245, where a man had been killed by a person who had become fixated with him. Although there the European Court of Human Rights dismissed the case, it examined the positive obligation of the State to protect life under Art. 2.

First, the positive obligation on the State to protect life is not an absolute one (and answer A is therefore incorrect). Other factors should be taken into consideration, such as the source and degree of danger and the means available to combat it. The court said in *Osman* that it will be enough for the applicant to show that the authorities did not do all that could reasonably be expected of them to avoid a real and immediate risk to life of which they have or ought to have knowledge. Answer B is incorrect, as there is no need to show that the State actually saw the risk and failed to act upon it. Answer C is incorrect, as the 'reasonable person' test is not mentioned in this ruling.

General Police Duties, para. 4.4.5.2

Answer 4.6

Answer **B** — In *Ireland* v *United Kingdom* (1978) 2 EHRR 25 it was held that the behaviour envisaged by Art. 3 goes far beyond the traditional image of 'torture' and its three features can be identified as having the following broad characteristics:

- torture—deliberate treatment leading to serious or cruel suffering;
- inhuman treatment—treatment resulting in intense suffering, both physical and mental;
- degrading treatment—treatment giving rise to fear and anguish in the victim, causing feelings of inferiority and humiliation.

In *Ribitsch* v *Austria* (1995) 21 EHRR 573 it was held that where an individual was alleged to have been punched and kicked by police officers and pulled along by his hair, there had been a violation of Art. 3 in the form of inhuman and degrading treatment. These cases demonstrate that Art. 3 *may* be breached by isolated physical assaults, depending on the circumstances, and therefore answer A is incorrect.

However, in a case where a French police officer kneed a prisoner, causing a ruptured testicle, the European Court of Human Rights accepted that general exceptions to criminal offences, such as self-defence, can apply (*RIVAS* v *France* (2004) Crim LR 305). Answer D is incorrect, because the circumstances in the question mirror those in *RIVAS* and this is not 'definitely' torture.

Finally, torture is a specific criminal offence under s. 134 of the Criminal Justice Act 1988; however, while that offence has a statutory defence of 'lawful authority, justification or excuse', the prohibition contained in Art. 3 is absolute. This means that Art. 3 overrules the provisions in s. 134 and not the other way around. Answer C is therefore incorrect.

General Police Duties, para. 4.4.6

Answer 4.7

Answer **B** — Under Art. 5 of the European Convention on Human Rights, every person has the right to liberty and security of person. When it comes to unauthorised entry into the country and deportation/extradition matters, a detainee is *still* afforded protection by virtue of Art. 5(1)(f). Answer D is therefore incorrect.

However, the House of Lords has ruled that unlike Art. 5(1)(c), Art. 5(1)(f) does not require the detention to be necessary to be justified (see *R (On the application of Saadi)* v *Secretary of State for the Home Department* [2002] UKHL 41).

In that case it was held that the temporary detention of asylum seekers pending their application to remain in the United Kingdom was not unlawful simply by reason of it not being necessary. Answers A and C are therefore incorrect.

In *Owalabi* v *Court Number Four at the High Court of Justice in Spain* [2005] EWHC 2849 (Admin), it was held that where a person was being extradited to Spain, the hearing was entitled to conclude that the delay of over five years between the individual's arrest and their extradition did not render the extradition unjust or oppressive. Answer C is also incorrect for this reason.

General Police Duties, paras 4.4.7, 4.4.7.7, 4.4.7.8

Answer 4.8

Answer **C** — 'Reasonable suspicion' will be assessed objectively and the court will look for 'the existence of facts or information which would satisfy an *objective observer* that the person may have committed the offence' (see *Fox* v *United Kingdom* (1991) 13 EHRR 157).

Answers A, B and D are therefore incorrect.

General Police Duties, para. 4.4.7.4

Answer 4.9

Answer **A** — Article 6(1) of the European Convention on Human Rights states that

> In the determination of his civil rights and obligations or of any criminal charge against him, everyone is entitled to a fair and public hearing within a reasonable time by an independent and impartial tribunal established by law.
>
> Judgment shall be pronounced publicly but the press and public may be excluded from all or part of the trial in the interest of morals, public order or national security in a democratic society, where the interests of juveniles or the protection of the private and family life of the parties so require, or to the extent strictly necessary in the opinion of the court in special circumstances where publicity would prejudice the interests of justice.

Since there are several reasons for determining whether a case can be heard in private, answers C and D are incorrect.

Article 6(1) does not distinguish between civil and criminal cases; therefore, answer B is incorrect.

Note that even where the press and/or the public have been excluded from all or part of the trial, the judgment must always be pronounced publicly.

General Police Duties, para. 4.4.8

Answer 4.10

Answer **B** — Article 8 of the European Convention on Human Rights states:

1. Everyone has the right to respect for his private and family life, his home and his correspondence.
2. There shall be no interference by a public authority with the exercise of this right except such as is in accordance with the law and is necessary in a democratic society in the interests of national security, public safety or the economic wellbeing of the country, for the prevention of disorder or crime, for the protection of health or morals, or for the protection of the rights and freedoms of others.

The provisions of Art. 8 extend a right to respect for a person's correspondence (as well as their private life, family life and home). Answer C is therefore incorrect.

Whilst the main aim of the Article is to protect these features of a person's life from arbitrary interference by 'public authorities', the State *does* have a positive obligation to prevent others from interfering with an individual's right to his or her private and family life (see *Stjerna* v *Finland* (1994) 24 EHRR 194), and this duty extends beyond simply maintaining public safety. Answers A and D are therefore incorrect.

General Police Duties, para. 4.4.10

Answer 4.11

Answer **A** — Under Art. 10 of the European Convention on Human Rights, everyone has a right to freedom of expression. However, as with all aspects of human rights, this has to be balanced against other social needs. In the case of *Hutchinson* v *DPP* The Independent, 20 November 2000, a conviction for criminal damage was upheld when it was decided that there were other ways in which the defendant could have expressed her opinions without committing a crime. Answer B is incorrect for this reason.

Because his actions were probably not proportionate, CLAYTON would not be able to use Art. 9 as a 'shield' for the same reasons noted previously (making answer C incorrect).

A person's belief, no matter how genuine, that his or her rights had been interfered with, will not provide an automatic defence to a criminal offence if that belief is not proportionate to the crime committed. Answer D is therefore incorrect.

General Police Duties, para. 4.4.11

Answer 4.12

Answer **C** — Under Art. 11 of the European Convention on Human Rights, everyone has the right to freedom of peaceful assembly. Therefore, the protestors had the right to protest, provided they were going about it peacefully. They do not appear to have interfered with the rights of the members of the hunt or the farm owner on these facts. Answer B is incorrect for this reason.

The State (or public authority) has two main obligations in these circumstances. In the first instance, it must not interfere with the protestors' rights to peaceful assembly. However, equally as important, it has a positive duty to prevent others from interfering with that right (which is why answer C is correct).

Therefore, even though the officers at the scene did not actively prevent the protest, arguably they should have acted to stop the marshals from doing so (which is why answers A and D are incorrect).

General Police Duties, para. 4.4.12

Answer 4.13

Answer **A** — Article 14 of the European Convention on Human Rights states that

> The enjoyment of the rights and freedoms set forth in this Convention shall be secured without discrimination on any ground such as sex, race, colour, language, religion, political or other opinion, national or social origin, association with a national minority, property, birth or other status.

Article 14 simply provides a guarantee that access to the Convention's other provisions must be enjoyed equally by everyone under the jurisdiction of the particular State. The list set out in the Article is not exhaustive and other categories of people or grounds of discrimination may be added by the courts (and have been added by the European Court of Human Rights). It does cover a wider range of behaviour than simply discrimination based on a person's race, colour, language or religion. Answer C is therefore incorrect.

A person claiming a breach of Art. 14 must show that his/her own individual circumstances are similar to those of another person who has been treated differently in relation to the enjoyment of Convention rights.

The open-ended wording of Art. 14 means that a wide range of categories of people who can be grouped by reference to their status may be protected. That protection certainly extends to a person's sexuality (see *Mendoza* v *Ghaidan* [2004] UKHL 30). Answer B is therefore incorrect.

However, it does not make express provision for *indirect* discrimination and the Divisional Court has expressed considerable doubt as to whether Art. 14 provides protection against indirect, as opposed to direct, discrimination (see *R (On the application of Barber)* v *Secretary of State for Work and Pensions* [2002] EWHC 1915 (Admin)). Answer D is therefore incorrect.

General Police Duties, para. 4.4.13

Answer 4.14

Answer **B** — First of all, we need to examine whether PUGACH had a right of occupation of the premises. The Criminal Law Act 1977, s. 7(1), states that,

> subject to the following provisions of this section and to section 12A(9) below, any person who is on any premises as a trespasser after having entered as such is guilty of an offence if he fails to leave those premises on being required to do so by or on behalf of—
> (a) a displaced residential occupier of the premises; or
> (b) an individual who is a protected intending occupier of the premises.

By obtaining written evidence that PUGACH was a protected intending occupier of the premises, the police could certainly have dealt with the squatters for a criminal offence.

However, this question mainly deals with whether or not PUGACH's human rights were violated by the police's failure to take action on his behalf. Protocol 1, Art. 1 to the Convention states that every natural or legal person is entitled to the peaceful enjoyment of his possessions.

An example of how this right might be used against a public authority can be seen in *AO* v *Italy* (2001) 29 EHRR CD 92. In that case the Italian police were held to have violated the applicant's right to peaceful enjoyment of his property when they continually failed to send any officers to his flat, which he was trying to repossess from squatters. This case shows that this right can be violated even in circumstances where the police have no direct contact with an individual's property (and answer A is therefore incorrect).

Although the action for repossession in *AO* v *Italy* had been going on for over four years, the case also illustrates one way in which private law matters can become issues of liability for public authorities such as police services. Answer D is therefore incorrect.

Finally, this Protocol *does* cover premises and the term 'possessions' can be interpreted very widely and, under European case law, has extended to land, contractual rights and intellectual property. Answer C is therefore incorrect.

General Police Duties, paras 4.4.15, 4.15.8.4

5 | Powers of Arrest (including Code G Codes of Practice) and Other Policing Powers

STUDY PREPARATION

The areas covered in this chapter could hardly be more important. In practical terms, this chapter contains the police officer's tool kit—and if it is relevant in practice, it is highly relevant in preparing for an examination or course of study.

In deciding what to do in any given situation, it is vital that you know what you are *empowered* to do. Following on from the previous chapter, it is also important to realise that each police power equals a reduction of, or interference with, someone's human rights. As holders of such powers, police officers are under a duty to exercise them properly—lawfully, proportionately and fairly.

An understanding of s. 24 of PACE and Code G of the PACE Codes of Practice is critical for operational officers, in respect of what constitutes a lawful arrest and when an arrest is 'necessary'.

QUESTIONS

Question 5.1

Constable HORNER was on patrol when she came across a large group of people outside a pub. The people were talking loudly and the officer approached them. Constable HORNER established that MINTON, who was standing amongst the group, had been arguing with another person and although no violence had been used,

MINTON was in an agitated state. Constable HORNER turned away from the group to call for back-up and while she was waiting for colleagues to arrive, she was struck on the back of her head. Constable NEARY was first to arrive on the scene and found Constable HORNER on the floor, conscious, but with a head injury. The group of people was still present, but they refused to say who had assaulted Constable HORNER; the officer was unable to identify the person herself. Constable NEARY decided to arrest MINTON to prevent a breach of the peace, with a view to seeking CCTV evidence relating to the assault on Constable HORNER.

Was Constable NEARY's arrest of MINTON lawful in the circumstances?

A Yes, provided the officer had reasonable grounds for suspecting that MINTON had actually committed the substantive offence.

B Yes, while the officer sought reasonable grounds for suspecting that MINTON had committed the substantive offence.

C No, arresting a person for a 'holding' offence would be deemed unlawful.

D No, the officer should have arrested MINTON formally for the offence of assault, otherwise the case would fail in court.

Question 5.2

PERRY entered a large retail clothing shop and whilst being watched by IQBAL, a store detective, PERRY hid a pair of jeans in her carrier bag. PERRY left the store without paying and was stopped outside by IQBAL. IQBAL decided that it was necessary to arrest PERRY for theft.

Does IQBAL have to inform PERRY of the grounds for the arrest, under s. 28 of the Police and Criminal Evidence Act 1984?

A Yes, unless it is made impracticable by her escaping arrest before the information could be given.

B No, IQBAL would only have to inform PERRY of the fact that she was under arrest.

C No, s. 28 applies to police officers only.

D Yes, unless it is impracticable due to her condition or behaviour.

Question 5.3

Constable POTTER was called to a domestic disturbance at the home of HENDERSON and LeBOW. On the officer's arrival, HENDERSON was shouting loudly at LeBOW and making threats. Constable POTTER arrested HENDERSON for a breach of the peace and HENDERSON began struggling violently. Constable POTTER later recorded the facts in a pocket notebook, noting that HENDERSON had not been cautioned at the time of the arrest because of the violent struggle.

Which of the following statements is correct in relation to the requirement to caution a person, according to the PACE Codes of Practice?

A There was a requirement for Constable POTTER to caution HENDERSON because she was not cautioned immediately before the arrest.

B There was no requirement for Constable POTTER to caution HENDERSON at the time of arrest, because she was not being arrested for an offence.

C Constable POTTER was required to caution HENDERSON at the time of arrest, because she was not in the process of escaping from the officer.

D There was no requirement for Constable POTTER to caution HENDERSON at the time of arrest, because of her behaviour; however, the officer was required to caution her as soon as practicable afterwards.

Question 5.4

DOWNEY worked as a security guard in a shopping centre and saw FENTON walking towards the public car park outside. It was clear to DOWNEY that FENTON was drunk from the way she was staggering. DOWNEY saw FENTON approach a car with the keys in her hand and decided to detain her, before she could drive the vehicle. DOWNEY made a 'citizen's arrest' on FENTON as she stood alongside the car and then contacted the police on his mobile phone.

Did DOWNEY have the power to arrest FENTON in these circumstances?

A Yes, provided it was not reasonably practicable for a constable to make the arrest instead.

B No, a member of the public only has the power to arrest a person to prevent a person from committing an indictable offence.

C Yes, regardless of whether there was a constable available to make the arrest instead.

D No, a member of the public only has the power to arrest a person when an indictable offence is being committed, or has been committed.

Question 5.5

Constable FRENCH, an officer from Dumfries and Galloway Constabulary, was pursuing a vehicle which was stolen from the Dumfries and Galloway Constabulary area. The vehicle crossed the Scottish border into Cumbria Constabulary's area, in England, where it eventually stopped. Before officers from Cumbria Constabulary arrived at the scene, Constable FRENCH arrested the driver, KELLEY.

What action should now be taken, in respect of KELLEY?

A KELLEY must be taken to the nearest designated station in Scotland, where the original offence took place.

B KELLEY must be taken to the nearest designated station in England, where the arrest took place.

C KELLEY must be taken to the nearest designated station in Scotland or to the nearest designated police station in England.

D KELLEY should be further arrested by an officer from Cumbria Constabulary and be taken to the nearest designated station in England.

Question 5.6

DC SHARPE was interviewing HUNTER for a burglary. The officer suspected that HUNTER had committed more than one burglary, but only had reasonable grounds to arrest him for the one offence. In the interview, HUNTER provided DC SHARPE with reasonable grounds to suspect he should be arrested for two other offences. At that time, the officer made a decision that HUNTER would be further arrested for those offences, but not until after the interview. HUNTER was actually arrested for the further offences two hours after the interview concluded.

Considering s. 31 of the Police and Criminal Evidence Act 1984, which of the following statements is correct in relation to the timing of HUNTER's arrest?

A HUNTER should have been arrested when DC SHARPE had reasonable grounds to suspect him of further offences; the officer has acted unlawfully.

B HUNTER should have been arrested when DC SHARPE made the decision to arrest him for the further offences; the officer has acted unlawfully.

C HUNTER should have been arrested before the end of the interview; the officer has acted unlawfully.

D DC SHARPE has acted lawfully; there was no requirement to arrest HUNTER before the officer did so.

Question 5.7

Constable SHAW was searching in the vicinity of a recent burglary, when she saw CARSON, who matched the description of the suspect. The officer arrested CARSON and radioed for transport. While they were waiting, CARSON told Constable SHAW that he could not have committed the burglary, as he was at home at the time. The transport was being driven by SANTOS, a designated escort officer. Constable SHAW asked SANTOS to take CARSON to his home address, while she attended there in her own vehicle, to check out his alibi. There was no reply at the address and SANTOS then took CARSON to the station.

Which of the following statements is correct in relation to s. 30(10) of the Police and Criminal Evidence Act 1984 (delay in taking an arrested person to a police station)?

A The delay in taking CARSON to the station was unlawful; SANTOS only has the authority to convey a person directly to a police station.

B The delay in taking CARSON to the station was lawful, provided the investigation into his alibi was conducted immediately.

C The delay in taking CARSON to the station was lawful, provided the investigation into his alibi was conducted as soon as reasonably practicable.

D The delay in taking CARSON to the station was unlawful; checking out an alibi would not amount to an 'investigation' as permitted under s. 30.

Question 5.8

Inspector TORRES is working a night shift and has been informed that the custody officer has reported sick. Inspector TORRES has made inquiries with neighbouring areas but no other sergeants are available to act as custody officer. There are five detainees in the cells. Inspector TORRES has asked Constable AVERY to return to the station urgently to act as custody officer. Constable AVERY is an experienced officer and is qualified to the rank of sergeant.

Has Inspector TORRES acted correctly by requiring Constable AVERY to act as the custody officer?

A Yes, as no other custody officer is available.

B No, Inspector TORRES should contact a superintendent, who may authorise Constable AVERY to act as custody officer.

C No, the custody office should be closed down and the detainees transferred to another custody office, as no other sergeant is available.

D Yes, provided no superintendent is available to make the decision and a custody officer is required urgently.

Question 5.9

SPEARS is aged 14 and has been issued with a disorder penalty notice under s. 2 of the Criminal Justice and Police Act 2001 for throwing fireworks on a main road.

Who would be liable for paying the fine attached to such a notice; should SPEARS accept liability for this offence?

A SPEARS only, as the person responsible for the offence.

B SPEARS's parent or guardian, because of her age.

C Either SPEARS or her parent or guardian.

D Neither SPEARS nor her parent or guardian; she should not have been issued with a notice because of her age.

Question 5.10

Magistrates have issued a warrant under s. 135(1) of the Mental Health Act 1983 in relation to SHORT, whose family has been concerned that his mental health has deteriorated significantly recently. The warrant authorises SHORT to be removed to a place of safety.

Which of the following statements is correct, in relation to the execution of the warrant issued by the court?

A The warrant must be executed by a constable, who must be accompanied either by a mental health professional or a registered medical practitioner.

B The warrant must be executed either by a mental health professional or a registered medical practitioner, who may ask for a constable to be present if there is reason to believe SHORT may become violent.

C The warrant may be executed either by a constable or a mental health professional, who must be accompanied by a registered medical practitioner.

D The warrant must be executed by a constable, who must be accompanied by a mental health professional and a registered medical practitioner.

Question 5.11

Constable TOWNSEND has attended single-crewed to assist LIANG, a mental health professional, and BAIG, a registered medical practitioner. The officer has been asked to assist in executing a warrant under s. 135(1) of the Mental Health Act 1983 in relation to PHELPS, whose mental health has caused some concern recently. They were granted access to PHELPS's home by a family member and Constable TOWNSEND assisted in taking him outside to a waiting vehicle; however, without any warning, PHELPS escaped before being placed securely inside. Constable TOWNSEND gave chase but lost sight of PHELPS in a busy shopping centre. Some four hours later, PHELPS was seen on CCTV walking along the High Street and officers are making their way to the scene.

Which of the following statements is correct, in relation to re-taking PHELPS under s. 138 of the Mental Health Act 1983?

A Because the warrant has been executed, the police will only have the power to remove PHELPS to a place of safety under the power of a new warrant.

B The police will have the power to remove PHELPS to a place of safety in these circumstances without a warrant.

C The police will have the power to remove PHELPS to a place of safety in these circumstances under the power of the existing warrant, which has not yet been executed.

D Because PHELPS was detained under a warrant, officers will have to apply the principles of s. 136(1) if they are to remove PHELPS to a place of safety.

Question 5.12

PCSO DALTON was on patrol when she was approached by HOUGHTON who came out of a nearby house. HOUGHTON asked her for assistance—she had been visiting her brother who lived in the house and stated that he suffered from severe alcohol problems. Her brother had fallen over in the house and cut his head; he was conscious but bleeding heavily. HOUGHTON had called 999, but had been told that there would be a delay in an ambulance attending; she wanted to take him to hospital herself but he was refusing. PCSO DALTON walked to the front door with HOUGHTON and could see her brother in the hallway. When he saw her, HOUGHTON's brother started shouting, 'Get her away from my house, I'm not going anywhere.' He was covered in blood and the head wound appeared to be serious. PCSO DALTON wanted to enter the house and help HOUGHTON take her brother to the hospital, because she believed it was in his best interests.

Considering powers under the Mental Capacity Act 2005, which of the following statements is correct?

A PCSO DALTON could enter the house in order to help remove HOUGHTON's brother to the hospital.

B PCSO DALTON could not enter the house in order to remove HOUGHTON's brother unless she was accompanied by a police officer.

C PCSO DALTON does not have the authority to enter the house for the purposes of this Act; only a police officer would be able to do so in these circumstances.

D Neither PCSO DALTON nor any police officer could deal with HOUGHTON's brother under this Act because he is not in a public place; the officer attending must use powers under s. 17(1) of PACE (entry to save life or limb).

Question 5.13

Constable ROBERTS attended a large retail store, where the occupants of a green 4×4 vehicle had been captured on closed circuit television (CCTV) as they entered the store and stole two bottles of wine from within. The vehicle was seen to make off immediately prior to Constable ROBERTS's arrival. Constable ROBERTS contacted the control room and asked the duty sergeant to authorise an urgent road check, under s. 4 of the Police and Criminal Evidence Act 1984, for the vehicle and its occupants.

Can the officer's request be granted in these circumstances?

A Yes, but Constable ROBERTS could have authorised the road check himself.

B Yes, provided the sergeant authorises it.

C No, only an inspector may authorise a road check in urgent circumstances.

D No, only a superintendent may authorise a road check in any circumstances.

Question 5.14

Superintendent HAYES has provided written authorisation for a road check to take place. Officers in Superintendent HAYES's area are investigating a case of causing death by dangerous driving and the suspect was believed to have driven away from the scene without stopping in a red Nissan motor vehicle. The superintendent has authorised that all red vehicles of a similar size and colour are to be stopped at the location of the incident, at the approximate time of day, for the next seven days. No useful information was gleaned during the initial period of seven days and the officer in the case has asked Superintendent HAYES to extend the period.

If Superintendent HAYES agrees to extend this period, what would be the maximum period that may be granted beyond the initial seven days?

A One further period of seven days.

B Two further periods of seven days.

C Three further periods of seven days, to a maximum period of 28 days.

D Unlimited period, provided the authorisations are for seven days at a time.

Question 5.15

Detective Constables COPE and FRIEDEL received information from NEWMAN, a security guard at a private flying club based in a small airport, who suspected the importation of drugs was taking place. NEWMAN stated that every Saturday morning, a car attended the club and met a light aircraft and people loaded packages into the car. They tasked NEWMAN to keep an eye out and one Saturday, NEWMAN called them, reporting the car was at the airport. On their arrival, they saw WILLARD standing near the suspected car.

What powers, if any, did the officers have to search WILLARD or the car, in these circumstances, utilising powers under s. 24B of the Aviation Security Act 1982?

A None, they were not in uniform.
B None, the power relates to searching aircraft only.
C They may search WILLARD and the vehicle.
D None, this Act relates to commercial airports, not private ones.

ANSWERS

Answer 5.1

Answer **A** — The practice of arresting someone on a 'holding' offence was accepted by the Court of Appeal in *R* v *Chalkley* [1998] QB 848 *provided the arresting officers had reasonable grounds for suspecting that the person had actually committed that offence.* If that suspicion is present then the fact that the officers making the arrest are doing so with the intention of investigating another, more serious offence does not render the arrest unlawful. If, however, there are no such grounds to suspect that the person had in fact committed the offence, or the officers know at the time of the arrest that there is no possibility of the person actually being charged with it, the arrest will be unlawful. Therefore, while Constable NEARY was entitled to arrest MINTON to prevent a breach of the peace, it would not be lawful to do so to allow the officer to *seek* reasonable grounds for suspecting the person: the reasonable grounds for suspicion must be present before the arrest takes place. Answers B and C are therefore incorrect.

The Divisional Court has held that, where officers who had arrested a man for a breach of the peace failed to arrest him formally for the further offence of assault on the police, their omission did not impact on the magistrates' decision that there was a case to answer in respect of the assault charge (*Blench* v *DPP* [2004] EWHC 2717 (Admin)). Answer D is therefore incorrect.

General Police Duties, paras 4.5.2, 4.5.10

Answer 5.2

Answer **A** — Section 28(1) of the Police and Criminal Evidence Act 1984 states that subject to subs. (5), where a person is arrested, otherwise than by being informed that he or she is under arrest, the arrest is not lawful unless the person arrested is informed that he or she is under arrest as soon as is practicable after his or her arrest.

Under s. 28(3), subject to subs. (5), no arrest is lawful unless the person arrested is informed of the ground for the arrest at the time of, or as soon as is practicable after, the arrest. This subsection applies to arrests made by members of the public as well as police officers; therefore, answers B and C are incorrect.

Section 28(5) states that nothing in this section is to be taken to require a person to be informed—

(a) that he or she is under arrest; or
(b) of the ground for the arrest,

if it was not reasonably practicable for him or her to be so informed by reason of his or her having escaped from arrest before the information could be given.

Answer D is therefore incorrect.

General Police Duties, para. 4.5.2.1

Answer 5.3

Answer **B** — Code C, para. 10.4 of the PACE Codes of Practice requires that a person must be cautioned on arrest or further arrest. There are exceptions to the requirement to administer the caution and these are

* where it is impracticable to do so by reason of the person's condition or behaviour at the time; or
* where he/she has already been cautioned immediately before the arrest in accordance with Code C, para. 10.1 (requirement to caution where there are grounds to suspect commission of an offence).

However, consideration also needs to be given to Code G, para. 4, Note for Guidance 1A, which states that the Code will not apply where a person is being arrested for a warrant or other matters, such as a breach of bail. It also states that the Code does not apply when a person is being arrested under a common law power to stop or prevent a breach of the peace. The caution should be given if it is intended to question a person about an 'offence' and since this is not a requirement for an arrest which is meant to simply place a person before the court, a caution is not required regardless of any other exceptions in Code C. Answers A and C are therefore incorrect.

Section 28(5) of PACE allows that a person need not be informed of the reason or grounds for their arrest if it was not reasonably practicable by reason of his/her having escaped from arrest before the information could be given. However, this exception is not listed in Code C, para. 10.4, which relates to cautions. Answer C is incorrect for this reason also.

There is nothing in Code C requiring a person to be cautioned as soon as practicable after their arrest, if they were not cautioned at the time, and therefore answer D is incorrect.

General Police Duties, paras 4.5.4.1, 4.5.5

Answer 5.4

Answer **D** — Under s. 24A of the Police and Criminal Evidence Act 1984 certain powers of arrest are provided for any person. Section 24A states:

(1) A person other than a constable may arrest without a warrant—
  (a) anyone who is in the act of committing an indictable offence;
  (b) anyone whom he has reasonable grounds for suspecting to be committing an indictable offence.
(2) Where an indictable offence has been committed, a person other than a constable may arrest without a warrant—
  (a) anyone who is guilty of the offence;
  (b) anyone whom he has reasonable grounds for suspecting to be guilty of it.
(3) But the power of summary arrest conferred by subsection (1) or (2) is exercisable only if—
  (a) the person making the arrest has reasonable grounds for believing that for any of the reasons mentioned in subsection (4) it is necessary to arrest the person in question; and
  (b) it appears to the person making the arrest that it is not reasonably practicable for a constable to make it instead.
(4) The reasons are to prevent the person in question—
  (a) causing physical injury to himself or any other person;
  (b) suffering physical injury;
  (c) causing loss of or damage to property; or
  (d) making off before a constable can assume responsibility for him.

Section 24A(4)(d) of PACE does allow a member of the public to make a 'citizen's' arrest, where it is not reasonably practicable for a constable to make it instead; however, unlike the powers of arrest available to police officers (which apply to all offences), the 'citizen's' power of arrest only applies where the relevant offence is *indictable*. Answers A and C are therefore incorrect.

Under s. 24A, a person other than a constable may make such an arrest when an arrestable offence *is* being committed, or *has* been committed; the power to make a preventative arrest (i.e. where an indictable offence is *about* to be committed) only applies to police officers. Answer B is therefore incorrect.

General Police Duties, para. 4.5.7

Answer 5.5

Answer **C** — The Criminal Justice and Public Order Act 1994 (ss. 136 to 140) makes provision for officers from one part of the United Kingdom to go into another part of the United Kingdom to arrest someone there in connection with an offence committed within their jurisdiction, and gives them powers to search on arrest.

A Scottish officer may arrest someone suspected of committing an offence in Scotland who is found in England, Wales or Northern Ireland if it would have been lawful to arrest that person had he or she been found in Scotland. Since this power is granted to Constable FRENCH, there is no requirement for an officer from an English police force to further arrest KELLEY and therefore answer D is incorrect.

Where a Scottish officer has arrested someone suspected of committing an offence in Scotland, who is found in England, the officer must take the person to the nearest convenient designated police station in Scotland *or* to the nearest convenient designated police station in England or Wales (see s. 137(7)).

Section 137(7) goes on to say that the person must be taken to the police station as soon as reasonably practicable. This would suggest that the arrested person should be taken to the nearest police station if the distance to one or another is too great. Since the arresting officer has a choice of police stations, answers A and B are incorrect.

General Police Duties, para. 4.5.8.5

Answer 5.6

Answer **D** — Section 31 of the Police and Criminal Evidence Act 1984 states that where:

(a) a person—
   (i) has been arrested for an offence; and
   (ii) is at a police station in consequence of that arrest; and
(b) it appears to a constable that, if he were released from that arrest, he would be liable to arrest for some other offence,
he shall be arrested for that other offence.

In *R v Samuel* [1988] QB 615, the Court of Appeal said that the purpose of the s. 31 requirement was to prevent the release and immediate rearrest of an offender—therefore, the court noted, s. 31 did not prevent any further arrest from being delayed until the release of the prisoner for the initial arrest was imminent.

Therefore, there was no requirement to arrest HUNTER at any time before he was actually arrested. The only obligation under s. 31 is that the person should not be released from police detention and then rearrested, when there were sufficient grounds to arrest him/her before he or she was released. Answers A, B and C are therefore incorrect.

General Police Duties, para. 4.5.10

Answer 5.7

Answer **B** — Section 30(10) of the Police and Criminal Evidence Act 1984 allows a police officer to delay taking an arrested person to a police station where his/her presence elsewhere is necessary in order to carry out such investigations as it is reasonable to carry out *immediately*. This was confirmed in the case of *R* v *Kerawalla* [1991] Crim LR 451, when it was decided that the delay permitted under s. 30(10) will only apply if the matter requires *immediate* investigation; if it can wait, the exception will not apply and the person must be taken straight to a police station. Therefore, answer C is incorrect.

The provisions allowing a delay in taking the prisoner to a police station (s. 30(10)) will also apply to any exercise of the powers by a designated escort officer (see the Police Reform Act 2002, sch. 4, pt 4). Answer A is therefore incorrect.

Taking an arrested person to check out an alibi before going to a police station may be justified in some circumstances (see *Dallison* v *Caffery* [1965] 1 QB 348). Answer D is therefore incorrect.

Note that where there is such a delay, the reasons for it must be recorded when the person first arrives at the police station (s. 30(11)).

General Police Duties, para. 4.5.11

Answer 5.8

Answer **A** — Under s. 36(3) of the Police and Criminal Evidence Act 1984, custody officers must be appointed and be of at least the rank of sergeant.

However, under s. 36(4), an officer of any rank may perform the functions of a custody officer at a designated police station if a custody officer is not readily available to perform them. The case of *Vince* v *Chief Constable of Dorset Police* [1993] 1 WLR 415, made it clear that this should only be an exception. Answer C is therefore incorrect.

There is nothing in s. 36(4) stating that a person performing the function in these circumstances must be authorised (whether by an inspector or a superintendent). Answers B and D are therefore incorrect.

General Police Duties, para. 4.5.13

Answer 5.9

Answer **B** — Under s. 2 of the Act, a disorder penalty notice may be issued to a person who is 10 years or over, where there is reason to believe the person has committed a s. 1 offence (previously the age limit was 16 years). Answer D is therefore incorrect.

Where the recipient of a notice is under 16, the relevant chief officer of police must notify such parent or guardian as he/she sees fit (see Penalties for Disorderly

Behaviour (Amendment of Minimum Age) Order 2004 (SI 2004/3166)). Where a parent or guardian of a young penalty recipient is notified in this way, then they are liable to pay the penalty under the original notice (see art. 5). Answers A and C are therefore incorrect.

General Police Duties, paras 4.5.14, 4.5.14.2

Answer 5.10

Answer **D** — Under s. 135(1) of the Mental Health Act 1983, where there is reasonable cause to suspect that a person believed to be suffering from a mental disorder—

(a) has been, or is being ill-treated or neglected, or
(b) is unable to care for himself/herself and is living alone,

a warrant may be issued by a magistrate authorising a *constable* to enter any premises specified and to remove the person to a place of safety. Answers B and C are therefore incorrect.

In doing so, the officer *must* be accompanied by an approved mental health professional and a registered medical practitioner. Answer A is therefore incorrect.

General Police Duties, para. 4.5.15.2

Answer 5.11

Answer **B** — Section 138 of the Mental Health Act 1983 provides a power to re-take people who have been in legal custody under the 1983 Act, who subsequently escape while being taken to or detained in a place of safety. This power applies whether or not the person was removed to a place of safety under s. 136 or whether they were removed under a warrant (under s. 135). Also, this will be a simple matter of detaining the person because he or she has escaped—there is no requirement to consider whether the principles of s. 136(1) apply in the circumstances. Answer D is therefore incorrect.

There is no requirement for the police to utilise powers under the existing warrant, or apply for a new warrant, and therefore answers A and C are incorrect.

Note, there is also a power for a court to issue a warrant for the arrest of a convicted mental patient who is unlawfully at large (Criminal Justice Act 1967, s. 72(3)), but this is not applicable in these circumstances.

General Police Duties, para. 4.5.15.3

Answer 5.12

Answer **A** — Section 5 of the Mental Capacity Act 2005, states:

(1) If a person (D) does an act in connection with the care or treatment of another person (P), the act is one to which this section applies if—
    (a) before doing the act, D takes reasonable steps to establish whether P lacks capacity in relation to the matter in question, and
    (b) when doing the act, D reasonably believes—
        (i) that P lacks clarity in relation to the matter and
        (ii) that it will be in P's best interests for the act to be done.
(2) D does not incur any liability in relation to the act that he would not have incurred if P—
    (a) had had capacity to consent in relation to the matter, and
    (b) had consented to D's doing the act.

The Act was brought into force to provide a statutory framework to empower and protect vulnerable people who are not able to make their own decisions. Importantly, it can provide police officers with a power to act in a person's best interests, effectively as if they had the person's consent. However, the power is not just given to police officers but to *anyone* acting in the person's best interests. This would include PCSO DALTON or any other person (although you would anticipate the PSCO calling a police officer to the scene to assist). Answers B, C and D are incorrect for this reason.

There is no mention in s. 5 as to *where* the power may be exercised; therefore, it has to be assumed that it may be utilised anywhere. Similarly, the section does not mention whether or not the person assisting has a power to enter premises—therefore, provided the person is doing an act *in connection with the care or treatment of another person*, their actions will be lawful under s. 5. Answers B, C and D are also incorrect for this reason.

General Police Duties, para. 4.5.15.5

Answer 5.13

Answer **A** — Section 4 of the Police and Criminal Evidence Act 1984 states that a road check may be authorised only where the officer has reasonable grounds for believing that the offence committed is an indictable offence. Therefore, as the offence is one of shoplifting, which is indictable, a road check can be authorised. Generally speaking an officer of at least the rank of superintendent must authorise a road check.

In urgent cases the authorising officer may be any rank below the rank of superintendent, and in this case Constable ROBERTS could have authorised the check provided a written record is made and a superintendent informed as soon as possible; answers B, C and D are therefore incorrect as the officer could have authorised the road check himself.

General Police Duties, para. 4.5.16

Answer 5.14

Answer **D** — Section 4 of the Police and Criminal Evidence Act 1984 states that a road check may be authorised only where the officer has reasonable grounds for believing that the offence committed is an indictable offence. Generally the authorisation will be given by a superintendent; however, an officer of any rank may authorise the road check in urgent circumstances.

Section 4(11)(a) states that the authorising officer must specify a period, not exceeding seven days, during which the road check may continue. This period may be either continuous, or conducted at specified times during that period. If it appears to a superintendent that the road check ought to continue beyond the initial seven days, he/she may authorise a further period of seven days during which it may continue. There is no limit as to how many road checks may be authorised, provided each period does not exceed seven days. Answers A, B and C are therefore incorrect.

General Police Duties, para. 4.5.16.1

Answer 5.15

Answer **C** — Under s. 24B of the Aviation Security Act 1982 (policing of airports or aerodromes), a police constable may stop and search, without warrant, any person, vehicle or aircraft in any area of an airport (excluding a dwelling house). Answer B is therefore incorrect.

The search may be conducted if the constable has reasonable grounds to suspect that he or she will find stolen or prohibited articles. There is no mention of the constable having to be in uniform; therefore, answer A is incorrect.

The term aerodrome, as defined by s. 38(1) of the 1982 Act, is used rather than airport, as it has a wider meaning and covers major airports as well as airfields used only by private flying clubs. Answer D is incorrect.

General Police Duties, para. 4.5.17

6 Stop and Search

STUDY PREPARATION

One of the main functions of the police service is to prevent and detect crime. A key power given to police officers is the ability to stop and search individuals, or the vehicles they are in, to establish whether they are in possession of articles which are either stolen, or which may be used to commit crimes.

The police service has for years struggled to strike a balance between a pro-active approach to the use of these powers for these reasons, and a proportionate response to the needs of our diverse communities.

The Police and Criminal Evidence Act 1984 (PACE) and the accompanying Codes of Practice provide the main legislative basis for police officers' use of stop and search powers; it is for line managers to ensure that they are used proportionately and in a non-discriminatory manner.

This chapter also covers the extended search powers available under the Criminal Justice and Public Order Act 1994 and the Aviation Security Act 1982.

QUESTIONS

Question 6.1

Constable GUTHRIE was on patrol on a night shift when observations were passed for a vehicle which had just been stolen in the vicinity. Constable GUTHRIE was aware that stolen vehicles were suspected of being taken to a derelict house in the neighbourhood, owned by MENCE. The intelligence suggested that MENCE did not live at the house, but stored the stolen vehicles at the location overnight, returning the following day to collect them. Constable GUTHRIE drove directly to the suspect house and on arrival saw that it was clearly unoccupied. The dwelling was surrounded by a high wall, but by climbing to the top, the officer could see two vehicles in the garden. Constable GUTHRIE identified one as the stolen vehicle, but there were no keeper details for the second one. The officer decided to search the second vehicle, believing it belonged to MENCE, for articles that could have been used to take the stolen vehicle.

Would Constable GUTHRIE have been entitled to search the second vehicle in these circumstances?

A No, because the vehicle was in the garden of a dwelling.

B Yes, because MENCE did not reside at the premises.

C No, because the premises were owned by MENCE, even though the suspect did not reside there.

D Yes, because MENCE, the owner of the dwelling, was not present on the premises.

Question 6.2

Constable TALLAC was on patrol when he heard a message on his radio describing a male person who had broken into a car. The description had been given by an anonymous caller to the control room. Constable TALLAC saw PEARSON walking along the street and realised that his clothing was similar to that of the person described in the radio message. Constable TALLAC intended stopping PEARSON in order to search him for prohibited articles.

Would Constable TALLAC be entitled to search PEARSON, based on the information from the radio message alone?

A No, anonymous information would not provide reasonable grounds for suspicion to conduct the search.

B Yes, provided a reasonable person would think that there were reasonable grounds for suspicion to conduct the search.

C No, the anonymous information would amount to hearsay, which would not provide reasonable grounds for suspicion to conduct the search.

D Yes, regardless of whether a reasonable person would think that there were reasonable grounds for suspicion to conduct the search.

Question 6.3

Constable HOLT was on patrol in a neighbourhood which is renowned for gangs of young people being involved in dealing drugs. As a member of the Neighbourhood Policing Team, Constable HOLT was aware that one of the main gangs in the area wore distinctive blue hoodies with a target on the rear of the garment as a means of their identification. The officer saw a group of young people outside a leisure centre, which was the usual location for dealing in the area, wearing clothing that identified them as part of the gang. Constable HOLT called for the assistance of other officers to approach the individuals and conduct a stop search.

A stop and search under s. 1 of PACE generally requires the officer to have 'reasonable grounds' to stop and search a person. Would the distinctive clothing the gang is wearing provide such grounds?

A No, the reasonable grounds cannot be based on generalisations or stereotypical images of certain groups, such as wearing distinctive clothing.

B Yes, the distinctive clothing may provide Constable HOLT with the reasonable grounds for a search.

C Yes, the distinctive clothing would automatically provide Constable HOLT with the reasonable grounds to search all people wearing such clothing.

D No, the reasonable grounds can be based on personal factors, such as wearing distinctive clothing, but only if Constable HOLT anticipates discovering offensive weapons or other dangerous instruments.

Question 6.4

A football match is due to take place in Inspector CARTER's area, and she is the officer in charge of a support unit positioned outside the train station. Intelligence has suggested that approximately 200 away supporters will be arriving, and staff on the train have reported seeing several weapons being carried by fans. Inspector CARTER is considering searching all supporters before they leave the train station.

In relation to the powers to authorise searches under s. 60 of the Criminal Justice and Public Order Act 1994, which statement is correct?

A The inspector may authorise the searches, but only if she suspects there will be incidents involving serious violence.

B The inspector may authorise the searches, but only of those suspected of carrying weapons.

C The inspector may authorise the search of any of the fans, in these circumstances alone.

D The inspector may not authorise the searches; this power is restricted to superintendents.

Question 6.5

An authorisation is in place in a Eastshire Police area under s. 60 of the Criminal Justice and Public Order Act 1994. There were serious riots and looting on the Friday night when the authorisation was granted. On the Saturday night, intelligence suggests that further riots will take place over the whole weekend and into the following week, with gang members carrying knives and other weapons. Superintendent LEACH is the senior officer in charge of policing for the area and is considering whether or not the s. 60 authorisation should be extended.

In relation to such an extension, which of the following statements is correct?

A Superintendent LEACH may extend the authorisation period, for up to seven days, depending on the intelligence.

B Superintendent LEACH may extend the authorisation period once, for 24 hours; further use of the powers would require a new authorisation.

C Superintendent LEACH may extend the authorisation period for 24 hours; further extensions may take place for 24-hour periods, up to a maximum of seven days.

D Superintendent LEACH may extend the authorisation period twice, for two 24-hour periods; further use of the powers would require a new authorisation.

Question 6.6

Constable WILLIS was on patrol in uniform in the early hours of the morning in an area where there had recently been outbreaks of serious public disorder between two gangs, who were known to carry weapons. An order was in force, under s. 60 of the Criminal Justice and Public Order Act 1994, to stop and search persons in the locality. Constable WILLIS saw MOORE walking in the street wearing a ski mask, which was concealing his face.

In what circumstances could Constable WILLIS ask MOORE to remove his mask?

A If he reasonably believed that MOORE was likely to be involved in violence.

B No further circumstances are required, as an order is in force under s. 60.

C If he reasonably believed that MOORE was attempting to conceal his identity.

D If he reasonably believed that MOORE was carrying a dangerous instrument or an offensive weapon.

Question 6.7

Eastshire Constabulary control room received a report of a suspicious vehicle driving around at night. The informant stated that there were four male persons in the vehicle and that they were all wearing masks covering their faces. Constable BUNCE was on mobile patrol and heard the observations for the vehicle. Shortly afterwards, the officer spotted the vehicle and began following it. Constable BUNCE was aware that there had recently been incidents of serious public disorder in the locality and that there was an order in force, under s. 60 of the Criminal Justice and Public Order Act 1994, to stop and search persons for weapons. It was dark and Constable BUNCE could not tell whether the occupants were wearing masks or not, but the officer intended stopping the vehicle to establish if they were.

What powers would be available to Constable BUNCE under s. 60AA(1) of the Criminal Justice and Public Order Act 1994 (requirement to remove items worn for the purpose of concealing identity), in these circumstances?

A Constable BUNCE has the power to stop the vehicle under s. 60AA(1), in order to require the occupants to remove their masks.

B Constable BUNCE would have to use the general power under s. 163 of the Road Traffic Act 1988 to stop the vehicle; however, there is a power to search a vehicle for items used to conceal a person's identity under s. 60AA(1).

C Constable BUNCE has the power to stop the vehicle under s. 60AA(1), in order to require the occupants to remove their masks, or to search the vehicle for such items, if they are not wearing any.

D Constable BUNCE would have to use the general power under s. 163 of the Road Traffic Act 1988 to stop the vehicle; there is no power to search a vehicle for items used to conceal a person's identity under s. 60AA(1).

Question 6.8

Constable SAXTON stopped and searched KELLY, using powers under s. 1 of the Police and Criminal Evidence Act 1984, whilst on foot patrol in the early hours of the morning. It was the middle of winter at the time of the stop and it was pouring with rain. KELLY had been stopped previously by the police and requested that Constable SAXTON make a record of the search there and then and asked for a copy.

What does Code A, para. 3 of the Codes of Practice state, about making a written record of the search?

A Constable SAXTON must make a record at the time, if it is reasonably practicable to do so.

B Constable SAXTON must make a record at the time, unless it is wholly impracticable to do so.

C Constable SAXTON must make a record at the time; there are no exceptions.

D Constable SAXTON must make a record at the time, unless KELLY is drunk, violent or likely to become violent.

Question 6.9

Constable NORTON has arrested BLOOM for possession of Class A drugs, following a successful stop and search. BLOOM has now been taken to a designated police station and is being booked in by the custody officer.

Which of the following statements is correct, in respect of the details which must be recorded on BLOOM's custody record?

A Constable NORTON must complete a search form and make sure the details of the search are noted on BLOOM's custody record.

B Constable NORTON must complete a search form and the custody officer must make sure the details of the search are noted on BLOOM's custody record.

C Constable NORTON must make sure that the search record forms part of BLOOM's custody record; there is no requirement to complete a separate form.

D Either Constable NORTON or the custody officer may ensure that the search record forms part of BLOOM's custody record; there is no requirement to complete a separate form.

Question 6.10

Constable LIPINSKI conducted a stop and search of GRANTHAM, who was driving a motor vehicle on a road, and the vehicle itself. The officer correctly provided GRANTHAM with a copy of the stop/search form. GRANTHAM was not the owner of the vehicle and indicated that MORLING, the actual owner, would probably wish to have a copy at some stage.

Which of the following statements is correct, in relation to MORLING being allowed a copy of the stop/search record?

A If MORLING requests a copy, one should be provided within three months of the date of the search.

B MORLING is not entitled to a copy; Constable LIPINSKI has correctly supplied GRANTHAM with one as the driver of the vehicle and the person searched.

C MORLING must be provided with a copy within three months of the date of the search.

D If MORLING requests a copy, one should be provided within 12 months of the date of the search.

Question 6.11

Constable BAIRD attended a suspicious incident reported by POOLE, a closed circuit television (CCTV) operator. POOLE saw two men acting suspiciously near a 4×4 vehicle, and saw one of the men hand the other a bag of white powder. He believed the bag was placed inside the cover of the spare wheel attached to the rear door of the vehicle. As a result of this information, Constable BAIRD searched the spare wheel, but found nothing inside.

Is Constable BAIRD required to supply a notice of this search, under s. 2 of the Police and Criminal Evidence Act 1984?

A Yes, it should be placed on the vehicle, and a copy sent to the registered owner.

B No, a notice is not required as the inside of the vehicle was not searched.

C Yes, it should be placed inside the vehicle, which may be entered by force to do so.

D Yes, a notice must be placed somewhere on the vehicle.

ANSWERS

Answer 6.1

Answer **B** — Powers to stop, search and seize are essentially intended for use in public places, meaning places to which the public, or any section of the public, has access, on payment or otherwise, as of right or by virtue of express or implied permission, or any other place to which people have ready access at the time when it is proposed to exercise the powers but which is not a dwelling (s. 1(1)(a) and (b) of the Police and Criminal Evidence Act 1984). However, although powers to stop and search may not be exercised in a dwelling house, they may be exercised in a garden or yard of a house in certain circumstances. Under s. 1(4) of PACE:

> If a person is in a garden or yard occupied with and used for the purposes of a dwelling or on other land so occupied and used, a constable may not search him in the exercise of the power conferred by this section unless the constable has reasonable grounds for believing—
> (a) that he does not reside in the dwelling; and
> (b) that he is not in the place in question with the express or implied permission of a person who resides in the dwelling.

Similar provisions apply under s. 1(5), relating to the search of a vehicle which is in a garden or yard of a dwelling, and therefore answer A is incorrect.

However, the crux of this particular question rests with whether or not the dwelling itself was occupied. According to s. 1(5), if a vehicle is in a garden or yard *occupied with and used for the purposes of a dwelling*, a constable may not search the vehicle or anything in or on it in the exercise of the power conferred by this section unless he/she has reasonable grounds for believing that the person in charge of the vehicle does not reside in the dwelling and that the vehicle is not in the place in question with the express or implied permission of a person who resides in the dwelling.

The officer had reasonable grounds for believing that the person in charge of the vehicle (MENCE) did not reside in the dwelling, and that the premises themselves were unoccupied (which meant there was no one to give express or implied permission for the vehicle to be there). Therefore, Constable GUTHRIE would have been entitled to search the vehicle in these circumstances and therefore answer C is incorrect.

The search would have been lawful *regardless* of whether MENCE was present on the premises or not. Answer D is therefore incorrect.

General Police Duties, paras 4.6.4.1, 4.6.4.2

Answer 6.2

Answer **B** — In order to conduct a search under s. 1 of the Police and Criminal Evidence Act 1984, a constable must have 'reasonable grounds for suspecting' that he or she will find the required articles as a result of the search. Suspicion has been described as 'a state of conjecture or surmise when proof is lacking' (*Shaaban bin Hussein* v *Chong Fook Kam* [1970] AC 942). That suspicion can be based on any evidence, even if the evidence would be inadmissible in a trial (e.g. because of hearsay). Also, the courts have accepted that reasonable grounds for suspicion can arise from anonymous information (see *O'Hara* v *Chief Constable of the Royal Ulster Constabulary* [1997] 1 All ER 129). Answers A and C are therefore incorrect.

It must be shown that the grounds on which the officer acted would be enough to give rise to that suspicion in a 'reasonable person' (*Nakkuda Ali* v *Jayaratne* [1951] AC 66). This means that answer B is correct, and answer D is incorrect.

General Police Duties, para. 4.6.4.4

Answer 6.3

Answer **B** — Under s. 1(2) of PACE, a constable may search any person or vehicle, or anything which is in or on a vehicle, for stolen or prohibited articles, fireworks or any article to which subs. (8A) (articles in connection with burglary, theft, etc.). Section 1(3) states that a constable does not have a power to search a person or vehicle or anything in or on a vehicle unless he or she has reasonable grounds for suspecting that he/she will find such articles.

Code A, para. 2.2 outlines the objective basis for that suspicion based on facts, information and/or intelligence which are relevant to the likelihood of finding an article of a certain kind and goes on to state that reasonable suspicion cannot be based on generalisations or stereotypical images of certain groups or categories of people as more likely to be involved in criminal activity. However, under para. 2.6 of the Code:

> where there is reliable information or intelligence that members of a group or gang habitually carry knives unlawfully or weapons or controlled drugs, and wear a distinctive item of clothing or other means of identification to indicate their membership of the group or gang, that distinctive item of clothing or other means of identification may provide reasonable grounds to stop and search a person.

Therefore, the distinctive clothing and the officer's prior knowledge of the group *may* provide the required reasonable grounds to conduct a stop and search for controlled drugs and for this reason answers A and D are incorrect.

However, para. 2.6 does not provide an *automatic power to search all people wearing such clothing*. There would have to be an objective basis for the search and therefore answer C is incorrect.

General Police Duties, para. 4.6.4.3

Answer 6.4

Answer **C** — Under s. 60 of the Criminal Justice and Public Order Act 1994, if an inspector reasonably believes that incidents of serious violence may take place in his or her area, or that people are carrying dangerous instruments or offensive weapons, he or she may give an authorisation to stop any pedestrian and search him or her for offensive weapons or dangerous instruments.

The power used to be restricted to superintendents, but may now be exercised by an inspector (which is why answer D is incorrect). However, when the power is exercised by an inspector, he or she must inform an officer of the rank of superintendent as soon as is reasonably practicable.

The authorisation may be given either for incidents of serious violence *or* to search for dangerous instruments or offensive weapons (making answer A incorrect). The power is to search any pedestrian, and is not restricted to those who may be carrying dangerous instruments or offensive weapons (which is why answer B is incorrect).

General Police Duties, para. 4.6.4.5

Answer 6.5

Answer **B** — Under s. 60 of the Criminal Justice and Public Order Act 1994, if an inspector reasonably believes that incidents of serious violence may take place in his or her area, or that people are carrying dangerous instruments or offensive weapons, he or she may give an authorisation to stop any pedestrian and search him or her for offensive weapons or dangerous instruments.

It is for the authorising officer, who must be a superintendent, to determine the period of time during which the power may be exercised and in any event must not exceed 24 hours. The officer should set the minimum period he/she considers necessary to deal with the risk of violence, the carrying of knives or offensive weapons.

A direction to *extend* the period authorised under the power may be given only once. This extension is for a maximum period of 24 hours and thereafter further use of the powers requires a new authorisation. In the context of this question, the extension may be granted on the Saturday night, but if intelligence suggests further incidents will take place on the Sunday and Monday night, a new authorisation may be put in place on the Sunday, which can be extended to the Monday if necessary.

Answers A, C and D are incorrect for these reasons.

General Police Duties, para. 4.6.4.6

Answer 6.6

Answer **C** — Under s. 60AA(1) of the Criminal Justice and Public Order Act 1994, where an authorisation under s. 60 is in force, a constable in uniform may require any person to remove any item which the constable reasonably believes that person is wearing wholly or mainly for the purpose of concealing his or her identity. The power is not absolute, as the constable has reasonably to believe that the person is wearing the item to conceal his or her identity (therefore answer B is incorrect). There is no need, however, for the constable reasonably to believe that the person is carrying a dangerous instrument or an offensive weapon, or that the person is likely to be involved in violence, in order to exercise the power under s. 60AA(1). Those matters would have been considered before the authorisation was granted under s. 60. Answers A and D therefore incorrect.

General Police Duties, para. 4.6.4.9

Answer 6.7

Answer **D** — Under s. 60AA(1) of the Criminal Justice and Public Order Act 1994, where an authorisation under s. 60 is in force, a constable in uniform may require any person to remove any item which the constable reasonably believes that person is wearing wholly or mainly for the purpose of concealing his or her identity. However, unlike s. 60, there is no specific power under this section to stop vehicles and therefore answers A and C are incorrect.

There is also no power to search for face coverings etc. under s. 60AA(1). The Divisional Court has held that the predecessor to this power (the old s. 60(4A)) neither involved nor required a 'search' and that therefore the provisions of s. 2 of the Police and Criminal Evidence Act 1984 did not apply (*DPP* v *Avery* [2001] EWHC 748 (Admin)). The court went on to hold that, although the power amounted to a significant interference with a person's liberty, it was justified by the type of situation envisaged by the legislators, whereby the police may need to call upon the law. Clearly, if an item is found during a lawful search for other articles (say, under s. 60(4)) which does not require any 'reasonable belief' by the officer, face coverings and masks could then be seized under s. 60AA(2)(b). As there is no accompanying power of search under s. 60AA, answer B is incorrect.

Given that this is a power for police officers in uniform, the general power to stop vehicles under s. 163 of the Road Traffic Act 1988 could be used.

General Police Duties, paras 4.6.4.9, 4.6.4.13

Answer 6.8

Answer **B** — Section 3(1) of the Police and Criminal Evidence Act 1984 states that a written record of a search under s. 1 need not be made at the time, when it is not practicable to do so. However, Code A, para. 4.1 of the Codes of Practice narrows this exception to those occasions where it is wholly impracticable to make the record. Answer B reflects the wording of Code A; therefore answers A and D are incorrect. If the officer does not record the search at the time, he or she must do so as soon as reasonably practicable after the search has been completed.

This exception will be met only if there is virtually no chance of the officer being able to make the written record (e.g. the officer has been called to an emergency immediately after the search). Since an exception does exist, answer C is incorrect.

Note that when an officer makes a record of the stop and search electronically and is able to provide a copy at the time, he or she must do so (e.g. if the officer has access to a portable printer) and a copy of the record must be provided.

General Police Duties, para. 4.6.6

Answer 6.9

Answer **C** — Under Code A, para. 4.2B, where a person is arrested as a result of a stop and search and taken to a police station, the constable who carried out the search must ensure that the search record forms part of the person's custody record (rather than completing a separate form). Answers A and B are therefore incorrect.

In all other cases the constable must make the record of the search at the time it takes place or as soon as practicable after completion of the search.

The *custody officer* has responsibility for ensuring that the person is asked if they want a copy of the record and, if they do, that they are given a copy as soon as practicable. Answer D is therefore incorrect.

General Police Duties, para. 4.6.6

Answer 6.10

Answer **A** — Where a search record has been made, the person searched, the owner or the person who was in charge of any vehicle that was searched, will be entitled to a copy of the record. Answer B is therefore incorrect.

The person must be supplied with a copy *if he/she requests one*. Answer C is incorrect, as this will be supplied on request.

The Crime and Security Act 2010 reduced the entitlement from 12 months to three months; therefore, answer D is incorrect.

General Police Duties, para. 4.6.6.2

Answer 6.11

Answer **D** — Section 2(6) of the Police and Criminal Evidence Act 1984 states that 'on completing the search of an unattended vehicle, or anything in or on such a vehicle, a constable shall leave a notice'. Therefore, even though the spare tyre was not actually in the vehicle, a notice must be left, and for that reason answer B is incorrect.

There may be occasions when officers have to force entry into a vehicle in order to search it. On such an occasion, the officer must, if practicable, leave the vehicle secure (Code A, para. 4.10). However, where the vehicle has not been damaged during the search, s. 2(7) states that 'the constable shall leave the notice inside the vehicle unless it is not reasonably practicable to do so without damaging the vehicle'. Answer C is therefore incorrect.

There is no obligation on the officer to send a notice to the registered owner's address, and therefore answer A is incorrect.

General Police Duties, para. 4.6.6.2

7 | Entry, Search and Seizure

STUDY PREPARATION

In the previous chapter, we examined the powers to search people and vehicles for evidence of an offence. This chapter deals with the powers to enter and search *premises* either to seize evidence of an offence, or to arrest a person. These powers generally fall into two categories:

1. search of premises under the authority of a warrant;
2. search of premises without the authority of a warrant.

Knowing and understanding these powers leads to confidence, not just as a student or exam candidate but as a police officer generally.

Changes were made to PACE procedures by the Serious Organised Crime and Police Act 2005, in respect of the application and execution of warrants and the extent to which some non-warranted police staff may enter and search premises to seize evidence of an offence.

Part 2 of the Criminal Justice and Police Act 2001 provides a power allowing officers searching premises to seize documents and sift through them at a different location.

QUESTIONS

Question 7.1

DC HALL is investigating an allegation that FRISK, who owns a building company, paid bribes to officers in a local authority planning department over a number of years, to push through planning applications. DC HALL has recovered evidence from a search of FRISK's offices and anticipates seizing numerous documents and computers at the local authority offices. DC HALL is seeking a multiple entry search warrant, but is uncertain how many visits will be required to complete the evidence-gathering process.

Which of the following statements is correct, in relation to the type of warrant DC HALL is seeking?

A DC HALL must state the maximum number of entries desired in the application for the warrant.

B DC HALL may apply for a warrant authorising unlimited entries in these circumstances, because the maximum number is unknown.

C DC HALL is not required to specify the number of entries desired; the warrant will automatically authorise unlimited entries.

D DC HALL is not required to specify the number of entries desired; an inspector may authorise further entries if necessary.

Question 7.2

DC GRANT is investigating a case involving a series of frauds. The officer has obtained an all premises warrant which authorises the search of PEDERSON's office and home address. DC GRANT has recovered documents that suggest PEDERSON owns two other premises where evidence may be found.

Will the warrant in DC GRANT's possession authorise the search of the other two premises?

A Yes, provided entry to those premises is authorised by an inspector in writing.

B Yes, provided entry to those premises is authorised by a superintendent in writing.

C No, DC GRANT will have to apply to a magistrate for another all premises warrant to search those premises.

D Yes, provided entry to those premises is authorised by an inspector in writing, or if one is not readily available, the senior officer on duty.

Question 7.3

DC GOMEZ was the officer in charge of a search which was conducted at MALONEY's home address. Officers entered the premises by force under the authority of a warrant to search for property stolen from a recent burglary at a jeweller's shop. The search team found several items of jewellery matching the description of the stolen goods and these were seized as evidence. MALONEY was not present when the search took place and DC GOMEZ established that there was no other person available who appeared to be in charge of the premises; however, the officer forgot to leave a copy of the warrant in a prominent place in the premises.

Given that DC GOMEZ has failed to follow the requirements of s. 16(7) of PACE by not leaving a copy of the warrant in a prominent place, which of the following statements is correct?

A The search was unlawful; this may result in the exclusion of any evidence obtained under the warrant and officers could be made to return the jewellery to MALONEY.

B This is a minor deviation from the terms of the warrant which would not render the search unlawful or result in the exclusion of any evidence obtained.

C The search was unlawful; this may result in the exclusion of any evidence obtained under the warrant, but officers could not be made to return the jewellery to MALONEY.

D The search was unlawful, but a failure to follow the requirements of s. 16 will not result in the exclusion of any evidence obtained under the warrant.

Question 7.4

A number of raves have been taking place on weekends and officers suspect that COOKSLEY is the organiser. The location of the events changes every week and intelligence suggests that COOKSLEY is dealing Class A drugs from a tent that is erected at each venue, which also contains the sound equipment for the rave. Officers have information that COOKSLEY transports the equipment and drugs to the venues in the back of a van. They are considering applying for a warrant under the Misuse of Drugs Act 1971 to search the vehicle and tent for drugs. However, COOKSLEY's address is unknown and officers will have to wait until the following weekend for intelligence on the next venue.

Which of the following statements is correct, in relation to the officers' intentions?

A Only the tent is a 'premises' in respect of a search warrant; there is no power to apply for a warrant to search a vehicle in this way.

B Both the tent and the vehicle are 'premises' and officers could apply for a search warrant in respect of both.

C Neither the tent (which is a moveable structure) nor the vehicle are 'premises' in respect of a search warrant; officers will have to use other powers to search them.

D Officers will have to use other powers to search both the tent and the vehicle; a search warrant requires a location to be specified in it before one can be issued.

Question 7.5

Detective Constable PRICE is investigating a fraud case and has uncovered evidence that a number of solicitors from a local firm may be involved. The officer has applied to a justice of the peace for a warrant under s. 8 of the Police and Criminal Evidence Act 1984, to enter and search the solicitors' offices for evidence relating to the offence. Detective Constable PRICE has reasonable cause to believe that there may be communications between solicitors and clients referring to the fraud. The officer is aware that there may be a substantial amount of paper and computer records on the premises and is anticipating having to use powers under s. 50 of the Criminal Justice and Police Act 2001 to seize and sift evidence.

Which of the following statements is correct, in relation to items subject to legal privilege which may be on the premises?

A Any communication between solicitors and clients is subject to legal privilege and cannot be searched for or seized under the terms of a warrant.

B Any items found that relate to criminal offences are not subject to legal privilege and may be searched for or seized.

C A warrant cannot authorise a search for legally privileged material and if such material is inadvertently seized, it would render the search unlawful.

D The possession of a warrant under s. 8 authorises any material found on the premises to be seized and sifted.

Question 7.6

Detective Constable ULHAQ has been called to a house fire and is the first officer on scene; he is not in uniform. He is unsure if there are persons present in the building or not and is considering whether he has power to force entry, using s. 17 of the Police and Criminal Evidence Act 1984.

Which of the following is correct?

A The officer may enter immediately to save life and limb, whether he believes there are persons in there or not.

B The officer may enter immediately to save life and limb if he has reasonable cause to *suspect* there are persons in there.

C The officer may enter immediately to save life and limb if he has reasonable cause to *believe* there are persons in there.

D The officer may not enter using s. 17 as he is not in uniform.

Question 7.7

Constable WILSON attended a burglary in the early hours of the morning. A witness, COLE, had seen a man breaking into a shop and removing two DVD players. COLE saw the man enter a house next to the shop. A short while later COLE saw the same man emerge empty handed and walk up the street. Constable WILSON made a search of the area and arrested GREEN, who matched the description given, nearby within minutes.

Constable WILSON considered searching the house GREEN had been seen entering. What authority would she have to do so in these circumstances?

A She has no authority to search immediately and would have to seek permission under s. 18 of the Police and Criminal Evidence Act 1984.

B She would have authority to search any premises which GREEN was in at any time prior to his arrest under s. 32 of the Police and Criminal Evidence Act 1984.

C She would have authority to search any premises which GREEN was in immediately prior to his arrest under s. 32 of the Police and Criminal Evidence Act 1984.

D She would have authority to search any premises occupied or controlled by GREEN and which he was in immediately prior to his arrest under s. 32 of the Police and Criminal Evidence Act 1984.

Question 7.8

Constable AHMED has arrested GRANT for an offence of burglary. Constable AHMED has been advised to seek permission from the duty inspector to search GRANT's home address, under s. 18 of the Police and Criminal Evidence Act 1984.

In relation to where Constable AHMED may search, and what he may search for, which of the following statements is correct?

A Premises occupied or controlled by GRANT, for evidence related to the offence for which he is in custody, or another similar indictable offence.

B Premises suspected to be occupied or controlled by GRANT, for evidence related to the offence for which he is in custody, or other similar indictable offences.

C Premises occupied or controlled by GRANT, for evidence related to the offence for which he is in custody only.

D Premises occupied or controlled by GRANT, for evidence related to the offence for which he is in custody, or any other indictable offence.

Question 7.9

Constable ELLIS attended a dwelling burglary in progress at 2.00 am. On arrival, the officer was told that the householders had disturbed the suspect, who had escaped through the back door into the rear garden. They had seen the suspect carrying a bag, believed to have contained items stolen from their house. The victims' rear garden was enclosed and was adjacent to several other houses; it was believed that the suspect had climbed over fences and escaped through the other gardens, onto the main street nearby. Whilst making a search of the area, Constable ELLIS received a message that GRAFF had been arrested in a street nearby, by other officers, and that he matched the suspect's description. However, this person was not carrying a bag as described by the witnesses. Constable ELLIS intended returning to the crime scene to search the neighbours' gardens for the bag, to try to link it to GRAFF.

What authority would Constable ELLIS require, in order to search neighbours' gardens, in these circumstances?

A Constable ELLIS would require the occupiers' permission, unless she was in immediate pursuit of a suspect.

B Constable ELLIS would *not* require the occupiers' permission, as this may cause disproportionate inconvenience to the person concerned.

C Constable ELLIS would *not* require the occupiers' permission, as this may cause disproportionate inconvenience to the investigation.

D Constable ELLIS would require the statutory authority of a warrant or through PACE (s. 17, 18 or 32). Otherwise she would require the occupiers' permission.

Question 7.10

HUDSON was arrested by Constable BALL from the Stolen Vehicle Squad, following the execution of a warrant at HUDSON's garage, where several stolen vehicles were found. Constable BALL received intelligence that HUDSON had another vehicle, which was parked outside his house. Constable BALL suspected that this vehicle might also be stolen.

In relation to searching and seizing the vehicle or its contents under ss. 18 and 19 of the Police and Criminal Evidence Act 1984, what powers would be available to Constable BALL?

A The vehicle is 'premises', which cannot be seized; the officer may search it and seize any contents obtained as a consequence of the commission of an offence.

B The vehicle is not 'premises' and may not be searched under s. 18; the officer would have to use powers available under s. 1 of the Act.

C The vehicle may be searched and seized if it is suspected it was obtained as a consequence of the commission of an offence, or for intelligence purposes.

D The vehicle and its contents may be searched and seized if it is suspected they were obtained as a consequence of the commission of an offence.

ANSWERS

Answer 7.1

Answer **B** — Section 15(2)(iii) of the Police and Criminal Evidence Act 1984 states:

> if the application is for a warrant authorising entry and search on more than one occasion, the ground on which he applies for such a warrant, and whether he seeks a warrant authorising an unlimited number of entries, or (if not) the maximum number of entries desired.

Therefore, an officer will normally be required to specify the number of entries desired and the warrant will *not* automatically authorise unlimited entries. Answer C is therefore incorrect.

On the other hand, s. 15(2)(iii) does provide some flexibility in case the number of entries is unknown (answer A is therefore incorrect).

Section 16(3B) of the Act deals with the authority required from an inspector in relation to multiple entry warrants. Under this section, premises may not be entered or searched for the second or any subsequent time under a warrant which authorises multiple entries, unless a police officer of at least the rank of inspector has authorised that in writing. The section does not give an inspector the power to authorise multiple entries; on the contrary, it places a restriction on such warrants so that each entry must be authorised by an inspector, even when multiple entries have been authorised by a magistrate. Answer D is therefore incorrect.

General Police Duties, paras 4.7.3.1, 4.7.3.2

Answer 7.2

Answer **A** — Section 16 of the Police and Criminal Evidence Act 1984 states:

> (3A) If the warrant is an all premises warrant, no premises which are not specified in it may be entered or searched unless a police officer of at least the rank of inspector has in writing authorised them to be entered.

There is no provision under this section for a senior officer on duty to authorise entry to new premises if an inspector is not readily available and there is no requirement for a superintendent to sign the authorisation. Answers B and D are therefore incorrect.

Also, there will be no requirement for the officer to apply to a magistrate for another all premises warrant to search those premises. Answer C is therefore incorrect.

General Police Duties, para. 4.7.3.2

Answer 7.3

Answer **A** — Section 16(7) of PACE states that if there is no person present who appears to the constable to be in charge of the premises, he or she shall leave a copy of the warrant in a prominent place on the premises. There was a clear breach of the terms of the warrant by DC GOMEZ in this case, which means that any entry and search made under a warrant will be unlawful. Further, a failure to follow the requirements of ss. 15 and 16 of PACE may result in the exclusion of any evidence obtained under the warrant. Answer D is therefore incorrect.

Where officers failed to provide the occupier of the searched premises with a copy of the warrant, they were obliged to return the property seized during the search (*R v Chief Constable of Lancashire, ex parte Parker* [1993] QB 577). As this is a possibility, answer C is incorrect.

Very minor departures from the letter of the warrant will not render any search unlawful (*Attorney General of Jamaica v Williams* [1998] AC 351); however, *Parker* suggests that failing to provide a copy of the warrant would not be considered a *minor* departure from the requirement to do so under s. 16.

General Police Duties, paras 4.7.3.2, 4.7.3.6

Answer 7.4

Answer **B** — Section 23 of PACE states that 'premises' include any place, and in particular,

(a) any vehicle, vessel, aircraft or hovercraft;
(b) any offshore installation;
(c) any renewable energy installation;
(d) any tent or moveable structure.

Answers A and C are therefore incorrect.

Since 'premises' includes any place, officers are not restricted by the fact that they are not yet aware of the location of the rave and therefore answer D is incorrect.

General Police Duties, para. 4.7.3.3

Answer 7.5

Answer **B** — Section 10(1) of the Police and Criminal Evidence Act 1984 states that subject to subs. (2), 'items subject to legal privilege' means—

(a) communications between a professional legal adviser and his client or any person representing his client made in connection with the giving of legal advice to the client;

(b) communications between a professional legal adviser and his client or any person representing his client or between such an adviser or his client or any such representative and any other person made in connection with or in contemplation of legal proceedings and for the purposes of such proceedings; and

(c) items enclosed with or referred to in such communications and made—

(i) in connection with the giving of legal advice; or

(ii) in connection with or in contemplation of legal proceedings and for the purposes of such proceedings,

when they are in the possession of a person who is entitled to possession of them.

Generally, material which falls within the definition in s. 10(1) is subject to legal privilege, which means that it cannot be searched for or seized. However, items held with the intention of furthering a criminal purpose are no longer subject to this privilege (s. 10(2)). Occasions where this will happen are very rare, but could include instances where a solicitor's firm is the subject of a criminal investigation (see *R* v *Leeds Crown Court, ex parte Switalski* [1991] Crim LR 559). Answer A is therefore incorrect.

Although a warrant cannot authorise a search for legally privileged material, the fact that such material is inadvertently seized in the course of a search authorised by a proper warrant does not render the search unlawful (*HM Customs & Excise, ex parte Popely* [2000] Crim LR 388). Answer C is therefore incorrect.

Possession of a warrant under s. 8 does not authorise police officers to seize *all* material found on the relevant premises to be taken away and 'sifted' somewhere else (*R* v *Chesterfield Justices, ex parte Bramley* [2000] QB 576). Officers using seize and sift powers will have to be able to show that it was essential (rather than simply convenient or preferable) to do so. Answer D is incorrect.

General Police Duties, paras 4.7.3.7, 4.7.3.8, 4.7.8.7

Answer 7.6

Answer **A** — Section 17 of the Police and Criminal Evidence Act 1984 provides authority for a constable to enter premises to arrest a person in several circumstances.

Under s. 17(1)(e), a constable may enter premises for the purposes of saving life or limb, or preventing serious damage to property. When entering premises, including dwellings, to search for a person, the constable must have reasonable grounds for believing that the person he is seeking is on the premises (s. 17(2)(a)). This expression is narrower than 'reasonable cause to suspect' and you must be able to justify that belief before using this power (although see *Kynaston* v *DPP* (1988) 87 Cr App R 200, where the court accepted reasonable cause to suspect). Note, however, that 'having reasonable cause to believe' does not extend to the power to enter to save life and limb; answers B and C are therefore incorrect.

Some parts of s. 17 require the officer to be in uniform; these relate to arresting a person for offences specified in s. 17, but again do not extend to entry to save life and limb; answer D is therefore incorrect.

No doubt persons trapped in buildings that are on fire will thank the legislator for such a common-sense approach to powers of entry.

General Police Duties, para. 4.7.5.1

Answer 7.7

Answer **C** — Authority is provided under s. 32(2)(b) of the Police and Criminal Evidence Act 1984 for a constable to enter and search any premises in which the person was when arrested or immediately before being arrested, if the constable has reasonable grounds for believing that there is evidence on the premises in consequence of the commission of an offence. As COLE had been in the premises immediately before his arrest, the officer could use s. 32; answer A is therefore incorrect. The search may be conducted for the purpose of finding evidence relating to the offence for which the person was arrested. As the defendant in the scenario was arrested within minutes of leaving the premises, this would be classed as 'immediately' (although the term 'immediately' is open to interpretation).

Answer B is incorrect as the search relates to premises the person was in immediately prior to arrest.

The Divisional Court has held that where a person had not been in the relevant premises (where he did not live) for over two hours preceding his arrest, the power under s. 32 may not be used (see *Hewitson* v *Chief Constable of Dorset Police* [2003] EWHC 3296 (Admin)).

Answer D is incorrect, as s. 32 does not state that the premises must be ones which are occupied or controlled by the person arrested. (This requirement may be found in s. 18 of the Act.)

General Police Duties, para. 4.7.5.2

Answer 7.8

Answer **A** — Under s. 18 of the Police and Criminal Evidence Act 1984, a constable may enter and search any premises occupied or controlled by a person who is under arrest for an indictable offence, if there are reasonable grounds to suspect that there are items on the premises that relate to that offence, *or* to some other indictable offence which is connected with or similar to that offence.

Answer B is incorrect because the premises must be controlled or occupied by the person; it is not enough that the officer suspects or believes that they are.

Answers C and D are incorrect as the officer may search for evidence relating to either the offence for which the suspect has been arrested, or those which are similar.

General Police Duties, para. 4.7.5.3

Answer 7.9

Answer **B** — Generally, Code B of the PACE Codes of Practice deals with the search of premises through the statutory authority of a warrant or through PACE (s. 17, 18 or 32). However, para. 5 of this Code deals with searches with the consent of the occupier, or the person 'entitled to grant consent'.

Paragraphs 5.1–5.3 deal with how such consent should be obtained, however, para. 5.4 states that it is unnecessary to seek consent if this would cause disproportionate inconvenience *to the person concerned*. Answer C is incorrect, as it is the inconvenience to the occupier that matters.

Note for Guidance 5C outlines that para. 5.4 is intended to apply when it is reasonable to assume innocent occupiers would agree to, and expect, police to take the proposed action, e.g. if

- a suspect has fled the scene of a crime or to evade arrest and it is necessary quickly to check surrounding gardens and readily accessible places to see if the suspect is hiding;
- police have arrested someone in the night after a pursuit and it is necessary to make a brief check of gardens along the pursuit route to see if stolen or incriminating articles have been discarded.

Therefore, it would be reasonable for Constable ELLIS to search the gardens without the occupiers' permission, even though she was not in immediate pursuit of a suspect, because to have woken the entire street in the middle of the night to search for a bag may have seemed disproportionate in these circumstances. This search could have been conducted *without* the statutory authority of a warrant, or other powers derived from PACE. Answers A and D are therefore incorrect.

General Police Duties, paras 4.7.6, 4.7.6.1

Answer 7.10

Answer **D** — Under s. 18 of the Police and Criminal Evidence Act 1984, a constable may enter and search any premises occupied or controlled by a person who is under arrest for an indictable offence if there are reasonable grounds to suspect that there are items on the premises that relate to that offence, or to some other indictable offence which is connected with or similar to that offence. For the purposes of the section, a vehicle is 'premises'. (Therefore, answer B is incorrect.)

Under s. 19 of the 1984 Act, an officer may seize anything which is on premises, if he or she has reasonable grounds for believing that it has been obtained in consequence of the commission of an offence and that it is necessary to do so in order to prevent it from being concealed, lost, damaged, altered or destroyed. Section 19 does not allow the seizure of property for intelligence purposes, and answer C is incorrect for this reason.

Where the 'premises' searched is a vehicle (see s. 23), the vehicle can itself be seized (*Cowan* v *Commissioner of Police of the Metropolis* [2000] 1 WLR 254) (making answer A incorrect).

This power has now also been added to the PACE Codes of Practice, Code B, Note 7B.

General Police Duties, para. 4.7.8.1

8 | Harassment, Stalking, Hostility and Anti-social Behaviour

STUDY PREPARATION

The focus on community safety within the whole criminal justice process has been sharply defined since the Crime and Disorder Act 1998. A range of statutory measures exist, giving the police (and other agencies) duties in relation to community safety and powers to help them take positive action and work together to deal with harassment and intimidation.

The Anti-social Behaviour Act 2003 provided the police and statutory partners further tools in the tool kit to protect the community from fear, intimidation and anti-social behaviour. The Anti-Social Behaviour Bill, when enacted, will overhaul the current system of ASBOs and introduce further offences as well as greater victim and community involvement.

The main legislation is supported by other enactments, such as the Fireworks Regulations 2004, the Noise Act 1996 and the Environmental Protection Act 1990 (litter). Taken together, these measures feature highly in regional and local policing strategies to tackle crime and the fear of crime. This makes them important, not only to police officers but also, as a result, to those training and examining police law.

Also covered in this chapter are the powers given to the police and the courts to deal with *personal* harassment, which are covered in various pieces of legislation such as the Protection from Harassment Act 1997 (which includes a new offence of stalking) and the Public Order Act 1986.

QUESTIONS

Question 8.1

MEREDITH is a racist. One day he was at home with several friends who share his beliefs, when COWANS, who is black, knocked on his door collecting money on behalf of charity. MEREDITH invited COWANS into his house on the pretext of looking for money. When they were in the living room of the house, MEREDITH began racially abusing COWANS in front of his friends. His intention all along was to stir up racial hatred. When COWANS eventually left the house, he contacted the police to report the incident.

Considering offences under s. 18 of the Public Order Act 1986 (using words or behaviour or displaying written material stirring up racial hatred), does the fact that the incident took place in a dwelling affect whether or not the police can take any action?

A No, the offence may be committed anywhere.

B Yes, the offence may only be committed in a public place.

C No, the offence may be committed in a public or private place.

D Yes, the offence may not be committed when both persons are in a dwelling.

Question 8.2

HAWKINS was walking through a city centre after a lunchtime drink one afternoon. At the time, a religious Hindu festival was taking place, involving people in traditional dress, who were walking to a place of worship nearby. HAWKINS began shouting, 'If these people want to live in our country, they should adopt a proper religion' and, 'Look at those stupid costumes they've got on, they're ridiculous.' HAWKINS's words were heard by pedestrians standing nearby, but not by the people in the procession. HAWKINS's intention was to insult the people taking part in the procession, because of their religious beliefs, and to stir up hatred amongst passers-by who did not share the same beliefs.

Would HAWKINS's behaviour amount to an offence under s. 29B of the Public Order Act 1986 (use of words or behaviour intended to stir up religious hatred)?

A Yes, as HAWKINS's intention was to stir up religious hatred.

B Yes, whether or not HAWKINS intended stirring up religious hatred.

C No, as HAWKINS's words were not threatening.

D No, as the people in the procession did not hear the comments.

Question 8.3

WADE lives in a small cul-de-sac and is openly homophobic. WADE became aware that two people of the same sex had bought a house in the street and the rumours amongst the neighbours were that the people were in a homosexual relationship. One day, neighbours noticed several posters in the front windows of WADE's house, on which were written, 'Sign my petition to get rid of sexual deviants from this street'. WADE's intention was to make the new neighbours uncomfortable about living in the area, so that they would move out.

Could WADE be guilty of an offence under s. 29AB of the Public Order Act 1986, of stirring up hatred against the neighbours, on the grounds of sexual orientation?

A No, WADE has not made threats to the neighbours, intending to stir up hatred on the grounds of their sexual orientation.

B Yes, WADE has used threatening, abusive or insulting words or behaviour, intending to stir up hatred on the grounds of their sexual orientation.

C No, this offence can only be committed where a person uses words or behaviour, and does not include the use of written materials.

D Yes, WADE has used threatening, abusive or insulting words or behaviour, intending to stir up hatred on the grounds of sexual orientation, or where hatred was likely to be stirred up.

Question 8.4

BERTRAND worked in the Information Department of Eastshire Police and specialised in computer programming. BERTRAND had previously been in a relationship with ROSS, a work colleague, which had ended recently. BERTRAND was upset at the break-up and became convinced that ROSS was now in a relationship with another colleague. BERTRAND managed to access ROSS's emails and monitored them remotely every day for about a month, to obtain information about the new relationship. ROSS suspected this was happening and asked BERTRAND to stop. BERTRAND was aware that ROSS was upset, but carried on accessing the emails.

Would BERTRAND's behaviour amount to stalking, under s. 2A(1) of the Protection from Harassment Act 1997?

A Yes, provided a course of conduct can be proved.

B No, this offence requires some positive action by the defendant and BERTRAND has not actually used the information for anything.

C Yes, regardless of whether a course of conduct can be proved.

D No, this offence requires some form of act or omission by the defendant, which has not occurred in these circumstances.

Question 8.5

When BERRY split up from her boyfriend, TROTT, he began posting abusive messages on his Facebook account, calling her a 'slut' and 'whore'. The abuse got worse and TROTT posted a number of photographs on his account of BERRY with no clothes on. Eventually, TROTT posted explicit photographs of the pair having sex. After each Facebook message or photograph, TROTT sent BERRY a message telling her to look at this account. BERRY was not concerned about her safety and initially ignored the abuse and photographs of her with no clothes on; however, she became extremely distressed because of the explicit photographs. Eventually, BERRY moved away from the area and changed her telephone number to avoid receiving messages from TROTT. She also stopped all contact with her family and friends because of the Facebook account.

Would TROTT's behaviour amount to stalking, under s. 4A of the Protection from Harassment Act 1997?

A No, TROTT has not threatened BERRY with violence.

B No, BERRY was not in fear that TROTT would use violence against her.

C No, BERRY only became extremely distressed when TROTT posted the explicit photographs; this was a single act and did not amount to a course of conduct.

D Yes, TROTT has pursued a course of conduct which has had a substantial adverse effect on BERRY's day-to-day activities.

Question 8.6

BARON has sent two threatening letters to his probation officer. However, the second letter was not received until four-and-a-half months after the first.

Could BARON be guilty of harassment contrary to ss. 1 and 2 of the Protection from Harassment Act 1997?

A No, as probation officers are unlikely to be distressed.

B No, owing to the length of time between the letters.

C Yes, but only if the probation officer is likely to be alarmed and distressed.

D Yes, but only if actual distress is caused to the probation officer.

Question 8.7

CRUTCHER and BOYCE are members of an animal rights extremist group and were targeting two companies, which CRUTCHER and BOYCE believed were suppliers to a third company, which tested its products on animals. Following a discussion between the two, CRUTCHER sent a threatening letter to the chief executive of one company and BOYCE sent a threatening email to the chief executive of the other. Their intention was to persuade both companies to stop supplying the third company with their products.

Given that the recipients are likely to be caused alarm and distress by the communications, would CRUTCHER and BOYCE's actions amount to a 'course of conduct' in respect of an offence under s. 1(1A) of the Protection from Harassment Act 1997?

A Yes, their conduct would be sufficient to amount to a 'course of conduct' in these circumstances.

B No, each person would have to send communications to at least two people.

C No, each person would have to send communications to at least two people from each company.

D No, because the communication they sent to each person was in a different form.

Question 8.8

COHEN is appearing in Crown Court, having been charged with an offence of harassment, contrary to s. 2 of the Protection from Harassment Act 1997. COHEN's solicitor has submitted to the court that the defendant suffers from mental health problems and the criterion that a person 'ought to know' that conduct amounted to harassment could not be met because of this illness.

Section 1(2) of the Protection from Harassment Act 1997 outlines a 'reasonable person' test in dealing with whether or not a person 'ought to know' that conduct amounted to harassment. Which of the following statements is true when considering this test, and COHEN's illness?

A The nature of COHEN's illness would provide a defence to this charge.

B The jury must consider COHEN's personal circumstances when deciding whether or not the criterion is met.

C The jury need only consider whether a reasonable person would think that COHEN's conduct amounted to harassment.

D In these circumstances, the jury would have to consider whether COHEN knew that the conduct amounted to harassment.

Question 8.9

STOCKWIN is infatuated with a female colleague from work; however, she has rejected his attempts to go out with her. STOCKWIN was upset and telephoned his colleague, threatening to burn her house down, but she was not concerned by his threats. A week later, STOCKWIN again telephoned his colleague and threatened to do the same thing and on this occasion, she was put in fear that he would carry out the threat and contacted the police.

Would STOCKWIN be guilty of an offence under s. 4 of the Protection from Harassment Act 1997 in these circumstances?

A Yes, as the work colleague was put in fear of violence on at least two occasions.

B No, as the work colleague was not put in fear of violence on at least two occasions.

C Yes, provided that it can be shown that violence was intended by STOCKWIN.

D Yes, provided that it can be shown that STOCKWIN actually knew that the work colleague was in fear of violence.

Question 8.10

Following the break-up of a long-term relationship with FRAMPTON, CLARKSON moved away to live with friends in Scotland. Before leaving, CLARKSON was convicted of harassment against FRAMPTON, contrary to s. 2 of the Protection from Harassment Act 1997. FRAMPTON has heard that CLARKSON intends returning to live nearby and has also been told by friends that CLARKSON is still angry about the break-up and will try to resume contact. FRAMPTON intends seeking a County Court injunction against CLARKSON, to avoid being subjected to further harassment.

Could a County Court issue an injunction in such circumstances, when there has been no evidence that CLARKSON has actually committed a further offence contrary to the Protection from Harassment Act 1997?

A No, only the High Court may issue an injunction in respect of an apprehended breach of the 1997 Act.

B No, an injunction may not be issued in respect of an apprehended breach of the 1997 Act.

C No, an injunction could only be issued in these circumstances if CLARKSON had previously been convicted of an offence contrary to s. 4 of the 1997 Act.

D Yes, the County Court could issue an injunction even for an apprehended breach of the 1997 Act.

Question 8.11

MURRAY had been involved in a long-standing dispute with her neighbour, WALTON, and had been made subject to a restraining order under s. 5(1) of the Protection from Harassment Act 1997. The order prohibited MURRAY from 'using abusive words or actions' towards WALTON. While the order was still in force, WALTON was visited by friends, who parked their car in the street outside the house. A short while later, WALTON observed MURRAY move her own car, which was also parked in the street, into such a position that it effectively blocked in WALTON's friends' car. WALTON contacted the police, claiming that MURRAY had breached the restraining order. When the officers arrived, MURRAY claimed that she was not aware that her behaviour amounted to a breach of the order.

Which of the following statements is correct, in respect of whether MURRAY could be found guilty of breaching the restraining order?

A MURRAY's behaviour was not serious enough to amount to harassment; therefore, the restraining order has not been breached.

B MURRAY's behaviour *may* have amounted to harassment, but she may have a defence if she could show that she honestly believed that her conduct did not breach the terms of the restraining order.

C MURRAY's belief is irrelevant; once the prosecution demonstrates that the restraining order was in place and the behaviour amounted to harassment, the court should find that the order has been breached.

D MURRAY's behaviour was not directed at WALTON; therefore, the restraining order has not been breached.

Question 8.12

STEPHENS, aged 19, was convicted by the magistrates' court for using threatening behaviour contrary to s. 5 of the Public Order Act 1986, towards an elderly resident living on an estate near his own home. He received a conditional discharge for the offence. Prior to issuing his sentence, the court heard that he had previously received both a reprimand and a final warning for the same offence, towards other residents in the area, while he was a youth. Although no application was made by the CPS, the magistrates took the decision to issue an ASBO against STEPHENS, utilising the evidence provided during his hearing, preventing him from entering the housing estate where the offences took place.

In relation to the ASBO issued, has the court acted within its powers in these circumstances?

A No, the court should not have issued an ASBO of its own volition; it may only respond to an application by a relevant authority.

B No, but the actions of the court *would* have been permissible if STEPHENS had not been given a conditional discharge for the offence.

C No, the evidence heard during the prosecution's case should not have been reused to support an ASBO.

D Yes, the court has acted properly in the circumstances, and the ASBO against STEPHENS will be lawful.

Question 8.13

GRIFFIN has been made subject to an ASBO by the magistrates' court. The court decided that because drug misuse had been a major cause of the behaviour that led to the ASBO being made, it would be appropriate for GRIFFIN to also receive an intervention order.

Over what period of time could GRIFFIN be made to comply with the intervention order?

A A minimum of three months.

B A minimum of six months.

C A maximum of six months.

D A maximum of 12 months.

Question 8.14

The police and local authority are holding a strategy meeting to discuss COLE, who is 9 years of age. Numerous referrals have been made to the anti-social behaviour co-ordinator over several months, showing evidence that COLE has been acting in an anti-social manner towards CHECK, an elderly next-door neighbour who lives alone.

Given that COLE has acted in an anti-social manner against CHECK, could an ASBO be applied for in these circumstances?

A No, because only one other household has been affected by COLE's behaviour.

B No, although the behaviour amounts to anti-social behaviour, an ASBO cannot be applied for because of COLE's age.

C Yes, the behaviour amounts to anti-social behaviour, and COLE's age is not relevant.

D No, because only one person in another household has been affected by COLE's behaviour.

Question 8.15

PENGELLI is 15 years of age and has been convicted of a burglary, which occurred during the night. The court has heard that PENGELLI has one unrelated previous conviction, but has recently taken up friendship with a group of young people who were the source of encouragement for the burglary. The court is considering making a Youth Rehabilitation Order (YRO), and the Probation Report has indicated that a curfew might be suitable to prevent PENGELLI from getting into further trouble.

Which of the following statements is correct, in relation to the proposal to implement a curfew as part of the YRO?

A PENGELLI is over 13 and can therefore be made subject to a curfew as part of the YRO.

B PENGELLI can be made subject to a curfew, as there are no restrictions on a person's age in respect of this type of intervention.

C PENGELLI is under 16 and cannot therefore be made subject to a curfew as part of the YRO.

D PENGELLI can be made subject to a curfew, as there are no restrictions on a person's age in respect of any intervention required by the court.

Question 8.16

REGAN is the subject of an exclusion order under s. 205 of the Criminal Justice Act 2003, preventing her from entering a shopping centre on weekends, due to previous anti-social behaviour. Constable MALIK has been called to the centre by security staff who are aware of the order and have spotted REGAN in the centre on CCTV.

What potential powers are available to Constable MALIK, to deal with REGAN in these circumstances?

A Constable MALIK may take REGAN's details and serve a written notice on her that she was in breach of the order. The officer may send a copy of the notice to the court.

B Constable MALIK may direct REGAN to leave the premises verbally; if she fails, she may be prosecuted.

C Constable MALIK may arrest REGAN for breach of the exclusion order.

D Constable MALIK may summons REGAN for breach of the exclusion order, unless an arrest is necessary.

Question 8.17

A Part 1A closure order has been issued in respect of a house, which is owned by RAWLINGS. RAWLINGS rents it out to a tenant, who only uses it on weekends to hold all-night parties. The parties have been the source of numerous complaints by residents because of the significant disorder they attract. The closure order was applied for by the police and Sergeant MEDINA wishes to secure the premises and post notices before the next party. Sergeant MEDINA has been in discussion with the manager of the local authority housing department about the best way to secure the premises.

Who does the closure order authorise to enter the premises to secure them in these circumstances—the police or the local authority?

A Only the police, because the premises are privately owned.

B Either organisation, provided they have consulted with each other about the order.

C Only the police, because the order was applied for by a police officer.

D Either organisation, but if force is to be used, a member of the local authority must be accompanied by a police officer.

Question 8.18

Constable ELSOM is part of a Neighbourhood Policing Team and has been liaising with the local authority about premises that have been subject to a number of complaints at public meetings because of persistent anti-social behaviour problems. Constable ELSOM is considering whether a Part 1A closure notice should be applied for in respect of the premises.

Which of the following statements best describes the 'persistent' element, which must be apparent before a closure notice may be made in respect of the premises?

A The premises must have been associated with significant and persistent disorder in the past 24 hours, or persistent serious nuisance in the preceding two months.

B The premises must have been associated with significant and persistent disorder in the past month, or persistent serious nuisance in the preceding three months.

C The premises must have been associated with significant and persistent disorder or persistent serious nuisance in the preceding two months.

D The premises must have been associated with significant and persistent disorder or persistent serious nuisance in the preceding three months.

Question 8.19

The police were concerned with the increasing number of calls they were receiving relating to loose horses on a main road. The horses were escaping from a field adjacent to the road and the problem was responsible for significant disruption, especially in the mornings and afternoons when people were on their way to work or taking children to school. The police have sought advice from the CPS as to whether the owner of the horses, PRICE, could be guilty of causing a public nuisance.

If PRICE were to be prosecuted for causing a public nuisance, what evidence would the court require in relation to the disruption caused to the community?

A It must be demonstrated that a representative cross-section of the community was affected by the problem.

B It must be demonstrated that the whole community was affected by the problem.

C Provided it can be shown there was danger to the public, the number of people affected by the problem is irrelevant.

D There is no requirement to demonstrate that disruption was actually caused to anyone; it must be shown that there was *potential* for a large part of the community to be affected by the problem.

Question 8.20

MULLER owns a company which organises large firework displays, for which he is authorised. He has several employees working for him, who help in his warehouse, accepting delivery of fireworks from the manufacturer and loading them into his van prior to displays. One such person is PLATT, who is 17 years of age. PLATT does not accompany MULLER to the displays; however, on a daily basis in the warehouse he handles large fireworks, which are specified as category 4 fireworks under the Fireworks Regulations 2004.

Does PLATT commit an offence under reg. 4(1) of the Fireworks Regulations 2004, by being in possession of fireworks that fall under category 4?

A Yes, as he is under the age of 18.

B No, as he is handling the fireworks as part of his work.

C Yes, regardless of his age.

D No, as he is not in a public place.

Question 8.21

COURT was hosting a party at his house on the evening of his son's wedding, on a warm evening in August. At midnight, COURT set off a series of fireworks in his garden to celebrate the wedding. The fireworks were of a standard type that he had bought in a supermarket the previous November and had kept aside for the occasion. COURT finished setting off the fireworks at about 30 minutes past midnight.

Regulation 7 of the Fireworks Regulations 2004 deals with the prohibition of use of fireworks at night time. In relation to these regulations, which of the following is correct?

A COURT has committed an offence because of the hour that he set the fireworks off.

B COURT has committed no offence because of the type of fireworks he set off.

C COURT may have committed an offence if local residents were disrupted or annoyed by the noise.

D COURT has committed an offence because of the hour that he set the fireworks off, but he could have avoided this by seeking permission from the local authority to do so.

Question 8.22

Whilst out on patrol at 2 am, Constable CLEAREY was approached by BERGEN, who was complaining about a noisy party being held at a house in the street. When standing outside BERGEN's house, Constable CLEAREY could hear very loud music coming from another house five doors away. The officer radioed the control room, asking them to contact the local authority's on-duty Environmental Health Officers, however, no one was available and on duty.

Given that the music emanating from the house may amount to 'excessive noise', which of the following statements is correct?

A The test for 'excessive' noise is whether or not it may be heard in a public place; however, evidence of acoustic measurements of the level of noise will always be required.

B The test for 'excessive' noise is whether or not it may be heard in another dwelling and evidence of acoustic measurements of the level of noise will always be required.

C The test for 'excessive' noise is whether or not it may be heard in another dwelling and while evidence of acoustic measurements of the level of noise is desirable, it is not essential.

D The test for 'excessive' noise is whether or not it may be heard in a public place and while evidence of acoustic measurements of the level of noise is desirable, it is not essential.

Question 8.23

Constable WHEELER was called to a local shopping centre because of a person causing annoyance. On arrival, Constable WHEELER saw GRAY sitting in a shop doorway, playing a guitar, busking for money. There were coins on a blanket in front of GRAY. At the officer's request, GRAY packed away the guitar and moved away from the doorway. However, the officer then observed GRAY approach a pedestrian and ask them for money.

Would GRAY's behaviour, as observed by Constable WHEELER, amount to an offence of begging, contrary to s. 3 of the Vagrancy Act 1824?

A No, GRAY's behaviour would not amount to begging in these circumstances.

B Yes, but only when GRAY asked for money; busking would not amount to begging.

C Yes, GRAY committed offences both when asking for money and whilst busking.

D Yes, but only when GRAY was busking; approaching one person to ask for money would not amount to begging.

ANSWERS

Answer 8.1

Answer **D** — An offence is committed contrary to s. 18(1) of the Public Order Act 1986, where a person uses threatening, abusive or insulting words or behaviour, intending to stir up racial hatred (or where it is likely to be stirred up). Certainly, the behaviour of the person in the question would meet these criteria. However, s. 18(2) states that the offence may be committed in a public or private place, but not when the words or behaviour used are not heard by persons other than those in that or another dwelling. The requirement is similar to those under ss. 4 and 5 of the same Act, and since both persons were in the same dwelling, no offence is committed, whatever MEREDITH's intentions! Answers A, B and C are incorrect for this reason.

General Police Duties, para. 4.8.2.1

Answer 8.2

Answer **C** — Section 29B(1) of the Public Order Act 1986 states that

> A person who uses threatening words or behaviour, or displays any written material which is threatening, is guilty of an offence if he/she intends thereby to stir up religious hatred or hatred on the grounds of sexual orientation.

This offence is similar to the one contained in s. 18 of the Act, where a person may be guilty of stirring up racial hatred by using threatening, abusive or insulting words or behaviour (or displays any written material) with intent to stir up racial hatred or where it is likely to be stirred up. One of the key differences between these offences is that under s. 29B, the words or behaviour must amount to some sort of threat. To reinforce this, s. 29J of the Act provides that the offences of stirring up religious hatred are not intended to limit or restrict discussion, criticism or expressions of antipathy, dislike, ridicule or insult or abuse of a particular religion or belief.

Therefore, even though HAWKINS's words were insulting and intended to stir up religious hatred, this particular offence would not be made out. (There may of course be a case to prosecute HAWKINS for an offence under s. 18 or even s. 4A of the Public Order Act 1986.) Answers A and B are therefore incorrect.

Since it is the defendant's intent that is relevant under this section, it is immaterial whether or not religious hatred was actually stirred up, or whether the people who were subject of the behaviour were actually concerned by it. Answer D is therefore incorrect.

General Police Duties, para. 4.8.2.5

Answer 8.3

Answer **A** — Section 29AB of the 1986 Act defines 'hatred on the grounds of sexual orientation'. The definition covers hatred against a group of persons defined by reference to their sexual orientation, be they heterosexual, homosexual or bisexual. The new ss. 29B to 29G of the 1986 Act have extended the various religious hatred offences in those sections to cover hatred on the grounds of sexual orientation. The offence may involve the use of words or behaviour or *display of written material* (s. 29B). Therefore, answer C is incorrect.

However, the offences differ from the offences of stirring up racial hatred in two respects. First, the offences apply only to 'threatening' words or behaviour, rather than 'threatening, abusive or insulting' words or behaviour. Answers B and D are incorrect, because the behaviour exhibited, whilst being very insulting, did not contain threats. The second difference is that in this section, the offences apply only to words or behaviour if the accused 'intends' to stir up hatred on grounds of sexual orientation. They do not apply in circumstances which are 'likely' to stir up hatred and answer D is incorrect for this reason also.

General Police Duties, para. 4.8.3

Answer 8.4

Answer **A** — Under section 2A(1) of the Protection from Harassment Act 1997, a person is guilty of an offence if:

- the person pursues a course of conduct in breach of s. 1(1) of the 1997 Act (i.e. a course of conduct which amounts to harassment); and
- the course of conduct amounts to stalking.

There are two matters, therefore, which need to be proved. Has the person pursued a course of conduct which amounts to harassment? Does the conduct amount to stalking? Answer C is incorrect because a course of conduct must be proved.

Section 2A(2) states that a course of conduct amounts to stalking of another person if it amounts to harassment and the person knows or ought to know that the course of conduct amounts to harassment of the other person. This section also states that the acts *or omissions* involved must be those that are associated with stalking; therefore, answer B is incorrect.

Section 2A(3) lists examples of behaviours associated with stalking, which include:

- following a person;
- contacting, or attempting to contact, a person by any means;
- publishing any statement or other material:
  (i) relating or purporting to relate to a person, or
  (ii) purporting to originate from a person;
- monitoring the use by a person of the internet, email or any other form of electronic communication;
- loitering in any place (whether public or private);
- interfering with any property in the possession of a person;
- watching or spying on a person.

Since simply *monitoring* a person's email amounts to an offence, answers B and D are incorrect.

General Police Duties, para. 4.8.4

Answer 8.5

Answer **D** — Section 4A of the Protection from Harassment Act 1997 prohibits a course of conduct relating to the offence of stalking involving fear of violence or serious alarm or distress. The first arm of the offence prohibits a course of conduct that causes the victim to fear, on at least two occasions, that violence will be used against them (which is similar to the existing s. 4 offence).

The second arm of the offence prohibits a course of conduct which causes 'serious alarm or distress' which has a 'substantial adverse effect on the day-to-day activities of the victim', which will include the victim moving home and changing the way they socialise. This is designed to recognise the serious impact that stalking may have on victims, even where an explicit fear of violence is not created by each incident of stalking behaviour. Answers A and B are incorrect as the offence may be committed when *either* of these outcomes is present and BERRY has most certainly changed her lifestyle as a result of TROTT's behaviour.

The issue of a 'course of conduct' relating to the s. 4 offence was addressed in *R (On the application of A) v DPP* [2004] EWHC 2454 (Admin). In this case, the defendant's conduct on the first occasion (e.g. a threat to burn the victim's house down) did not cause the victim undue concern, but a second threat some time later to do the same thing *did* put the victim in fear of violence, partly because this was the second time the threat had been made. The defendant argued that the victim had only been put in fear of violence by his threats to burn her house down on the second occasion and therefore there had been no course of conduct (i.e. the victim had only feared violence on one occasion, as opposed to the two occasions that were required by the section). The Divisional Court disagreed and held that the magistrates were entitled to find as a matter of fact that the two incidents had put the victim in fear of violence, notwithstanding her admission that, on the first occasion, she had not been too concerned. While this case relates to a different offence, the elements for a course of conduct will be the same for s. 4 and s. 4A and therefore answer C is incorrect.

General Police Duties, para. 4.8.4

Answer 8.6

Answer **D** — If an accused intends to cause alarm or distress and actually does so, that is likely to meet the requirements of s. 1 (*Baron* v *Crown Prosecution Service* (Divisional Court, 13 June 2000)), provided he follows a course of conduct. Course of conduct has been considered by the courts. In *Lau* v *DPP* [2000] 1 FLR 799, the Divisional Court held that although only two incidents are necessary, the fewer the number of incidents and the further apart they are, the less likely it is that there will be a finding of harassment. In *Baron*, the court accepted that the more spread out and limited in number the incidents and the more indirect their means of delivery (in this case by letter), the less likely it is that a course of conduct amounting to harassment will be found. However, there is no rule and it will depend upon the facts of each individual case. In *Baron*, two letters sent some four-and-a-half months apart could be a course of conduct amounting to harassment, and therefore answer B is incorrect.

Note it is alarm *or* distress; the court need only be satisfied that the behaviour involved one or the other (*DPP* v *Ramsdale* [2001] EWHC 106 (Admin)), and therefore answer C is incorrect.

Finally, the court in *Baron* refused to endorse the view that public service employees are less likely to be caused distress by threatening letters, and therefore answer A is incorrect.

General Police Duties, para. 4.8.4.1

Answer 8.7

Answer **A** — Under s. 1(1A) of the Protection from Harassment Act 1997, a person commits an offence if he/she pursues a course of conduct which involves harassment of two or more persons and which he/she knows or ought to know involves harassment of those persons and by which he/she intends to persuade any person not to do something which he or she is entitled or required to do, or to do something that he or she is not under any obligation to do.

Under s. 7(3)(b) of the Act, a course of conduct for this offence must involve, in the case of conduct in relation to two or more people, conduct on at least one occasion to each of those people. The fact that the letters were sent by two different people is irrelevant, because under s. 7(3A), a person's conduct may be aided and abetted by another, and both would commit this offence provided it can be shown they were acting together. Answer B is therefore incorrect.

Home Office Circular 34/2005 provides examples of offences which might be committed under s. 1(1A). In this guidance, it cites the example of an animal rights extremist sending a threatening email to an individual on one occasion working for one company and another similar letter to a different individual working for another company, with the intention of persuading them to stop supplying a third company with their products (similar to the circumstances in this question). Since the offence may be committed by sending different forms of communication to only one person from each company, answers C and D are incorrect (this is true even though the communications were sent by two different people).

General Police Duties, para. 4.8.4.1

Answer 8.8

Answer **C** — Section 1(2) of the Protection from Harassment Act 1997 states that for the purposes of this section

the person whose course of conduct is in question ought to know that it amounts to or involves harassment of another if a reasonable person in possession of the same information would think the course of conduct amounted to or involved harassment of the other.

This is an objective test as to whether that conduct was reasonable in the judgment of the jury/court—the test is not about whether the defendant 'knew' that the conduct amounted to harassment and therefore answer D is incorrect.

The Court of Appeal has held that no characteristics of the defendant can be attached to the word 'reasonable' (*R* v *Colohan* [2001] EWCA Crim 1251) and for that reason answer B is incorrect.

Although the defendant's mental illness may be relevant to sentence, the protective and preventive nature of the Act together with the objective nature of these tests means that such illness does not provide a defence. Answer A is therefore incorrect.

General Police Duties, para. 4.8.4.2

Answer 8.9

Answer **A** — For an offence of putting people in fear of violence contrary to s. 4 of the Protection from Harassment Act 1997, it has to be shown that a course of conduct caused a person to fear, on at least two occasions, that violence would be used against them. The Divisional Court examined this issue in the case of *R (On the application of A)* v *DPP* [2004] EWHC 2454 (Admin). In a case similar to the one in this question, the defendant argued that the victim had only been put in fear of violence by his threats to burn her house down on the second occasion; therefore the offence had not been made out. The Divisional Court disagreed and held that the magistrates were entitled to find that the two incidents had put the victim in fear of violence, notwithstanding her admission that, on the first occasion, she had not been too concerned. Answer B is therefore incorrect.

It must then be shown that the defendant knew or ought to have known that the victim would fear that violence would be used against them. Therefore, answer D is incorrect. This is not an offence of 'intent' but is subject to a test of reasonableness against the standard of an ordinary person in possession of the same facts as the defendant, and therefore answer C is incorrect.

General Police Duties, para. 4.8.4.7

Answer 8.10

Answer **D** — Under ss. 3 and 3A of the Protection from Harassment Act 1997, the High Court *or* a county court may issue an injunction in respect of civil proceedings brought in respect of an actual *or* apprehended breach of s. 1(1) and (1A). Answers A and B are therefore incorrect.

The effect of this is that a defendant may be made the subject of an injunction even though their behaviour has not amounted to an offence under the 1997 Act, or regardless of whether they were previously convicted of a s. 4 offence. Answer C is therefore incorrect.

General Police Duties, para. 4.8.4.9

Answer 8.11

Answer **B** — Section 5(5) of the Protection from Harassment Act 1997 states that if without reasonable excuse the defendant does anything which he/she is prohibited from doing by an order under this section, he/she is guilty of an offence.

The circumstances in this question are similar to those in *R v Evans (Dorothy)* [2004] EWCA Crim 3102. In that case the appellant had been convicted of harassing her neighbours and a restraining order had been made by the court. Among other things, the order prohibited the appellant from 'using abusive words or actions' towards her neighbours. Some time into the life of the order, the neighbour called a plumber out to her house and he parked his van in the street. It was alleged that the appellant then moved her own car, which was also parked in the street, into such a position that it effectively blocked the plumber's van. The appellant was convicted of the offence of breaching the order and appealed, partly on the basis that her conduct could not properly be said to have amounted to 'abusive action'.

The Court of Appeal held that such matters should be approached in the same way as specific legislation which outlaws abusive conduct, and that a jury was entitled to conclude that, as she had been motivated by spite, the appellant's actions *could* be 'abusive' for this purpose. This was regardless of whether MURRAY's behaviour was directed at WALTON, or a third party. Answers A and D are therefore incorrect.

However, in the *Evans* case, the Court of Appeal also considered the issue of 'reasonable excuse', when it came to the defendant's understanding of the terms of the order. The court held that harassment takes many forms and therefore the courts need to be able to prohibit conduct in fairly wide terms (e.g. in the wording of the order). It is, however, unclear just how far the defendant's subjective understanding of the terms of the order will be relevant. *If a defendant honestly believed that his/her conduct did not breach the terms of the order, this would certainly be relevant when considering whether or not he/she had a 'reasonable excuse'.* MURRAY's belief is therefore relevant, which makes answer B correct, and answer C incorrect.

General Police Duties, paras 4.8.4.11, 4.8.4.12

Answer 8.12

Answer **D** — Under s. 1C of the Crime and Disorder Act 1998, criminal courts may make an ASBO in respect of a defendant where he or she has been convicted of a criminal offence. The court can make an order of its own volition, irrespective of whether any specific application has been made by the relevant authority (which makes answer A incorrect). The order can only be made in addition to any sentence or conditional discharge (which makes answer B incorrect) (s. 1C(4)).

The issue of whether the same material should be used from a criminal trial to support the application of an ASBO was examined in the case of *S v Poole Borough Council* [2002] EWHC 244 (Admin). In this case, the defendant had been convicted of several offences under the Education Act 1996, and objected to the same material being used from his criminal trial to support the application of an ASBO. He argued that the use of the ASBO had been intended as an alternative to prosecution. The Divisional Court did not find in favour of the appellant, and it held that it was 'perfectly proper' to use the same material in this way and that an ASBO is akin to an injunction in a civil court. Answer C is therefore incorrect.

General Police Duties, paras 4.8.5, 4.8.5.1

Answer 8.13

Answer **C** — The Drugs Act 2005 inserted ss. 1G and 1H into the Crime and Disorder Act 1998, and the sections relate to intervention orders. This type of order can be made alongside an ASBO when drug misuse has been a cause of the behaviour that led to the ASBO being made.

An intervention order sets out the specified activities and attendance requirements of a defendant, and the duration of the order cannot exceed six months (s. 1G). The breach of an order is a summary offence (s. 1H).

Answers A, B and D are therefore incorrect.

General Police Duties, para. 4.8.5.1

Answer 8.14

Answer **B** — Section 1(1) of the Crime and Disorder Act 1998 states that an application for an ASBO may be made by a relevant authority if it appears to the authority that the following conditions are fulfilled with respect to any person *aged 10 or over*. Answer C is therefore incorrect.

Under s. 1(1), the relevant authority must also show—

(a) that the person has acted in an anti-social manner, that is to say, in a manner that caused or was likely to cause harassment, alarm or distress to one or more persons not of the same household as himself/herself; and

(b) that such an order is necessary to protect relevant persons from further anti-social acts by him/her.

Since the behaviour must amount to harassment, alarm or distress to *one or more* persons not of the same household as himself/herself, answer D is incorrect. Further, there is no requirement for more than one *household* to be affected and therefore answer A is incorrect.

General Police Duties, para. 4.8.5.1

Answer 8.15

Answer **B** — Section 1(1) of the Criminal Justice and Immigration Act 2008 provides that where a person aged under 18 is convicted of an offence, the court by or before which the person is convicted may make a Youth Rehabilitation Order (YRO), which can impose on the person any one or more of a number of requirements. The Order has a number of potential requirements each of which can operate as a stand-alone requirement or be combined with other requirements under the YRO. Examples of the type of requirements that may be made under a YRO include a supervision requirement, drug treatment requirement, curfew or unpaid work requirement.

The Act specifies that a person may only be made subject to an unpaid work requirement if he or she is 16 or 17 years of age. Answer D is incorrect as there *are* restrictions on a person's age for some interventions.

However, there are no such restrictions in respect of a curfew requirement and therefore answers A and C are incorrect.

General Police Duties, para. 4.8.5.2

Answer 8.16

Answer **B** — Exclusion orders may be granted under s. 205 of the Criminal Justice Act 2003 prohibiting a person from entering a place specified in the order, for a period specified but for a period of no more than two years. The order may specify different places for different periods or days.

Under s. 112(1) of the Serious Organised Crime and Police Act 2005, a constable may direct a person to leave a place if he or she believes, on reasonable grounds, that the person is in breach of an order.

A person who knowingly contravenes a direction given to him under this section is guilty of a summary offence (see s. 112(5)). Since the offence is committed when the person fails to comply with the direction (not when they simply breach the order), answers C and D are incorrect.

A direction under this section may be given orally (see s. 112(4)). Answer A is incorrect as there is no requirement to send a notice in writing.

General Police Duties, paras 4.8.5.4, 4.8.5.5

Answer 8.17

Answer **C** — Part 1A of the Anti-social Behaviour Act 2003, added by the Criminal Justice and Immigration Act 2008, makes provision for closure orders in respect of premises associated with persistent disorder or nuisance. Either the police or the local authority may apply for a closure order, provided they consult with each other.

If a closure order is applied for by the police, a constable (or a person authorised by the chief officer of police) may enter the premises and secure them against entry by any other person, using reasonable force if necessary. If the order has been applied for by the local authority, a person authorised by that authority may enter the premises and secure them against entry by any other person. Answers B and D are incorrect because entry must be made by the organisation which applied for the order, using reasonable force if necessary.

Section 11A(2) requires that the authorising officer must be satisfied that the local authority has been consulted and that reasonable steps have been taken to identify those living on the premises or with an interest in them before the authorisation for a closure notice is issued. However, the fact that the premises are privately owned will not bar the local authority from becoming involved, therefore answer A is incorrect.

General Police Duties, para. 4.8.5.10

Answer 8.18

Answer **D** — Part 1A of the Anti-social Behaviour Act 2003, added by the Criminal Justice and Immigration Act 2008, makes provision for closure notices in respect of premises associated with persistent disorder or nuisance. Either the police or the local authority may issue a closure notice, provided they consult with each other.

There must be reasonable grounds for believing that a person has engaged in anti-social behaviour on the premises *in the preceding three months* and that the premises are associated with significant and persistent disorder or persistent serious nuisance. The timescale is the same for both types of anti-social behaviour; therefore, answers A, B and C are incorrect.

General Police Duties, para. 4.8.5.10

Answer 8.19

Answer **A** — The behaviour of the defendant must interfere with the material rights enjoyed by a class of Her Majesty's subjects (*R v Johnson* [1997] 1 WLR 367). Answer D is therefore incorrect.

Although there is no 'magic number' of people who must suffer from the annoyance or obstruction in order for it to amount to a *public nuisance*, you must show that the act or omission affected the public in general as opposed to a small group of people (such as the employees of a firm). Therefore, in *R* v *Madden* [1975] 1 WLR 1379, where a person made a hoax bomb call to an organisation, it was held that such behaviour could in theory amount to a public nuisance, although in *Madden* it did not as the annoyance/obstruction was limited in its effect.

Further, in Lord Denning's view (*Attorney General* v *PYA Quarries Ltd (No. 2)* [1957] 2 QB 169), a nuisance would need to be 'so widespread in its range or so indiscriminate in its effect' that it would not be reasonable to expect one person to bring proceedings on his/her own to put a stop to it. Therefore, the number of people affected by the problem *is* relevant, and the number must be significant, regardless of how much danger is caused to the community. Answer C is therefore incorrect.

On the other hand, it was also held in the *PYA Quarries Ltd* case that it is *not* necessary to prove that every member within a class of people in the community has been affected by the defendant's behaviour; simply that a representative cross-section has been so affected. Answer B is therefore incorrect.

General Police Duties, paras 4.8.6.1, 4.8.6.2

Answer 8.20

Answer **B** — There are two offences covering *possession* of fireworks under the Fireworks Regulations 2004. First, an offence is committed by a person under the age of 18, who is in possession of an adult firework in a public place (reg. 4(1)). Adult fireworks are ordinary fireworks, which may be purchased by people over the age of 18, and will usually be used for families at their own homes on Bonfire Night. The second offence is committed where any person is in possession of a category 4 firework anywhere (reg. 5). Fireworks listed under category 4 are those which are more powerful than the ordinary ones referred to previously, and are used in large displays.

However, both of these offences are subject to the exception listed in reg. 6, which states that possession will not be unlawful if a person is in possession of fireworks in the course of his or her work or business, or where he or she has been properly authorised to conduct displays. Therefore, even though PLATT may not be authorised to conduct displays, he will be in possession of the fireworks as part of his work and does not commit the offence. Answer C is therefore incorrect. Also, because of this exception, it is irrelevant that he is under 18 (and answer A is therefore incorrect). Answer D is incorrect, as PLATT has a defence not because he is not in a public place, but because of the exception noted earlier.

General Police Duties, para. 4.8.6.7

Answer 8.21

Answer **B** — Regulation 7(1) of the Fireworks Regulations 2004 states that subject to para. (2), no person shall use an adult firework during night hours (11pm–7am).

Paragraph (2) lists the exceptions to this offence, which include setting fireworks off on 'permitted fireworks nights', such as Bonfire Night, during Diwali and on New Year's Eve; however, reg. 7 prohibits the setting off of *adult* fireworks, in other words, category 4 fireworks, which are generally only for sale to fireworks (or pyrotechnic) professionals. The type of fireworks bought by COURT in the supermarket are not affected by reg. 7, which is why answers A, C and D are incorrect.

General Police Duties, para. 4.8.6.8

Answer 8.22

Answer **C** — The Noise Act 1996 provides powers for local authorities to tackle the problems of noise within their community. Sections 2 and 3 of the Act allow for the serving of warning notices in relation to 'excessive noise' emanating from one house which can be heard in another at night (which is defined as being between 11 pm and 7 am). Since the test is that noise is emanating from one house which can be heard in another, answers A and D are incorrect.

The noise level should be measured using an 'approved device' (s. 6) and any warning must be served on the person who appears to be responsible for the noise or by leaving the warning notice at the 'offending premises' (s. 3(3)). However, under the Environmental Protection Act 1990 there is no requirement for evidence of acoustic measurements and a court may convict on other evidence, for example evidence from an environmental enforcement officer of excessively loud music being played (see *Lewisham Borough Council* v *Hall* [2002] EWHC 960 (Admin)). Answers A and B are also incorrect for this reason.

Note that s. 2(2)(b) of the 1996 Act includes noise emitted from any premises in respect of which a premises licence or a temporary event notice has been issued under the Licensing Act 2003, that can be heard in a dwelling.

General Police Duties, para. 4.8.6.11

Answer 8.23

Answer **A** — Section 3 of the Vagrancy Act 1824 creates the ancient offence of begging or gathering alms in streets and public places. A single act of approaching one person and asking for money is not, without more, enough to raise a *prima facie* case of begging (*R* v *Dalton* [1982] Crim LR 375). Answers B and C are therefore incorrect.

Where the person seeking money is doing something in exchange, such as singing as a busker, it has been held that this conduct does not amount to begging either (see *Gray* v *Chief Constable of Greater Manchester Police* [1983] Crim LR 45). Answers C and D are incorrect for this reason.

General Police Duties, para. 4.8.6.13

9 | Offences Involving Communications

STUDY PREPARATION

In the previous chapter, we studied the effects of more direct forms of harassment and anti-social behaviour. This chapter deals with perhaps more subtle communications, forming a more personal type of abuse, which can be equally distressing for the victim. The legislation covering these offences is varied, encompassing the Postal Services Act 2000 and the Malicious Communications Act 1988, and deals with harassment by letter, telephone call, text and email.

The chapter also covers offences of communicating false information, under the Anti-terrorism, Crime and Security Act 2001 and the Criminal Law Act 1977, with the intention of inducing fear that people's lives are at risk.

QUESTIONS

Question 9.1

CORTEZ belonged to a hardline group, which was protesting against the occupation of Middle Eastern countries by Western governments. At a pre-arranged time during a demonstration, CORTEZ along with some other demonstrators sprayed liquid in the faces of officers policing the demonstration, shouting that the substance was acid. In fact, the substance was a mild irritant, which produced no long-term effects.

What would the prosecution have to show in relation to CORTEZ and the others' states of mind, in order to convict them of an offence under s. 114 of the Anti-terrorism, Crime and Security Act 2001 (noxious substances etc.)?

A They intended that any person would fear either that his/her life was endangered, or that there would be a serious risk to human health.

B Only that they intended any person to fear that his/her life was endangered.

C They intended either to endanger life, or to create a serious risk to human health.

D They intended a particular person, or a particular group of people, to fear that their life/lives would be endangered.

Question 9.2

Until recently, MELLOR worked for a company that owned five night clubs and was the manager of one of the clubs; however, MELLOR was sacked after falling out with the owner, BOYD. On a busy Saturday night, between midnight and 12.30 am, MELLOR rang the receptionist at each of the five clubs stating that there was a bomb at one of the premises. MELLOR then texted BOYD with the same message. MELLOR was deliberately unspecific about the location, intending to cause maximum disruption, hoping that each premises would be evacuated.

Which of the following statements is correct in relation to MELLOR's liability under s. 51(2) of the Criminal Law Act 1977 (communicating false information)?

A Provided the intention was to cause the receptionist at each premises to fear that a bomb was likely to explode, MELLOR could be guilty of this offence.

B Provided the intention was to cause any person to fear that a bomb was likely to explode, MELLOR could be guilty of this offence.

C Provided the intention was to cause BOYD to fear that a bomb was likely to explode, MELLOR could be guilty of this offence.

D This section requires the offender to be specific about the location of the alleged threat; MELLOR could not be guilty of this offence as the message was too vague.

Question 9.3

FENWICK was due to go on a skiing holiday; however, leading up to the holiday, significant snowfall caused the airport to close down and flights were delayed. Three days before FENWICK was due to go on holiday, he posted a tweet on his Twitter account which stated, 'Airport still closed! They've got three days to get their act together or I'm blowing the airport sky high!!' The tweet was posted as a joke and was read by several hundred people; the comment received several replies, all of which were of a humorous nature. However, a week after it was posted, the tweet was read by a member of staff who worked at the airport, YOUNG, who considered that the matter was serious enough to make a report to the police.

Could FENWICK be liable for an offence in these circumstances, under s. 127 of the Communications Act 2003 (improper use of public electronic communications network)?

A Yes, even though the message was posted as a joke, it was menacing in its nature.

B Yes, although the message was not menacing in its nature, FENWICK sent a message which he knew to be false, causing needless anxiety to another (YOUNG).

C No, the message was not of a menacing character and FENWICK had no intention of causing needless anxiety to another.

D No, but FENWICK could be guilty of an offence under s. 51(2) of the Criminal Law Act 1977 (hoax bomb calls).

Question 9.4

ANDREWS runs a general store on a housing estate. The shop contains a counter within the premises that acts as an agent for the Post Office, providing a general postal service. LIMOUTH is a local resident whom ANDREWS had previously banned from the premises for shoplifting. LIMOUTH entered the store one day to use the post office counter to pay a bill. ANDREWS threatened to call the police if LIMOUTH did not leave immediately.

Which of the following statements is correct in relation to the power to remove a person from premises, under s. 88(4) of the Postal Services Act 2000?

A ANDREWS has the power to remove LIMOUTH under s. 88(4) at this point, before the arrival of the police.

B Section 88(4) does not create a power for members of the public to remove people from premises; however, the police may do so when they arrive.

C ANDREWS does not have the power to remove LIMOUTH under s. 88(4), because these premises are not covered by the Postal Services Act 2000.

D ANDREWS does not have the power to remove him under s. 88(4), without any further adverse behaviour by LIMOUTH.

Question 9.5

FOSTER runs a post office and recently had problems with CHILTON because FOSTER had refused to cash a cheque that CHILTON had presented. CHILTON then refused to leave the Post Office and the police were called. CHILTON was removed from the premises and told by FOSTER not to attend there again. CHILTON has just walked into the premises and been told by FOSTER, 'I've already banned you; I want you to leave now.'

Which of the following statements is correct, in relation to s. 88 of the Postal Services Act 2000?

A FOSTER is entitled to remove CHILTON from the premises if he refuses to leave.

B FOSTER is entitled to remove CHILTON from the premises in these circumstances alone.

C FOSTER is entitled to remove CHILTON from the premises if she suspects him of committing any offence under the Postal Services Act 2000.

D FOSTER is entitled to remove CHILTON from the premises if he refuses to leave and FOSTER suspects him of committing an obstruction.

Question 9.6

BOLIN was expecting an important parcel, but was out of the house when it arrived. BOLIN drove into the street as a van belonging to a national parcel delivery service was being driven away. BOLIN followed the van to the next delivery address and approached the driver, QUINLAN, asking whether she had a parcel for him. QUINLAN stated that parcels could only be delivered to an address and that if BOLIN's was on the van, it would be delivered the next day. BOLIN became angry and blocked in QUINLAN's van, refusing to move until she handed over his parcel. QUINLAN called the police and Constable NORTON arrived a short while later.

Considering offences and powers under s. 88 of the Postal Services Act 2000, which of the following statements is correct?

A Constable NORTON is required under this section to remove BOLIN from the scene, or assist QUINLAN to do so.

B Constable NORTON is required under this section to remove BOLIN, or assist QUINLAN; however, QUINLAN had the power to do so herself.

C BOLIN has committed an offence under this section by obstructing QUINLAN; however, the power to remove people only applies in a post office or related premises.

D BOLIN has committed no offence under this section; the offence only relates to an obstruction caused in a post office or related premises.

Question 9.7

GARNER was recently fired by TOGHILL, the manager of the company GARNER worked for. GARNER was upset at the dismissal and in order to get revenge, arranged for a ton of horse manure to be delivered to TOGHILL's home address and dumped on the front lawn.

Considering the offence under s. 1 of the Malicious Communications Act 1988, which of the following statements is correct?

A Provided it can be shown that it was GARNER's intention to cause distress or anxiety to TOGHILL, the offence is complete.

B GARNER's behaviour would not amount to 'sending a communication'; the offence relates to sending letters or electronic communications.

C GARNER's behaviour would not amount to 'sending a communication', because the 'message' was delivered by someone else.

D The offence is complete in these circumstances alone, regardless of GARNER's intention.

Question 9.8

HEALD was infatuated with his neighbour, FARR and continually asked her out on dates. FARR was flattered and not at all threatened by this, but refused to go out with him. HEALD then made an indecent phone call to FARR in an effort to 'turn her on'. HEALD did not, however, intend FARR to be distressed by these calls. She was not threatened and found it all mildly amusing.

Consider the offence outlined in s. 127 of the Communications Act 2003 of improper use of a public electronic communications network. Has HEALD committed this offence?

A Yes, but only if it can be proved the phone call was grossly offensive.

B Yes, even though HEALD did not intend to cause distress and FARR was not distressed by the call.

C No, HEALD did not make persistent use of a public electronic communications network.

D No, FARR was not caused annoyance, inconvenience or needless anxiety by the call.

ANSWERS

Answer 9.1

Answer **A** — Under s. 114(1) of the Anti-terrorism, Crime and Security Act 2001, a person is guilty of an offence if he/she—

(a) places any substance or other thing in any place; or
(b) sends any substance or other thing from one place to another (by post, rail or any other means whatever);

with the intention of inducing in a person anywhere in the world a belief that it is likely to be (or contain) a noxious substance or other noxious thing and thereby endanger human life *or* create a serious risk to human health. Answer B is therefore incorrect.

You do not have to show that the defendant had any particular person in mind in whom he/she intended to induce the belief in question (see the Anti-terrorism, Crime and Security Act 2001, s. 115(2) and the Criminal Law Act 1977, s. 51(3)). Answer D is therefore incorrect.

The key element to this offence is *not* any actual endangering of life or risk to human health, or an intention to do so; it is committing an act with the intention that someone else would believe such a thing would happen. Answer C is therefore incorrect.

General Police Duties, para. 4.9.2

Answer 9.2

Answer **B** — Under s. 51(2) of the Criminal Law Act 1977, a person who communicates any information which he or she knows or believes to be false to another person with the intention of inducing in him/her or any other person a false belief that a bomb or other thing liable to explode or ignite is present in any place or location whatever is guilty of an offence.

There is no need for the person making the communication to have any particular person in mind at the time the threat is made (s. 51(3)); therefore, answers A and C are incorrect.

It has been held that while the information communicated need not be specific, a message saying that there is a bomb somewhere has been held to be enough, even though no location was given (*R* v *Webb* (1995) 92(27) LSG 31). Answer D is therefore incorrect.

General Police Duties, para. 4.9.3

Answer 9.3

Answer **C** — The Communications Act 2003, s. 127 states:

(1) A person is guilty of an offence if he—
    (a) sends by means of a public electronic communications network a message or other matter that is grossly offensive or of an indecent, obscene or menacing character; or
    (b) causes any such message or matter to be so sent.
(2) A person is guilty of an offence if, for the purpose of causing annoyance, inconvenience or needless anxiety to another, he—
    (a) sends by means of a public electronic communications network, a message that he knows to be false;
    (b) causes such a message to be sent; or
    (c) persistently makes use of a public electronic communications network.

Communications under this Act take in public social media systems such as Twitter (see *Chambers* v *DPP* [2012] EWHC 2157 (Admin)). This case involved a man posting a joke on his Twitter account about a bomb hoax at an airport, who was arrested and charged under s.127. *However*, while the Divisional Court confirmed that a message posted on Twitter would fall within the remit of s. 127, it overturned Chambers's conviction on the grounds that the message itself was not menacing in its nature in the context that it was posted—the circumstances were similar to those in this question. Answer A is therefore incorrect.

If an offence under s. 127(1) is ruled out, has an offence been committed under s. 127(2)? While the member of staff who worked at the airport, YOUNG, was caused anxiety, s. 127(2) requires that the offender sent the message 'for the *purpose* of causing annoyance, inconvenience or needless anxiety to another'. This intent is not present in the circumstances outlined; therefore, answer B is incorrect.

Finally, under s. 51(2) of the Criminal Law Act 1977, a person who communicates any information which he or she knows or believes to be false to another person with the intention of inducing in him/her or any other person a false belief that a bomb or other thing liable to explode or ignite is present in any place or location whatever is guilty of an offence. However, the wording of the 1977 Act offence is in the present tense, which suggests that a message threatening to place a bomb etc. sometime in the future would not suffice. Answer D is therefore incorrect.

General Police Duties, paras 4.9.3, 4.9.6

Answer 9.4

Answer **D** — Under s. 88(1) of the Postal Services Act 2000, a person commits an offence if, without reasonable excuse, he or she obstructs a person engaged in the business in connection with the provision of a universal postal service, or obstructs the course of business of any universal postal service post office or related premises.

Under s. 88(3), a person commits a further offence if without reasonable excuse, he/she fails to leave a universal postal service post office or related premises when required to do so by a person who is engaged in the business of a universal service provider, and reasonably suspects him of committing an offence under subs. (1).

Section 88(4) provides that a person who commits an offence under subs. (3) may be removed by any person engaged in the business of a universal service provider.

This needs to be viewed as a step-by-step process; a person may be removed from premises using the power under s. 88(3) when he/she has first committed an offence under s. 88(1) *and* then refused to leave the relevant premises having committed an offence under s. 88(3). Returning to the scenario in this question, LIMOUTH has neither caused an obstruction nor has he failed to leave at this stage. Therefore, without any further adverse behaviour by him, there is no power to remove him from the premises at this stage. Answer A is therefore incorrect.

Anyone failing to leave when properly required to do so under subs. (3) may be removed by the post office staff but also, subs. (5) provides that *'any constable shall on demand remove, or assist in removing, any such person'*. Whilst this places a clear duty on individual police officers to help in removing offenders under these circumstances, post office staff may do so independently of the police and answer B is therefore incorrect.

Finally, 'related premises' are any premises belonging to a universal postal service post office *or* used together with any such post office (s. 88(6)), which would cover the type of premises in this scenario. Answer C is therefore incorrect.

General Police Duties, para. 4.9.4.2

Answer 9.5

Answer **D** — Under s. 88(3) of the Postal Services Act 2000, a person commits an offence if without reasonable excuse, he/she fails to leave a universal postal service post office or related premises when required to do so by a person who is engaged in the business of a universal service provider, and the person reasonably suspects him/her of committing an offence under subs. (1).

A person who commits an offence under subs. (3) may be removed by any person engaged in the business of a universal service provider (s. 88(4)(b)).

Offences under s. 88(1) relate to obstructing a person engaged in the business of a universal service provider in the execution of his or her duty, or obstructing a person while in any universal postal service post office or related premises. There is no power under this section to remove a person who has committed *any* offence under the Postal Services Act 2000 and answer C is therefore incorrect.

The power to remove a person is triggered only when the person who is engaged in the business of a universal service provider reasonably suspects that the person has committed an offence of obstruction *and* the person has failed to leave the premises. In the given scenario, the person has done neither and this power does not apply in the circumstances. Answers A and B are therefore incorrect.

General Police Duties, para. 4.9.4.2

Answer 9.6

Answer **C** — Under s. 88(1) of the Postal Services Act 2000, a person commits an offence if he/she obstructs a person engaged in the business of a universal service provider in the execution of his/her duty in connection with the provision of a universal postal service, *or* obstructs, while in any universal postal service post office or related premises, the course of business of a universal service provider. Since the obstruction offence may be committed in either of these circumstances, answer D is incorrect.

Under s. 88(5), a constable *shall* on demand remove, or assist in removing, any person who has committed an obstruction under this section and has without reasonable excuse failed to leave when required to do so by someone engaged in the postal provider's business. However, the power to remove a person only applies when he or she has committed an obstruction in a post office or related premises, and has refused to leave there. Answer A is therefore incorrect (although, of course, there may be offences committed under other Acts of Parliament).

Finally, under s. 88(4), a person who commits an offence under subs. (3) *may* be removed by any person engaged in the business of a universal service provider. Again, this power only relates to an offence committed on post office or related premises and therefore answer B is incorrect.

General Police Duties, para. 4.9.4.2

Answer 9.7

Answer **A** — Under s. 1(1)(a) of the Malicious Communications Act 1988, any person who sends to another person a letter, electronic communication or article of any description which conveys—

(i)   a message which is indecent or grossly offensive;
(ii) a threat; or
(iii) information which is false and known or believed to be false by the sender;

commits an offence. GARNER's behaviour would not amount to an offence under s. 1(1)(a), because this subsection relates to the sending of a 'message'. However, under s. 1(1)(b), the sending of any *article* or electronic communication which is, in whole or part, of an indecent or grossly offensive nature amounts to an offence. GARNER's behaviour *would* be covered by this subsection, and for this reason answer B is incorrect.

Under s. 1, a person is guilty of an offence if his/her purpose, or one of his/her purposes, in sending it is that it should, so far as falling within para. (a) or (b), cause distress or anxiety to the recipient or to any other person to whom he intends that it or its contents or nature should be communicated. 'Purposes' is simply another way of saying 'intention' and since the prosecution would be required to prove intent, answer D is incorrect.

The offence can be committed by using someone else to send or transmit a message, or deliver an article (see s. 1(3)). Answer C is therefore incorrect.

General Police Duties, para. 4.9.5

Answer 9.8

Answer **B** — Section 127 of the Communications Act 2003 contains two separate offences. Under s. 127(1), a person is guilty of an offence if he/she—

(a) sends by means of a public electronic communications network a message or other matter that is grossly offensive or of an indecent, obscene or menacing character; or
(b) causes any such message or matter to be so sent.

Since the offence may be committed by sending a message that is grossly offensive *or* of an indecent character, answer A is incorrect.

The offence under subs. (1) is designed to deal with nuisance calls, and the offence is complete when the defendant sends the relevant message or other matter that is, as a matter of fact, indecent, obscene or menacing. There is no need to show intention on the part of the defendant, nor any resultant distress caused (answer D is therefore incorrect). The offence is complete by simply making an indecent phone call.

The separate offence under s. 127(2) of the Act *does* deal with causing annoyance, inconvenience or needless anxiety to another. Under this section, a person is guilty of an offence when they send or cause a message by means of a public electronic communications network that he/she knows to be false, or persistently makes use of such a network. However, since the behaviour of the person in this scenario is covered by s. 127(1), the offence is complete and answer C is incorrect.

General Police Duties, para. 4.9.6

10 | Terrorism and Associated Offences

STUDY PREPARATION

The law on terrorism contained in this chapter relates to the Terrorism Act 2000, the Terrorism Act 2006, the Counter-Terrorism Act 2008, the Terrorism Prevention and Investigation Measures Act 2011 and the, still relevant, offences under the Explosive Substances Act 1883.

Areas covered in this chapter include the greatly extended definition of 'terrorism' and a 'terrorist' and police powers to deal with someone suspected of being one, as well as the obligations placed on members of the public to assist the authorities in identifying and dealing with terrorism.

Finally, the chapter deals with the policing powers derived from the Serious Organised Crime and Police Act 2005 to deal with campaigners opposed to experiments with animals.

QUESTIONS

Question 10.1

MEAH arranged a private meeting in a hotel room between HASSAN, who is a member of a proscribed organisation, and SAIF, who is not. The intention of the meeting was to allow HASSAN to persuade SAIF, who is a wealthy businessman, to provide funds for the organisation. MEAH himself is not a member of the proscribed organisation and was not present at the meeting.

In these circumstances, has MEAH committed an offence under s. 12(2) of the Terrorism Act 2000 (arranging a meeting to further the activities of a proscribed organisation)?

A No, the meeting did not occur in a public place.

B No, the meeting only took place between two people.

C Yes, at least two people were present at the meeting.

D No, MEAH was not present at the meeting.

Question 10.2

GIRVAN is an employee of a well-known high street bank. Over the last few months she has become increasingly suspicious of a customer's account and has started to collect information which she suspects demonstrates links between the customer's account and an animal rights group. She suspects, but has no evidence, that the customer is providing money that will be used for acts of terrorism. However, she has collected information relating to his personal bank account that she suspects to be important.

In relation to disclosing her suspicions to the police, which of the following statements is correct?

A She should disclose the information as soon as it amounts to admissible evidence.

B She must disclose the information now even if it does not amount to admissible evidence.

C She should disclose only her suspicions now: the information she collected is confidential.

D There is no obligation to disclose: it is a matter of choice.

Question 10.3

CHARTERIS lived in a flat in London and believed that the person living in the opposite flat was a wanted terrorist. CHARTERIS's suspicions were based on a picture released by the police of a person who escaped after attempting to blow up a bus. CHARTERIS is too scared to contact the authorities.

Could CHARTERIS commit an offence under s. 38B(2) of the Terrorism Act 2000, by failing to disclose information about the person living in the opposite flat?

A Yes, CHARTERIS must disclose this information to a police officer as soon as reasonably practicable.

B Yes, CHARTERIS must disclose this information to a police officer or a member of Her Majesty's forces as soon as reasonably practicable.

C No, CHARTERIS did not come into possession of the information through work or employment.

D No, this offence is only committed if a person fails to disclose information about an offence involving the commission, preparation or instigation of an act of terrorism.

Question 10.4

The police received information about a person who is suspected to be assisting in the commission of a terrorist act. The informant stated that a person had been seen covertly photographing a crowded shopping centre and that their behaviour was extremely suspicious. A surveillance operation took place and ZAFAR was identified and detained in the shopping centre. Officers confiscated a laptop and a camera, which contained hundreds of photographs of crowded areas and iconic sites.

The Terrorism Act 2000 creates a number of different offences. Which of the following statements is true in relation to s. 58 of the Act (collecting or making a record of information relating to terrorism)?

A It must be shown that the photographs were in ZAFAR's possession to encourage the commission of terrorist acts by any person.

B It must be shown that the photographs were in ZAFAR's possession to provide practical assistance to any person in relation to terrorist acts.

C There is no requirement to prove any intent on ZAFAR's behalf; simply being in possession of the photographs in these circumstances is an offence.

D It must be shown that the photographs were in ZAFAR's possession to provide practical assistance to himself in relation to terrorist acts.

Question 10.5

GUL is appearing in the Divisional Court, having appealed against a conviction for encouraging acts of terrorism under s. 1(2) of the Terrorism Act 2006. The circumstances of the case were that GUL was accused of uploading videos on YouTube of scenes showing attacks on soldiers of the Coalition forces in Iraq and Afghanistan by insurgents. GUL did not deny posting the videos, but argued that there had been no 'encouragement' in the form of words or a statement and that the videos were not depicting scenes of terrorism, since they were showing scenes of a war.

Which of the following statements is correct, in relation to the term 'encourage-ment', in regard to an offence under s. 1(2) of the Terrorism Act 2006?

A Communication without words or any other statement (such as posting a video) would amount to 'encouragement' under the Act and the conviction should be upheld.

B Communication without words or any other statement would amount to 'encour-agement'; however, the scenes shown were not depicting scenes of terrorism.

C The defendant has not made an oral 'statement', therefore, this does not amount to 'encouragement'.

D The defendant has not made a 'statement', whether written or otherwise, there-fore, this does not amount to 'encouragement'.

Question 10.6

FARR has become associated with people who are in the process of being radicalised by a terrorist group. Some of the people have been sent to a training camp in the UK and FARR has been invited. Although FARR has not been directly involved in pre-paring for acts of terrorism, he suspects that the purpose of the training camp may be for his friends to receive instructions on bomb-making equipment and that he has been invited as a test of his loyalty.

If FARR does attend the training camp, what more would need to be shown regarding his intent, in order for him to be guilty of an offence under s. 8(1) of the Terrorism Act 2006 (attending a place used for terrorist training)?

A That FARR knew that at least one other person was present to receive training for the commission or preparation of acts of terrorism.

B That FARR knew the training was being delivered for the commission or prepar-ation of acts of terrorism.

C That it would have been obvious to a reasonable person that the training was being delivered for the commission or preparation of acts of terrorism.

D That FARR knew or believed the training was being delivered for the commission or preparation of acts of terrorism, or that he could not reasonably have failed to understand the purpose of the training.

Question 10.7

The police have been investigating five individuals suspected of preparing for acts of terrorism, and intelligence has been received that they are in possession of bomb-making equipment. In the early hours of the morning, their address is cordoned off, following a designation under s. 33 of the Terrorism Act 2000. Officers entered the address and arrested four of the five suspects. Intelligence is received that the fifth suspect is at an address—a nearby block of four flats—which was previously unknown to the investigation team. While an arrest team is en route to the address, further intelligence is received that the fifth person is in possession of the equipment. The Bronze Commander, Inspector BENSON, has contacted the Operational Commander, Chief Inspector CAWLEY and asked for authorisation to cordon off the new location immediately. Inspector BENSON has asked that the block of flats be included in the authorisation, so that other residents may be removed from any danger presented by the bomb-making equipment.

Which of the following statements is correct, in relation to an urgent authorisation under s. 33 of the Terrorism Act 2000?

A Chief Inspector CAWLEY does not have the power to make such a designation urgently, only a superintendent may do so in these circumstances.

B Inspector BENSON could make such a designation if it is required as a matter of urgency.

C The designation must be made by a superintendent, unless there are reasonable grounds to suspect that an act of terrorism is about to take place in the locality.

D Inspector BENSON could make such a designation if it is required as a matter of urgency. However, the power relates to the removal of vehicles or pedestrians and not to people in dwellings.

Question 10.8

MALIK was arrested along with ten other suspects during an operation which identified a terrorist cell, believed to be preparing for acts of terrorism in the City of London. Following an extensive investigation, nine of the suspected terrorists were charged with offences under the Terrorism Act 2000; however, there was insufficient evidence to charge MALIK. The Assistant Commissioner responsible for SO15, Counter Terrorism Command, has been meeting with the Secretary of State to provide an update on the operation. The Assistant Commissioner has expressed concerns about MALIK being released without charge, because he presents a significant risk to the public because of his suspected terrorism-related activities. They discussed whether or not it would be suitable to serve a Terrorism Prevention and Investigation Measures (TPIM) notice on MALIK, to restrict his movements.

Which of the following statements is correct, in relation to the service of such a notice on MALIK in these circumstances?

A The Secretary of State may authorise a TPIM notice to be served on MALIK if the matter is urgent; otherwise, the permission of the court must be sought.

B The Secretary of State must seek permission of the court in every case, before a TPIM notice can be served on MALIK.

C The Assistant Commissioner may authorise a TPIM notice to be served on MALIK if the matter is urgent; otherwise, the permission of the Secretary of State must be sought.

D The Secretary of State may authorise a TPIM notice to be served on MALIK, without reference to the court.

Question 10.9

Constable ALLEN has attended SAYEED's home address to serve him with a Terrorism Prevention and Investigation Measures (TPIM) notice, under s. 2 of the Terrorism Prevention and Investigation Measures Act 2011, to restrict his movements because of his suspected links to terrorism. The TPIM requires SAYEED to reside at the address on the notice and prohibits him from travelling overseas. The notice also contains a list of people that SAYEED is not to contact. On serving the notice, Constable ALLEN decided that SAYEED's address should be searched to discover anything that might breach any measures specified in the TPIM notice.

Which of the following statements is correct, in relation to whether Constable ALLEN may search SAYEED's address?

A A search of premises in connection with a TPIM notice may only be made under warrant.

B A search of premises may only be made in connection with a TPIM notice, where the person has absconded.

C A search of premises may only be made in connection with a TPIM notice, where there are concerns for public safety.

D A search of premises may be made at the time of serving a TPIM notice, for the purpose of discovering anything that might breach any measure specified in the notice.

Question 10.10

TELLER created a home-made pipe bomb, using explosives drained from a number of fireworks, having found out how to do so on the Internet. TELLER boasted about making the pipe bomb on a social networking site and the police were informed. A warrant was executed at TELLER's house and the bomb was found. TELLER was subsequently prosecuted for an offence under s. 4 of the Explosive Substances Act 1883, but pleaded not guilty on the grounds that the bomb was made out of mere curiosity and there was no criminal intent.

What might the court take account of, when deciding whether or not TELLER was guilty of this offence?

A That the bomb was capable of being detonated.

B That the bomb was in TELLER's possession for a criminal purpose.

C That the bomb was in TELLER's possession unlawfully.

D That TELLER or some other person intended that the bomb should be detonated in some way.

Question 10.11

HIGGINS is a campaigner opposed to the exploitation of animals. HIGGINS has managed to arrange a meeting with O'SULLIVAN, the CEO of Eastshire Holdings, a company which HIGGINS believes is about to supply products to Westshire Sciences Institute (WSI). WSI is known to conduct experimentation work with animals. At the meeting, HIGGINS intends to peacefully persuade O'SULLIVAN not to enter into a contract with WSI on moral grounds.

Would HIGGINS commit an offence under s. 145(1) of the Serious Organised Crime and Police Act 2005, in these circumstances?

A Yes, HIGGINS has tried to induce O'SULLIVAN into not entering a contract.

B No, this offence does not apply to contractual issues between companies.

C No, the offence would only be complete if HIGGINS had tried to persuade O'SULLIVAN to break a contract already in place.

D No, HIGGINS's peaceful behaviour would mean that no offence has been committed in these circumstances.

ANSWERS

Answer 10.1

Answer **B** — There are a number of serious terrorist offences arising out of proscribed organisations. In summary, these are:

- belonging or professing to belong to a proscribed organisation (s. 11(1));
- inviting support for a proscribed organisation (s. 12(1));
- arranging or managing (or assisting in doing so) a meeting of three or more people (in public or private) which the defendant knows is:
  - to support a proscribed organisation,
  - to further the activities of a proscribed organisation, or
  - to be addressed by a person who belongs or professes to belong to a proscribed organisation (s. 12(2));
- addressing a meeting to encourage support for a proscribed organisation or to further its activities (s. 12(3)).

Clearly, MEAH has arranged a meeting to support a proscribed organisation and/or further the activities of a proscribed organisation; however, the conditions listed previously are not all present. First, the meeting must be attended by three or more people; therefore, answer C is incorrect.

There is no requirement for the person who arranged the meeting to actually be present to commit the offence and therefore answer D is incorrect.

Finally, the meeting may take place in public or private. Answer A is therefore incorrect.

General Police Duties, para. 4.10.2.1

Answer 10.2

Answer **B** — There are a number of offences contained in the Terrorism Act 2000, and some relate to money and its use for the purposes of terrorism. GIRVAN's suspicions about the customer's activities, if proved to be true, would amount to such an offence. Section 19 of the 2000 Act places a statutory duty on people who form a suspicion about activities they believe amount to the offences outlined here, if that belief/suspicion is based on information that comes to their attention in the course of their employment. The duty is to inform the police without delay of those suspicions, and answers A and D are therefore incorrect. They must also disclose the information on which it is based, and therefore answer C is also incorrect. Failure to comply with this duty is an offence, punishable with five years' imprisonment.

General Police Duties, para. 4.10.4.1

Answer 10.3

Answer **A** — The Terrorism Act 2000, s. 38B states:

(1) This section applies where a person has information which he knows or believes might be of material assistance—
 (a) in preventing the commission by another person of an act of terrorism, or
 (b) in securing the apprehension, prosecution or conviction of another person, in the United Kingdom, for an offence involving the commission, preparation or instigation of an act of terrorism.

A person commits an offence if he/she does not disclose the information as soon as reasonably practicable (s. 38B(2)). This would include disclosing information which would lead to the arrest of a person for an offence involving the commission, preparation or instigation of an act of terrorism and therefore answer D is incorrect.

In England, Wales or Scotland, disclosure must be made to a constable, whereas in Northern Ireland, disclosure must be made to a constable or a member of Her Majesty's forces (s. 38B(3)). Answer B is therefore incorrect.

Section 19 of the Act places a statutory duty on people who form a suspicion about terrorism offences, based on information that comes to their attention in the course of their employment. However, this is not the case for disclosure under s. 38B. Answer C is therefore incorrect.

Note that it is a defence for a person charged with an offence under s. 38B(2) to prove that they had a reasonable excuse for not making the disclosure (s. 38B(4)).

General Police Duties, para. 4.10.4.3

Answer 10.4

Answer **B** — Section 58 of the Terrorism Act 2000 creates an offence of collecting or making a record of information (including photographs and electronic records) of a kind likely to be useful to a person committing or preparing an act of terrorism, or possessing a document or record containing information of that kind (s. 58). Since the offence relates to the collection etc. of documents for any person, answer D is incorrect.

The document etc. concerned must be of a kind that is likely to provide practical assistance to a person, rather than simply encouraging the commission of terrorist acts (*R* v *K* [2008] EWCA Crim 185 and *R* v *Muhommed* [2010] EWCA Crim 227). Answer A is therefore incorrect.

Finally, simply possessing such documents etc. will not amount to an offence in itself and answer C is for that reason incorrect.

Note that in *R* v *Brown* [2011] EWCA Crim 2751, it was held that s. 58 did not infringe the appellant's right to free speech under ECHR, Art. 10.

General Police Duties, para. 4.10.5

Answer 10.5

Answer **A** — An offence may be committed under s. 1(2) of the Terrorism Act 2006 when a person publishes a statement to encourage the commission, preparation or instigation of acts of terrorism or Convention offences ('Convention offences' include those in relation to explosives, biological weapons, chemical weapons, nuclear weapons, hostage-taking, hijacking, terrorist funds, etc.).

Section 3(1) provides that the offence can be committed by publishing a statement electronically, i.e. via the Internet and 'statement' includes a communication of any description, including a communication without words consisting of sounds or images or both (s. 20(6)). Answers C and D are therefore incorrect.

In *R* v *Gul* [2012] EWCA Crim 280, the defendant's conviction was upheld by the Divisional Court after he had uploaded videos onto the Internet of scenes showing attacks on soldiers of the Coalition forces in Iraq and Afghanistan by insurgents. The court held that the videos *were* depicting scenes of terrorism within the definition of s. 1 of the Terrorism Act 2000 and therefore answer B is incorrect.

General Police Duties, para. 4.10.6.1

Answer 10.6

Answer **D** — For the purposes of the Terrorism Act 2006, offences are grouped into three specific areas: encouragement etc. of terrorism, preparation of terrorist acts and terrorist training, and offences involving radioactive devices and materials and nuclear facilities and sites. The offences within the *preparation of terrorist acts and terrorist training* group are:

- preparation for terrorist acts (s. 5(1));
- providing instruction or training in any of the skills mentioned for the commission or preparation of acts of terrorism or Convention offences (s. 6(1));

- receiving instruction or training in any of the skills mentioned for the commission or preparation of acts of terrorism or Convention offences (s. 6(2));
- attendance at a place used for terrorist training (s. 8(1)).

In relation to the offences of providing or receiving instruction or training under s. 6, the skills mentioned include the making, handling or use of a noxious substance; the use of any method or technique for doing anything capable of being done for the purposes of terrorism; and the design or adaptation for the purposes of terrorism of any method or technique for doing anything.

In *R* v *Da Costa* [2009] EWCA Crim 482, it was held that the person delivering the training had to know that one or more of those receiving it intended to use it for a terrorist purpose. However, this was the *mens rea* required to prove an offence by the person delivering training and not the person receiving it and therefore answer A is incorrect.

In order to prove an offence under s. 8(1), it must be shown that the person *either knew or believed that the instruction or training was wholly or partly for purposes connected with the commission or preparation of acts of terrorism, or that the person could not reasonably have failed to understand the purpose of such instruction or training* (s. 8(2)). This is wider than simply 'knowing' the purpose of the training, and therefore answer B is incorrect.

There is no mention of what would have been obvious to a reasonable person; therefore, answer C is incorrect.

General Police Duties, para. 4.10.6.2

Answer 10.7

Answer **B** — Section 33 of the Terrorism Act 2000 provides the power to cordon off areas. Generally, the power to make such a designation is limited to a police officer who is of at least the rank of superintendent (s. 34(1)). However, s. 34(2) states that a constable who is not of the rank required by subs. (1) may make a designation if he considers it necessary by reason of urgency. Answer A is therefore incorrect.

Section 33(2) states that a designation may be made only if the person making it considers it expedient for the purposes of a terrorist investigation. Neither of these sections require the authorising officer to have reasonable grounds to believe that an act of terrorism is about to take place in the locality, even if the matter is urgent, and therefore answer C is incorrect.

Section 36(1) of the Act outlines the actions a constable in uniform (or PCSO) may take in a cordoned area. They may order a person in a cordoned area to leave it immediately, order the driver or person in charge of a vehicle to move it from the area immediately, remove a vehicle in such an area or prohibit or restrict access to a cordoned area by pedestrians or vehicles. Under s. 36(1)(b) a power is given to order a person *immediately to leave premises which are wholly or partly in or adjacent to a cordoned area*. Answer D is therefore incorrect.

General Police Duties, paras 4.10.7.5, 4.10.7.6, 4.10.7.7

Answer 10.8

Answer **A** — Terrorism Prevention and Investigation Measures (TPIM) are a civil preventative measure, issued under s. 2 of the Terrorism Prevention and Investigation Measures Act 2011, which are intended to protect the public from the risk posed by suspected terrorists who can be neither prosecuted nor, in the case of foreign nationals, deported, by imposing restrictions intended to prevent or disrupt their engagement in terrorism-related activity.

The Secretary of State may impose requirements, restrictions and other provision which may be made in relation to an individual by serving a TPIM notice on him or her if certain conditions are met (s. 2(1)). There are five conditions listed in s. 3, which must be met before a notice may be served. The first four, conditions A to D, generally relate to the reasonable belief of the Secretary of State that the notice is necessary to prevent or restrict the individual's involvement in terrorism-related activity.

Condition E states that a TPIM notice may be served if—

(a) the court gives the Secretary of State permission under section 6, *or*
(b) the Secretary of State reasonably considers that the urgency of the case requires terrorism prevention and investigation measures to be imposed without obtaining such permission.

Therefore, the Secretary of State *may* impose requirements, restrictions and other provision which may be made in relation to an individual by authorising a TPIM notice to be served on him or her, providing the matter is urgent; and answer B is therefore incorrect. However, unless the circumstances are urgent, the permission of the court must be sought. Answer D is therefore incorrect.

There is no facility under s. 3 for a TPIM notice to be authorised by an Assistant Commissioner and for that reason answer C is incorrect.

General Police Duties, para. 4.10.8

Answer 10.9

Answer **D** — Terrorism Prevention and Investigation Measures (TPIM) are a civil preventative measure, issued under s. 2 of the Terrorism Prevention and Investigation Measures Act 2011, which are intended to protect the public from the risk posed by suspected terrorists who can be neither prosecuted nor, in the case of foreign nationals, deported, by imposing restrictions intended to prevent or disrupt their engagement in terrorism-related activity.

Section 24 gives effect to sch. 5. The schedule provides for powers of entry, search, seizure and retention in a number of scenarios relating to TPIM notices. These include:

Without a warrant:

• entry and search of premises to locate an individual for the purpose of serving a TPIM notice (or other specified notices) on that individual;
• search of an individual or premises at the time of serving a TPIM notice for the purpose of discovering anything that might breach any measure specified in the TPIM notice;
• search of premises on suspicion that an individual subject to a TPIM notice has absconded; and
• search of an individual subject to a TPIM notice for public safety purposes.

With a warrant:

• search of an individual or premises for purposes of determining whether the individual is complying with the measures specified in the TPIM notice.

Therefore, searches *may* take place without a warrant, *or* where the person has absconded or where there are concerns for public safety.

Answers A, B and C are therefore incorrect.

General Police Duties, para. 4.10.8.2

Answer 10.10

Answer **C** — Section 4(1) of the Explosive Substances Act 1883 states:

Any person who makes or knowingly has in his possession or under his control any explosive substance under such circumstances as to give rise to a reasonable suspicion that he is not making it or does not have it in his possession or under his control for a lawful object, shall, unless he can show that he made it or had it in his possession or under his control for a lawful object, be guilty of a felony...

Whether a person's purpose in having the items prohibited by these offences is a 'lawful object' will need to be determined in each case (see *R* v *Fegan* (1971) 78 Cr App R 189 and *R* v *G* [2009] UKHL 13).

In *R* v *Riding* [2009] EWCA Crim 892, a person alleged they had made a pipe bomb out of mere curiosity, using explosives drained from a number of fireworks. The defence contended that 'lawful object' meant the absence of a criminal purpose rather than a positive object that was lawful. However, the court was satisfied it meant the latter and mere curiosity could not be a 'lawful object' in making a lethal pipe bomb.

There is no requirement to show that the bomb was capable of being detonated, that it was in a person's possession for a criminal purpose, or that the defendant or some other person intended that the bomb should be detonated in some way. Answers A, B and D are therefore incorrect.

General Police Duties, para. 4.10.9

Answer 10.11

Answer **D** — A person commits an offence under s. 145(1) of the Serious Organised Crime and Police Act 2005 if, with the intention of harming an animal research organisation, he or she:

(a) does a relevant act, or
(b) threatens that he or she or somebody else will do a relevant act,
in circumstances in which that act or threat is intended or likely to cause a second person to take any of the steps in subsection (2).

A 'relevant act' is an act amounting to a criminal offence, or a tortious act causing the other party to suffer loss or damage of any description.

The steps referred to in subs. (2) are:

(a) not to perform any contractual obligation owed to a third person (whether or not such non-performance amounts to a breach of contract); or
(b) to terminate any contract; or
(c) not to enter into a contract with a third person.

Since the circumstances in the question are covered by s. 145(2)(c), answers B and C are incorrect.

Under s. 145(3)(b), no offence is committed if the only relevant tortious act is an inducement to break a contract. This means that no offence is committed by people peacefully arguing, or representing, that one person should cease doing business with another on the basis of the other's involvement with an animal research organisation. Answer A is therefore incorrect.

General Police Duties, para. 4.10.11.1

QUESTIONS

Question 11.1

DENNIS owns an off-licence and had just closed the premises late at night, locking the door. HUDSON arrived at the premises in a drunken state demanding to be let in to buy a bottle of wine. DENNIS refused to allow HUDSON in and HUDSON began shouting, 'If you don't let me in, I'll smash all these windows.' HUDSON then sat on the wall waiting for DENNIS to open the shop door.

Assuming that an arrest may be necessary in these circumstances, does DENNIS have the power to arrest HUDSON for a breach of the peace, contrary to common law?

A No, the threats were made towards DENNIS's property, not DENNIS.

B Yes, provided DENNIS reasonably believed HUDSON would carry out the threat.

C Yes, provided DENNIS reasonably believed HUDSON was capable of carrying out the threat.

D No, only a police officer has the power of arrest to prevent a breach of the peace that has not yet occurred.

Question 11.2

Constable PIENAAR attended a domestic disturbance at DEMETRIOU's home. All was quiet on arrival; however, DEMETRIOU was extremely drunk and had been involved in a heated argument with his father before the officer arrived. Although no violence had been used or threatened, DEMETRIOU's father was in fear for his safety if DEMETRIOU carried on drinking after Constable PIENAAR left. DEMETRIOU offered to go and stay with a relative for the night; however, the officer feared that he might return to his parent's home and that a breach of the peace would occur. Consequently, Constable PIENAAR arrested DEMETRIOU to prevent a breach of the peace from occurring in the future.

Would Constables PIENAAR's use of this preventative power of arrest be lawful in these circumstances?

A No, the offer by DEMETRIOU to leave the premises would have negated the 'immediacy' required to use this power and the arrest was unlawful.

B Yes, Constable PIENAAR did not need to believe that a breach of the peace may occur in the 'immediate' future; a belief that one might occur sometime in the future would be sufficient.

C No, DEMETRIOU had not used any violence; Constables PIENAAR's belief that a breach of the peace may occur in the future would not satisfy the 'immediacy' required and the arrest was unlawful.

D Yes, Constable PIENAAR was required to believe that a breach of the peace may occur in the 'immediate' future; this requirement is satisfied in these circumstances.

Question 11.3

A group of 20 people have been charged with the offence of riot, following a serious incident of disorder on a housing estate. The Crown Prosecution Service intends introducing evidence that at least 15 of the defendants were threatening violence towards people from a minority ethnic group, while five defendants actually used violence towards them. Other evidence shows that at least ten other people were gathered near those charged. These people did not take part in the threats or violence, but their presence added to the intimidation.

According to s. 1 of the Public Order Act 1986, who can be found guilty of riot in these circumstances?

A Any of the people present who were not victims of the incident.

B Any of the defendants who used or threatened to use unlawful violence.

C The five defendants who actually used unlawful violence.

D None of the people present, as only five defendants actually used violence.

Question 11.4

A large group of people are appearing in Crown Court to answer a charge of riot, contrary to s. 1(1) of the Public Order Act 1986. The court has heard objections from the defence relating to the evidence provided by the Crown Prosecution Service regarding the defendants' 'common purpose'.

What evidence would the court require, relating to the issue of a 'common purpose'?

A That the defendants used simultaneous violence for a common purpose.

B That the defendants had an agreed common purpose.

C That the defendants had an unlawful common purpose.

D Only that the defendants had a common purpose.

Question 11.5

HOWLEY has been charged along with a number of other people, with an offence of violent disorder, under s. 2 of the Public Order Act 1986. HOWLEY intends to use the defence that he was intoxicated at the time of the incident, and that he was not aware of his actions.

What does s. 6 of the Public Order Act 1986 state in relation to the defence of intoxication?

A It cannot be used as a defence in relation to this offence, or an offence under s. 1.

B HOWLEY *may* use this defence if he can show either that his intoxication was not self-induced, or it was caused solely by taking a substance in the course of medical treatment.

C HOWLEY *may* use this defence, but only if he can show that his intoxication was not self-induced.

D HOWLEY *may* use this defence, but only if he can show that his intoxication was caused solely by taking a substance in the course of medical treatment.

Question 11.6

WORTON, CAMERON and MAHROOF appeared in Crown Court for violent disorder, contrary to s. 2 of the Public Order Act 1986, following a fight in a pub. After hearing the evidence, the jury acquitted WORTON of the offence.

Could CAMERON and MAHROOF still be convicted of the offence in these circumstances?

A Yes, only two people are required to have used or threatened unlawful violence for this offence.

B No, when a defendant is acquitted of this offence, all other defendants must also be acquitted.

C Yes, when a defendant is acquitted of this offence, the other defendants may still be convicted.

D Only if it can be shown that CAMERON and MAHROOF actually used violence (as opposed to threatening violence).

Question 11.7

Constable CARLISLE attended a report of a stolen vehicle being driven around a housing estate. On arrival, the officer saw SALTER getting out of the stolen vehicle. Constable CARLISLE arrested SALTER, who began violently to resist arrest. While the officer was waiting for back-up, a crowd of about eight people gathered around and each of them threatened violence towards Constable CARLISLE. Some of the people then started to punch and kick the officer to aide SALTER's escape.

Has an offence of violent disorder, under s. 2 of the Public Order Act 1986, been committed in these circumstances?

A Yes, if it can be shown that the people were present together, using or threatening unlawful violence.

B Yes, but only in respect of the people who were present together, using unlawful violence.

C Yes, if it can be shown that the people were present together, using or threatening unlawful violence simultaneously.

D Yes, if it can be shown that SALTER and the other people were deliberately acting together, to use or threaten unlawful violence.

Question 11.8

WEBB and CAHILL were in dispute about a boundary between their gardens. One day, CAHILL returned from work as WEBB was about to cut down a tree, which was in the disputed boundary area. CAHILL, who owned an Alsatian dog that lived in a kennel in the rear garden, saw what was happening and shouted at WEBB, 'Stop that or I'll set the dog on you and it will cause you serious injury.' The dog was still in the kennel, but WEBB was genuinely in fear that CAHILL would carry out the threat. At the time, WEBB was alone in one enclosed garden, and CAHILL was alone in the other. There were no other people present at the scene.

Could CAHILL be guilty of an offence under s. 3 of the Public Order Act 1986 (causing an affray) in these circumstances?

A No, there was no likelihood of another person being present at the scene, who would fear for their safety.

B Yes, CAHILL threatened WEBB with immediate personal violence.

C No, CAHILL would have to threaten or use personal violence towards WEBB, rather than making a threat with the dog.

D Yes, had a person of reasonable firmness been at the scene, they would have feared for their safety.

Question 11.9

HAWKER was drunk and was standing at the bar in a busy pub waiting to be served when HUGHES appeared alongside him. A bar staff member served HUGHES before HAWKER and he became very angry, shouting at HUGHES for pushing in. HUGHES made a sarcastic comment before moving away with his drinks. HAWKER continued drinking at the bar, brooding about the incident with HUGHES. Eventually, HAWKER saw HUGHES leaving the pub and followed him outside. HAWKER came up behind HUGHES and threw a punch, which completely missed, but would have caused serious injury had it connected. HAWKER was so drunk that he fell over before being able to follow up the punch. Constable DEANS was outside the pub and witnessed the incident. Because HUGHES was uninjured, the officer arrested HAWKER for an offence under s. 4 of the Public Order Act 1986.

Has Constable DEANS correctly arrested HAWKER for an offence contrary to s. 4 of the Public Order Act 1986 in these circumstances?

A No, HAWKER intended to take HUGHES by surprise, so that HUGHES would not have been aware of the assault until the act had occurred.
B No, because HUGHES did not believe that immediate and unlawful violence would be used against him.
C No, because HUGHES was not in fear that immediate and unlawful violence would be used against him.
D Yes, HAWKER intended to use immediate and unlawful violence against HUGHES.

Question 11.10

CONROY is appearing in court accused of using threatening behaviour towards Constable MERRECK, contrary to s. 4(1) of the Public Order Act 1986. CONROY has not denied using threatening behaviour, but is pleading not guilty on the grounds that the incident took place when both of them were inside a dwelling. The prosecution's solicitor has described the location of the alleged offence to the court: the incident took place in the hallway of a communal house that CONROY shares with seven other people. The hallway is accessed via a common front door, which has a digital keypad with the number restricted to the occupants. The residents have their own separate bedrooms with lockable doors and share other parts of the house, such as the lounge, kitchen and bathroom.

Would the location of the incident, as described by the prosecution's solicitor, qualify as a 'dwelling', under s. 8 of the Public Order Act 1986?
A No, where premises are shared by more than one person, no part of the structure can be classed as a dwelling as defined in s. 8.
B Yes, any part of a structure that is shared by more than one person will be classed as a dwelling as defined in s. 8.
C Yes, because the hallway could only be entered by way of a digital keypad and is restricted to the occupants, it will be classed as a dwelling as defined in s. 8.
D No, because this part of the premises is not occupied as a person's home it will not be classed as a dwelling as defined in s. 8.

Question 11.11

SADIQUE, who is Asian but from Uganda, has bought a product, which has failed to work. He returns it to the shop and is dealt with by AKANJI, a shop assistant who is Nigerian by birth. Less than happy with the service, SADIQUE calls AKANJI 'an African twat' and 'an African bitch'. AKANJI is very distressed by this and contacts the police.

Has SADIQUE committed an offence contrary to s. 31(1)(b) of the Crime and Dis-order Act 1998 (racially aggravated intentional harassment, alarm or distress)?

A No, as 'African' does not describe a racial group.

B No, as SADIQUE is from the same racial group as AKANJI.

C Yes, provided SADIQUE intended to distress AKANJI.

D Yes, there is no need to prove intent, provided distress is caused.

Question 11.12

Constable KELLEY stopped MAHER and his friend NEWTON, who were in a motor vehicle at night. Constable KELLEY had reasonable grounds to suspect they were in possession of stolen property and informed MAHER and NEWTON of his intention to search them and the vehicle. At the end of the search, which was negative, MAHER said to Constable KELLEY, 'I told you you wouldn't fucking find anything.'

Considering the requirements of s. 5 of the Public Order Act 1986 (using threaten-ing, abusive or insulting words or behaviour), is MAHER likely to have committed this offence?

A Yes, provided it can be shown that NEWTON heard MAHER's bad language.

B Yes, Constable KELLEY heard MAHER's bad language, which is sufficient to prove the offence.

C No, as it is unlikely that those present would have been caused any harassment, alarm or distress.

D Yes, if an innocent bystander had heard MAHER's bad language, that person may have been caused harassment, alarm or distress.

Question 11.13

Constable ROBINSON was on patrol in a shopping centre, when she saw INCE walking along, shouting and swearing in a loud voice. There were a number of shoppers in the area and Constable ROBINSON approached INCE and advised him to stop swear-ing and annoying people. INCE ignored Constable ROBINSON and walked away, con-tinuing to swear loudly at passers-by. Constable ROBINSON decided that it was necessary to issue INCE with a Disorder Penalty Notice for an offence contrary to s. 5 of the Public Order Act 1986.

What would have to be proved in relation to INCE's state of mind, for the offence under s. 5 to be made out?

A That he intended his behaviour to be insulting, or was aware that it was.

B That he intended his behaviour to be insulting.

C That he was aware that his behaviour was insulting, whether he intended it to be so or not.

D That he ought to have been aware that his behaviour was insulting.

Question 11.14

Inspector LOTT has been called to a residential property because a group of animal rights protesters have gathered outside. The group have followed PRICE to the house, believing that he lives there; however, he does not. The group is protesting against PRICE, who works at a local laboratory where they believe experiments take place involving animals. The group's intention is to intimidate PRICE into giving up his job at the laboratory. Also in the house is PRICE's friend, BLUNT, the house owner. BLUNT and PRICE have asked Inspector LOTT to move the protesters away from the premises.

What would Inspector LOTT reasonably have to believe in order to utilise his powers under s. 42 of the Criminal Justice and Police Act 2001, to direct the group to leave the area?

A That their presence amounts to, or is likely to amount to, the harassment of PRICE.

B That their presence amounts to, or is likely to amount to, the harassment of PRICE or BLUNT.

C That their presence amounts to, or is likely to amount to, the harassment of any person in the dwelling.

D That their presence amounts to, or is likely to amount to, the harassment of BLUNT.

Question 11.15

IRWIN was treated in the casualty department of a hospital, after falling and spraining a wrist. Although the injuries were not serious, IRWIN was convinced that the arm was broken. IRWIN returned to the hospital about four hours after being discharged and insisted on receiving further treatment. IRWIN began causing a disturbance and because the hospital staff were worried about their safety, they called the police. POWELL, the on-duty security guard, became aware of the disturbance and decided to deal with IRWIN before the police arrived. POWELL was a duly authorised NHS staff member.

Would POWELL have the authority to remove IRWIN from the premises before the arrival of the police?

A No, only a constable could do so, because IRWIN was a patient, waiting for medical advice.

B Yes, either POWELL, a constable or any NHS staff member could do so, because IRWIN was not a patient, waiting for medical advice.

C Yes, either POWELL or a constable could do so, because IRWIN was not a patient, waiting for medical advice.

D No, having received treatment less than eight hours ago, IRWIN may not be ejected from the premises.

Question 11.16

HALSTEAD is the chair of a city centre traders' association. Every Monday morning at 8.30 am, HALSTEAD organises a group of between 30–40 traders, who park their cars on the outskirts of the city centre and ride to work on bicycles. The group's aims are to highlight the harm caused by carbon emissions, and to ease traffic congestion. Due to the number of cyclists, some disruption is inevitably caused to vehicular traffic.

Considering s. 11 of the Public Order Act 1986 (public processions), as the organiser of the group, is HALSTEAD required to notify the local police?

A No, this legislation applies to demonstrations or protests; therefore, notice is not required.

B Yes, provided the bicycles follow a set route and a set time.

C Yes, this is a procession to publicise a cause or a campaign; therefore, notice is required.

D No, this legislation does not apply to commonly and customarily held processions, such as this.

Question 11.17

Constable JEFFERS, who is in full uniform, has been deployed to deal with a trespassory assembly, in respect of which an order under s. 14A of the Public Order Act 1986 has been obtained prohibiting it taking place. The officer is four-and-a-half miles from the monument where the assembly was due to take place, and is carrying out powers granted by s. 14C of the 1986 Act, preventing access to the site. The officer has stopped a vehicle, and has directed the occupants not to proceed in the direction of the assembly.

Are the officer's actions lawful?

A Yes, as the officer was in uniform the actions are lawful.

B Yes, the actions are lawful; it is immaterial that the officer was in uniform.

C No, the officer is outside the radius set by the Act at four miles.

D No, the officer has no power to stop vehicles under this section.

Question 11.18

Constable DONAHUE is the community beat officer on a housing estate, which has been suffering an ongoing youth annoyance problem outside a small shopping centre. One bank holiday weekend, the police were called to the location to deal with intimidation and annoyance towards shopkeepers and customers, on average 20 times a day. Constable DONAHUE was on duty on the bank holiday Monday and visited the shopping centre during the afternoon. There were two youths present who the officer knew were the main instigators. After speaking to the shopkeepers, Constable DONAHUE formed the opinion that there would be further harassment that afternoon and evening. Constable DONAHUE asked the control room if they could contact the on-duty superintendent, to consider whether an order should be given under s. 30 of the Anti-social Behaviour Act 2003, to disperse the two youths before the problem escalated again.

Would the on-duty superintendent be able to authorise such a request in the circumstances?

A No, because there are only two people present.

B Yes, because there are two or more people present.

C No, this power may not be used at such short notice.

D Yes, this is a significant and persistent problem; it is irrelevant how many people are present.

Question 11.19

A dispersal order under s. 30 of the Anti-social Behaviour Act 2003 is in place in a shopping centre, because of anti-social behaviour that had been caused by youths drinking excessively, intimidating shoppers and committing a number of robberies. One Saturday, a group of 20 people attended the shopping centre to stage a protest against America's involvement in Iraq. The group had not notified the police of their intention to protest. Their target was a large food hall area, which contained several American-owned fast food outlets. They intended preventing people from entering the shops and persuading them not to buy food there. They began shouting at shoppers who were entering the food hall and many people felt harassed and intimidated by their actions. The police were called to deal with the incident.

Would the officers attending the scene be able to use powers under s. 30(4) of the Anti-social Behaviour Act 2003 to disperse the protesters, by virtue of the order already in place?

A No, this would be an abuse of power; the order was in place for unrelated incidents of anti-social behaviour.

B Yes, but they would need the superintendent who gave the original order to extend the criteria to include the protest.

C No, a fresh dispersal order will need to be applied for by any superintendent to take in the behaviour by the protesters.

D Yes, the protesters may be dispersed using the powers granted by the first dispersal order.

Question 11.20

Constable DARCH was on patrol at 9.30 pm in a housing estate where, following incidents of significant and persistent anti-social behaviour, a dispersal order was in place. Constable DARCH saw PURSE, aged 15, staggering around shouting loudly and clearly drunk. PURSE refused to go home and even though there were no other young people in the area, Constable DARCH was concerned that PURSE would continue to act in an anti-social manner if left at the location.

Would Constable DARCH have the power to take PURSE home by force in these circumstances, utilising powers under s. 30(6) of the Anti-social Behaviour Act 2003 (power to remove people to their place of residence)?

A Yes, in order to prevent PURSE from committing anti-social behaviour.

B No, these powers only apply between the hours of 10 pm and 6 am.

C No, this power may only be used to protect young people at risk of anti-social behaviour by others.

D No, there is no power to use force under this section.

Question 11.21

The residents association on a housing estate has become increasingly concerned about gang-related activity in the area on most evenings. Young people have formulated into two rival gangs and there is evidence of regular violence taking place between them. Some of the gang members are as young as 12 years of age, and this has prompted members of the committee to approach the police to establish whether any action could be taken to prevent the gangs from continuing their activities.

Section 34 of the Policing and Crime Act 2009 deals with measures that can be taken to prevent gang-related activities. Which of the following statements is correct in relation to the members of the gang involved in the activities?

A Measures can be taken against any person under the age of 18.

B Measures can be taken against any person over the age of 14.

C Measures can be taken against any person who satisfies the conditions, regardless of their age.

D Measures can be taken against any person between the ages of 14 and 17.

ANSWERS

Answer 11.1

Answer **B** — A breach of the peace was defined specifically in *R* v *Howell* [1982] QB 416. A breach of the peace generally occurs when an act is done, or threatened to be done,

- which harms a person or, in his or her presence, his or her property; or
- which is likely to cause such harm; or
- which puts someone in fear of such harm.

Since DENNIS was in fear that harm would be done to the shop, answer A is incorrect. A constable or any other person may arrest without warrant any person:

- who is committing a breach of the peace;
- whom he or she reasonably believes will commit a breach of the peace in the immediate future; or
- who has committed a breach of the peace, where it is reasonably believed that a recurrence of the breach of the peace is threatened.

The power of arrest is given to a constable or any other person (answer D is therefore incorrect). There is no requirement for the person to reasonably believe that the person is capable of carrying out the threat, merely that the threat may be carried out. Answer C is incorrect.

General Police Duties, paras 4.11.2, 4.11.2.4

Answer 11.2

Answer **D** — A breach of the peace is defined in *R* v *Howell* [1982] QB 416; a case which stated that a breach of the peace generally occurs when an act is done, or threatened to be done

- which harms a person or, in his or her presence, his or her property; or
- which is likely to cause such harm; or
- which puts someone in fear of such harm.

A constable or any other person may arrest without warrant any person

- who is committing a breach of the peace;
- whom he or she reasonably believes will commit a breach of the peace in the immediate future; or

- who has committed a breach of the peace, where it is reasonably believed that a recurrence of the breach of the peace is threatened.

This means that if a constable (or other person) is to arrest a person where a breach of the peace has not yet occurred, but it is believed one will occur in the future (which is the case in this question), the arrest will only be lawful if it is reasonably believed that it will happen in the *immediate* future. Answer B is therefore incorrect.

Guidance on 'immediacy' in relation to conduct in a domestic setting is contained in *R (On the application of Wragg)* v *DPP* [2005] EWHC 1389 (Admin). In this case, police officers attending a domestic dispute found one of the parties, who had been in a heated argument with a relative also living in the house, to have consumed a large amount of alcohol. In relation to the immediacy or imminence test the police officers believed that a breach of the peace could take place in the house after they departed that night insofar as the other household member was at risk of immediate assault whilst the accused was still in drink. The arrest of the accused was held to be lawful. In *Demetriou* v *DPP* [2012] All ER (D) 165 (Apr) it was also held that an arrest was lawful if a person willing to leave premises but who an officer believed would return to cause violence gave rise to a reasonable basis for fearing imminent violence.

Answers A and C are incorrect for this reason.

General Police Duties, paras 4.11.2, 4.11.2.3, 4.11.2.4

Answer 11.3

Answer **C** — Under s. 1(1) of the Public Order Act 1986:

Where 12 or more persons who are present together use or threaten unlawful violence for a common purpose and the conduct of them (taken together) is such as would cause a person of reasonable firmness present at the scene to fear for his personal safety, each of the persons using unlawful violence for the common purpose is guilty of riot.

The offence of riot may be made out in these circumstances against the five defendants who actually used violence (answer D is therefore incorrect). However, only those defendants who actually used violence will be guilty and therefore answers A and B are incorrect. Of course, other defendants present may also be guilty of other serious Public Order Act offences.

General Police Duties, para. 4.11.4

Answer 11.4

Answer **D** — Under s. 1(1) of the Public Order Act 1986:

Where 12 or more persons who are present together use or threaten unlawful violence for a common purpose and the conduct of them (taken together) is such as would cause a person of reasonable firmness present at the scene to fear for his personal safety, each of the persons using unlawful violence for the common purpose is guilty of riot.

There must be a common purpose, but this need not be part of a predetermined plan, nor be unlawful in itself. Answers B and C are therefore incorrect.

Section 1(2) states that it is immaterial whether or not the 12 or more use or threaten unlawful violence simultaneously. Therefore, answer A is incorrect.

General Police Duties, para. 4.11.4

Answer 11.5

Answer **B** — Section 6(5) of the Public Order Act 1986 states:

For the purposes of this section a person whose awareness is impaired by intoxication shall be taken to be aware of that of which he would be aware if not intoxicated, unless he shows either that his intoxication was not self-induced or that it was caused solely by the taking or administration of a substance in the course of medical treatment.

The defence under s. 6(5) applies to all of the general Public Order Act offences; therefore, answer A is incorrect.

The defence may be raised either when the defendant claims intoxication was not self-induced or that it was caused solely by the taking or administration of a substance in the course of medical treatment. Answers C and D are therefore incorrect.

General Police Duties, para. 4.11.4.2

Answer 11.6

Answer **C** — Section 2(1) of the Public Order Act 1986 states:

Where 3 or more persons who are present together use or threaten unlawful violence and the conduct of them (taken together) is such as would cause a person of reasonable firmness present at the scene to fear for his personal safety, each of the persons using or threatening unlawful violence is guilty of violent disorder.

Section 2(1) requires three or more persons who are present together to use or threaten unlawful violence and therefore answer A is incorrect.

In order to convict any defendant of this offence, it must be shown that there were three or more people using or threatening violence. However, where two of the defendants are acquitted, the remaining defendant can be convicted (see *R v Mahroof* (1989) 88 Cr App R 317). Therefore, answer B is incorrect.

For an offence of riot, under s. 1 of the Act, only the persons who actually used violence may be convicted. This is not the case for an offence under s. 2; therefore, answer D is incorrect.

General Police Duties, para. 4.11.5

Answer 11.7

Answer **A** — Under s. 2(1) of the Public Order Act 1986, where three or more persons who are present together use or threaten unlawful violence and the conduct of them (taken together) is such as would cause a person of reasonable firmness present at the scene to fear for their personal safety, each of the persons using or threatening unlawful violence is guilty of violent disorder. Unlike the offence of riot (under s. 1 of the Act), for this offence each of the persons using *or* threatening unlawful violence may be guilty of the offence; therefore, answer B is incorrect.

Under s. 2, there is no requirement to show that the persons using or threatening unlawful violence did so simultaneously (unlike the offence under s. 1) and therefore answer C is incorrect.

The circumstances in this question are similar to the case of *R v NW* [2010] EWCA Crim 404. In that case, a person was violently resisting arrest by a police officer, during which time a crowd gathered and various members of the crowd used or threatened violence. The Court of Appeal held that for the purposes of this section, it was not necessary for a person to deliberately act in combination with at least two other people present at the scene, but that it is sufficient that at least three people be present, each separately using or threatening unlawful violence. Answer D is therefore incorrect.

General Police Duties, para. 4.11.5

Answer 11.8

Answer **A** — Under s. 3(1) of the Public Order Act 1986, a person is guilty of affray if he/she uses or threatens unlawful violence towards another and his/her conduct is such as would cause a person of reasonable firmness present at the scene to fear for his/her personal safety.

However, in order to prove this offence, the threat cannot be made by words alone (s. 3(3)). CAHILL has not committed an act of violence towards WEBB (either personally or with the dog) in these circumstances as the behaviour merely amounted to a verbal threat. Answer B is therefore incorrect.

The 'action' by the defendant *may* consist of utilising something else such as a dog to threaten the violence (*R* v *Dixon* [1993] Crim LR 579). Answer C is therefore incorrect.

Finally, for this offence to be complete, the House of Lords has held that, in order to prove the offence of affray, the threat of unlawful violence has to be towards a person (or persons) present at the scene (*I* v *DPP* [2001] UKHL 10). This means that there does have to be *someone* other than the defendant at the scene.

Once this element has been proved, it will be necessary to prove the second element, namely whether the defendant's conduct would have caused a hypothetical person present at the scene to fear for his/her personal safety (see *R* v *Sanchez* (1996) 160 JP 321 and *R* v *Carey* [2006] EWCA Crim 17).

However, where the likelihood of a hypothetical person of reasonable firmness being present was low this element of the offence was not satisfied. In *R (On the application of Leeson)* v *DPP* [2010] EWHC 994 (Admin) a woman had issued a drunken threat to kill her long-term partner whilst holding a knife, in a bathroom, in an otherwise unoccupied house. In these circumstances the court held that there was no possibility of a hypothetical bystander fearing for their safety.

The most recent case (*Leeson* noted previously) places a different perspective on the 'hypothetical' third person, and in the example given in this question, the two parties were in separate enclosed gardens, with very little likelihood of another person being affected by the behaviour (as opposed to a situation in a pub, for example, where several people could be injured). This makes answer A correct, and answer D incorrect.

General Police Duties, para. 4.11.6

Answer 11.9

Answer **A** — Under s. 4(1) of the Public Order Act 1986, a person is guilty of an offence if he—

(a) uses towards another person threatening, abusive or insulting words or behaviour, or

(b) distributes or displays to another person any writing, sign or other visible representation which is threatening, abusive or insulting,

with intent to cause that person to believe that immediate unlawful violence will be used against him or another by any person, or to provoke the immediate use of unlawful violence by that person or another, or whereby that person is likely to believe that such violence will be used or it is likely that such violence will be provoked.

Under s. 6(3) of the Act, a person is guilty of an offence only if he or she *intends* his or her words or behaviour to be threatening, abusive or insulting, or is aware that they may be. It is HAWKER's intent that counts, not whether HUGHES actually believed or even feared that immediate unlawful violence would be used against him. Answers B and C are therefore incorrect.

It is not possible to prove that the victim feared immediate unlawful violence, where it was the intention of the accused to take the victim by surprise so that they did not know they would be assaulted until the act had occurred. The court considered that the accused should have been charged with assault (*Hughes v DPP* [2012] EWHC 606 (Admin)). This case shows that if HAWKER simply intended to use immediate and unlawful violence against HUGHES without the required threats, the offence is not made out and therefore answer D is incorrect.

General Police Duties, para. 4.11.7

Answer 11.10

Answer **D** — An offence under s. 4(2) of the Public Order Act 1986 may be committed in a public or private place. However, no offence will be committed where the words or behaviour are used, or the writing, sign or other visible representation is distributed or displayed, by a person inside a dwelling and the other person is also inside that or another dwelling.

Section 8 of the Public Order Act 1986 provides the definition of a dwelling, which is:

> any structure or part of a structure occupied as a person's home or as other living accommodation (whether the occupation is separate or shared with others) but does not include any part not so occupied, and for this purpose 'structure' includes a tent, caravan, vehicle, vessel or other temporary or movable structure.

Therefore, it is not correct to say that where premises are shared by more than one person, no part of the structure can be classed as a dwelling. Living accommodation (such as a person's bedroom) will fall within the definition in s. 8, whether the occupation is separate or shared with others. Answer A is therefore incorrect.

On the other hand, it is also not correct to state that any part of a structure that is shared by more than one person will be classed as a dwelling as defined in s. 8. Even where accommodation is shared, any part of the premises not used as 'living accommodation' will not be classed as a dwelling. Answer B is therefore incorrect.

In *Le Vine v DPP* [2010] EWHC 1128 (Admin) a laundry room, commonly used by tenants in sheltered housing, did not form part of a dwelling. Similarly, communal landings which form access routes to separate dwellings have been held not to constitute part of a dwelling even though they could only be entered by way of an entryphone system (*Rukwira v DPP* [1993] Crim LR 882). Answer C is therefore incorrect.

Note that a police cell has been held not to be living accommodation for the purposes of s. 8 (*R v Francis* [2006] EWCA Crim 3323).

General Police Duties, para. 4.11.7.1

Answer 11.11

Answer **C** — This question loosely follows the circumstances of *R v White (Anthony Delroy)* [2001] 1 WLR 1352, where the Court of Appeal upheld White's conviction for this offence. The court held that the words used are to be construed as they are generally used in England and Wales; and on that basis the word 'African' described a racial group defined by reference to race and therefore answer A is incorrect. This offence can be committed towards people from the same racial group as the accused and answer B is therefore incorrect. This is a crime of 'specific intent' and as such does require the intent to be proven, and therefore answer D is incorrect.

General Police Duties, para. 4.11.8

Answer 11.12

Answer **C** — The Public Order Act 1986, s. 5 states:

A person is guilty of an offence if he—
(a) uses threatening, abusive or insulting words or behaviour, or disorderly behaviour, or
(b) displays any writing, sign or other visible representation which is threatening, abusive or insulting, within the hearing or sight of a person likely to be caused harassment, alarm or distress thereby.

There needs to be a person within whose sight or hearing the conduct takes place. This requirement was confirmed in *Taylor v DPP* [2006] EWHC 1202 (Admin), where it was held that there must be at least evidence that there was someone who could see, or could hear, at the material time, what the individual was doing. It would not be sufficient to show that an 'innocent bystander' may have been caused harassment, alarm or distress; there was no such person present and answer D is therefore incorrect.

The second element that has to be proved is that the person present was *likely* to have been caused harassment, alarm or distress by the defendant's conduct. In *Harvey v DPP* [2011] EWHC Crim B1 (Admin), the defendant had used bad language when detained by the police (saying, e.g. 'I told you you wouldn't find fuck all') and although this might have been considered abusive or insulting, there was no evidence that anyone involved, or any bystanders, had suffered or were likely to have been caused any harassment, alarm or distress. All those involved would have heard such language on many occasions and in consequence the Appeal Court quashed the conviction. Of course, each case will be different, but using the *Harvey* case as an example, it is likely that even if NEWTON had overheard the swearing, he would not have been caused harassment, alarm or distress by the words used by MAHER. The same would be the case in respect of Constable KELLEY and for that reason answers A and B are incorrect.

General Police Duties, para. 4.11.9

Answer 11.13

Answer **A** — Section 6 of the Public Order Act 1986 states that a person is guilty of an offence under s. 5 only if:

> he intends his words or behaviour, or the writing, sign or other visible representation, to be threatening, abusive or insulting, or is aware that it may be threatening, abusive or insulting, or (as the case may be) he intends his behaviour to be or is aware that it may be disorderly.

This is not an offence which relies only on the intent of the person exhibiting the behaviour; it can also be committed if a person is simply aware that their behaviour is threatening, abusive or insulting. Answer B is therefore incorrect. This is also a case of either/or: INCE would either have to intend his behaviour to be insulting, or he would have to be aware that it was; therefore, answer C is incorrect.

The fact that a person ought to have known that his or her behaviour was insulting is immaterial, making answer D incorrect. The person's state of mind is often ignored when it comes to charging people with offences under s. 5 (and s. 4). Occasionally, defence solicitors make a point of insisting that their client be interviewed before charge. While it may be impractical to interview all offenders for these offences, it may be worth considering when the facts are unclear.

General Police Duties, para. 4.11.9.1

Answer 11.14

Answer **D** — Section 42 of the Criminal Justice and Police Act 2001 gives the police certain powers to give directions in order to prevent intimidation or harassment. The legislation is designed to prevent protesters causing harassment to people in their own homes, as happened in this question. The most senior police officer present at the scene has discretionary powers to give directions to people in the vicinity, including a direction to leave the area.

In order to give a direction under s. 42, the officer must believe, on reasonable grounds, that the persons present are there for the purposes of persuading the resident or anyone else that they should not do something they are entitled or required to do, or that they should do something they are not obliged to do. The officer must also believe, on reasonable grounds, that the person's presence amounts to or is likely to result in the harassment of the resident, or is likely to cause alarm or distress to the resident. Therefore, in this question, even though the group's hostility is directed at PRICE, the outcome must be the harassment of BLUNT, the resident. Answers A, B and C are incorrect for this reason.

General Police Duties, para. 4.11.9.3

Answer 11.15

Answer **C** — Section 119(1) of the Criminal Justice and Immigration Act 2008 creates an offence of causing a nuisance or disturbance to an NHS staff member who is working on NHS premises and then failing to leave when required to do so by a constable or an NHS staff member. This section will only apply to people who are not on the NHS premises for the purpose of obtaining medical advice, treatment or care for themselves.

Section 120 of the 2008 Act provides a power for a constable or authorised person to remove a person who has committed an offence under s. 119. Although a non-authorised NHS staff member may ask a person to leave, this does not extend to a power of removal of a person who refuses. Answer B is therefore incorrect.

An authorised officer cannot remove the person if it is reasonably believed they are in need of medical advice etc. or that such removal would endanger their mental or physical health (s. 120(4)). However, a person ceases to be on NHS premises for the purpose of obtaining medical advice, treatment or care for himself or herself in the following two circumstances:

- once the person has received the medical advice (s. 119(3)(a));
- if the person has received the medical advice etc. during the last eight hours (s. 119(3)(b)).

Having received treatment less than eight hours previously, IRWIN is not a patient and may be ejected from the premises. Answers A and D are therefore incorrect.

It should be noted that this legislation is only in force in relation to NHS premises in England at this time (and not Wales).

General Police Duties, para. 4.11.10

Answer 11.16

Answer **D** — Section 11 of the Public Order Act 1986 places certain obligations on the organisers of public processions that are intended:

- to demonstrate support for, or opposition to, the views or actions of any person or body;
- to publicise a cause or campaign; or
- to mark or commemorate an event.

Since the legislation applies to processions that are intended to publicise a cause or campaign, or to mark or commemorate an event, in addition to demonstrations, answer A is incorrect.

If a public procession is to be held for any of these purposes, the organisers must give written notice, by delivering it to a police station in the relevant police area, unless it is not reasonably practicable to do so (s. 11(1) and (4)). Under s. 11(3), the notice must specify:

- the date and time of the proposed procession;
- the proposed route; and
- the name and address of the person(s) proposing to organise it.

If such a procession is held without compliance with these requirements, or if a procession takes place on a different date, time or route, each of the people organising it commits a summary offence (s. 11(7)).

However, it was held that this did not apply to commonly and customarily held processions, for example, an organised cycle ride that started at the same time and place on the last Friday of every month, even though there was no fixed, settled or predetermined route, end-time or destination (*R (On the application of Kay)* v *Commissioner of Police of the Metropolis* [2008] UKHL 69). Answers B and C are therefore incorrect.

General Police Duties, para. 4.11.11.1

Answer 11.17

Answer **D** — Under s. 14A of the Public Order Act 1986, the chief officer of police has the power, if he or she reasonably believes that it is intended to hold a trespassory assembly which may result in serious disruption to the life of the community or significant damage to land or a building or monument which is of historical, archaeological or scientific importance, to apply to the district council for an order prohibiting for a specified period the holding of all trespassory assemblies in the district or part of it. The order must not last for more than four days and must not apply to an area greater than that represented by a circle of five miles radius from a specified centre, and therefore answer C is incorrect. A constable, who must be in uniform, has power to stop someone he or she reasonably believes to be on his or her way to an assembly prohibited by an order under s. 14A and to direct him or her not to proceed in the direction of the assembly, and therefore answer B is incorrect. This power, however, does not apply to vehicles and is restricted to 'stop that person', and answer A is therefore incorrect. Other powers exist to stop the vehicle, however.

General Police Duties, paras 4.11.11.5, 4.11.11.6

Answer 11.18

Answer **C** — A written order may be given under s. 30 of the Anti-social Behaviour Act 2003, authorising the dispersal of groups of people if the relevant officer (a superintendent) has reasonable grounds for believing that any members of the public have been intimidated, harassed, alarmed or distressed as a result of the presence or behaviour of groups of two or more persons in public places. Answer A is incorrect, as an order may be given even if only two people are present. Answer D is incorrect as there must be at least two people present. The relevant officer must also be satisfied that the anti-social behaviour is a significant and persistent problem in the relevant locality (which would be the case in the circumstances given).

However, because of the implications of such an authorisation on the human rights of members of the public, further conditions are attached to the order; for example, the order may not be given without the consent of the local authority (s. 31(2)). More significantly, the authorisation must be given publicly, for example by notifying the local newspaper or by placing posters in a conspicuous place (s. 31(3)). The publicity must be given before the specified date on which the powers of dispersal are due to begin (see s. 31(2)).

Note that in accordance with the Crown Prosecution Service: Anti-Social Behaviour Guidance (May 2008), the validity of the authorisation must be proved at court, both as regards the reasons for making the authorisation and that proper publicity has been given (*Carter* v *Crown Prosecution Service* [2009] EWHC 2197 (Admin)).

Clearly, these powers may not be utilised in matters of urgency and appropriate planning must take place beforehand. Answer B is therefore incorrect.

General Police Duties, para. 4.11.12.1

Answer 11.19

Answer **D** — A written order granted by a superintendent must be in place before the police can act under s. 30(4) of the Anti-social Behaviour Act 2003 and order the group to disperse. If the order is in place, a constable in uniform, who has reasonable grounds for believing that the presence or behaviour of two or more persons in a public place has resulted, or is likely to result, in any members of the public being intimidated, harassed, alarmed or distressed, may issue directions:

(a) requiring the people in the group to disperse (either immediately or by such time and in such a way as the officer may specify);
(b) requiring any of those people whose place of residence is not within the relevant locality to leave the relevant locality (or any part of it) either immediately or by such time and in such a way as the officer may specify; and
(c) prohibiting any of those people whose place of residence is not within the relevant locality from returning to the relevant locality (or any part of it) for such period (not exceeding 24 hours) from the giving of the direction as the officer may specify.

In *R (On the application of Singh)* v *Chief Constable of West Midlands* [2005] EWHC 2840 (Admin), it was held that the use of s. 30(4) powers to disperse a group of protesters of two or more people who were causing harassment, alarm or distress to members of the public, was lawful even though the order which was already in force related to quite different anticipated anti-social behaviour. Therefore, the police in this question may use their powers to disperse the group, without applying to the superintendent who originally granted the order, or any other superintendent. Answers A, B and C are all incorrect for this reason.

In addition, because of the implications of such an authorisation for the human rights of members of the public, further conditions are attached to the order; for example, the order may not be given without the consent of the local authority (s. 31(2)). More significantly, the authorisation must be given publicly, for example by notifying the local newspaper or by placing posters in a conspicuous place (s. 31(3)). The publicity must be given before the specified date on which the powers of dispersal are due to begin (see s. 31(2)). This means that these powers may not be given in matters of urgency, as in the scenario, and that appropriate planning must take place beforehand. Answers B and C are also incorrect for this reason.

General Police Duties, paras 4.11.12.1, 4.11.12.2

Answer 11.20

Answer **A** — Section 30(6) of the Anti-social Behaviour Act 2003 states that if, between the hours of 9 pm and 6 am, a constable in uniform finds a person in any public place in the relevant locality whom he has reasonable grounds for believing:

(a) is under the age of 16; and

(b) is not under the effective control of a parent or a responsible person aged 18 or over,

he may remove the person to the person's place of residence unless he has reasonable grounds for believing that the person would, if removed to that place, be likely to suffer significant harm.

Since the incident occurred at 9.30 pm, it is within the timescales and answer B is therefore incorrect.

In *R (W)* v *Metropolitan Police Commissioner* [2006] EWCA Civ 458 it was held that the word 'remove' in s. 30(6) naturally and compellingly means 'take away using reasonable force if necessary'. However, this is not an arbitrary power and, within a designated dispersal area, a constable must only use this power (a) to protect children under 16 from the physical and social risks of anti-social behaviour by others, *or* (b) to prevent children from themselves participating in anti-social behaviour. Since force may be used in either of these circumstances, answers C and D are incorrect.

General Police Duties, para. 4.11.12.3

Answer 11.21

Answer **B** — The Policing and Crime Act 2009 provides courts with the power to grant injunctions in relation to gang-related violence. Under s. 34(1), a court may grant an injunction against a respondent aged *14 or over*, if the relevant conditions are met, relating to the prevention of the respondent from engaging in, or encouraging or assisting, gang-related violence, or alternatively, to protect the respondent from gang-related violence.

Answers A, C and D are therefore incorrect.

General Police Duties, para. 4.11.12.5

12 | Sporting Events

STUDY PREPARATION

The maintenance of public order at sporting events is an important area of responsibility for the police and the service has a far more sophisticated range of measures to help deal with football hooliganism than it did in the 1970s and 1980s. Large sporting events can tie up significant numbers of officers and the emphasis today is on more preventative measures to control spectators.

The Sporting Events (Control of Alcohol etc.) Act 1985 and the Football (Offences) Act 1991 create offences relating to drunkenness and rowdy behaviour at designated sporting events, while the Football Spectators Act 1989 provides the courts with significant powers to issue banning orders against those who are involved with football-related disorder, in connection with regulated football matches both inside and outside the United Kingdom.

The police rely heavily on football clubs to regulate the sale of tickets at major sporting events. The final part of the chapter deals with offences created by the Criminal Justice and Public Order Act 1994 to deal with 'ticket touts', whose actions can undermine attempts to separate home and away supporters.

QUESTIONS

Question 12.1

GUTHRIE was amongst a group of fans from a Premiership football club who were travelling to a designated football match. Their coach stopped at a service station 20 miles from the ground, approximately 90 minutes before the game was due to kick off. While they were there, they received news that the match had been called off due to a frozen pitch. Before they left to go home, another coach pulled into the service station, full of fans from the home team. GUTHRIE and the group of fans he was with took part in singing racist songs, aimed at fans from minority ethnic back-grounds who were sitting in the other coach.

Considering offences under s. 3(1) of the Football (Offences) Act 1991 (taking part in chanting of a racialist nature), which of the following statements is correct?

A The chanting did not take place within an hour of the kick off; therefore, the offence is incomplete.

B The chanting did not take place at a designated football match; therefore, the offence is incomplete.

C The chanting took place within two hours of the kick off; therefore, the offence is complete.

D The chanting must take place during the playing time at a designated football match; therefore, the offence is incomplete.

Question 12.2

REYNOLDS was arrested and charged with criminal damage and affray, following an incident which took place while he was on his way to a Premier League football match. REYNOLDS had been drinking heavily in a pub before the match and while he was walking to the ground before kick-off, he stopped at an off-licence to buy some cans of lager. The off-licence owner refused to serve him because he was drunk, and out of anger REYNOLDS caused significant damage to stock in the premises, and smashed a large window on his way out. In court, REYNOLDS admitted the offences and the magistrates were considering imposing a banning order. In response, REYNOLDS claimed that his behaviour was not actually connected to the football match he was attending.

Which of the following statements would be correct in relation to the imposition of a banning order, under s. 14A of the Football Spectators Act 1989?

A The court may decide not to consider a banning order, because REYNOLDS's behaviour was unrelated to the football match.

B The court need not consider a banning order, because REYNOLDS has not used violence towards another person.

C The court need not consider a banning order, because the incident did not take place at the ground.

D The court must consider a banning order, because REYNOLDS was on his way to a football match when he committed the offences.

Question 12.3

KELLY was 55 years of age and was attending the last game of the season of a Premier League club. At half-time, the club was losing 3–0 and KELLY lost his patience; he managed to find his way into the player's tunnel and confronted the manager. KELLY shouted, 'I've been supporting this club for 45 years and you've ruined it, you bastard!' The manager did not engage with KELLY but was visibly upset. Constable SWAIN witnessed the behaviour and attempted to calm KELLY down, but he refused to leave the area. Constable SWAIN arrested KELLY for an offence contrary to s. 5 of the Public Order Act 1986. KELLY was charged and pleaded guilty in court; the magistrates took into account his age, his lack of previous convictions and the mitigating circumstances. KELLY was given a two-year conditional discharge, with the proviso that he did not engage in such behaviour again.

Which of the following statements is correct, in relation to the court's duty to issue a banning order, under s. 14A of the Football Spectators Act 1989?

A There is no evidence that KELLY was drunk or engaged in violent behaviour, therefore the court may not issue a banning order in this case.

B The court may issue a banning order, but it is not absolutely necessary in these circumstances, despite KELLY's admission of guilt.

C The court must issue a banning order; there is no discretion not to do so because of the offence that KELLY has committed.

D KELLY was conditionally discharged for the offence; this is not a criminal justice outcome that would attract a banning order.

Question 12.4

CORTEZ is appearing in the magistrates' court due to his part in organising a violent confrontation during a European Champions League football match in Italy. As a result of an undercover operation, the police have been able to demonstrate that CORTEZ was the organiser of violence between fans from an English Premier League club and an Italian club. However, the police have been unable to produce evidence that CORTEZ actually took part in the violence in Italy. An application is being made for a banning order against CORTEZ.

Could such an order succeed in these circumstances?

A Yes, and if it makes an order, the court must require CORTEZ to surrender his passport.

B No, a banning order may only be made when the person has been convicted of a relevant offence.

C Yes, and if it makes an order, the court may require CORTEZ to surrender his passport.

D No; because the incidents of violence occurred abroad, the court must be satisfied that CORTEZ actually took part.

Question 12.5

The police have been looking for JENSEN to serve a notice on him prior to applying for a banning order against him, because of his violent behaviour at Premiership football matches. JENSEN has so far evaded the police, however, officers working at a home tie of a UEFA Champions League match have been circulated his photograph. JENSEN is spotted outside the ground at the end of the game by Constable BARNETT and because the next game for the club is in two weeks' time, which is the return leg abroad, the officer is keen to detain JENSEN before he disappears again.

Would Constable BARNETT be entitled to detain JENSEN in these circumstances, using powers under s. 21A(2) of the Football Spectators Act 1989?

A No, there is no power of detention at this time because this is not within the control period.

B Yes, JENSEN could be detained for up to a maximum of six hours while a decision is being made whether to serve a notice on him.

C No, JENSEN has not yet been served with a notice outlining that a banning order is to be applied for.

D Yes, JENSEN could be detained for up to a maximum of four hours while a decision is being made whether to serve a notice on him.

Question 12.6

HUNTER was driving a public service vehicle containing a number of passengers who support an English Premier League club. HUNTER was driving the supporters home from a match against another Premier League club. The vehicle was stopped on the motorway by the police, who found that many of the passengers were either in possession of alcohol or drunk. HUNTER admitted stopping at a shop, to allow the passengers to buy alcohol, which they brought onto the vehicle.

Which of the following statements is correct, in relation to offences that may have been committed under the Sporting Events (Control of Alcohol etc.) Act 1985?

A No offences were committed under this Act, as the supporters were not on their way to a designated sporting event.

B HUNTER committed the offence, along with anyone who was drinking alcohol in the vehicle.

C HUNTER committed the offence, along with anyone who was drunk in the vehicle.

D HUNTER committed the offence, along with anyone who was in possession of alcohol or who was drunk in the vehicle.

Question 12.7

CRIBBINS supports an English Premier League club, which has reached the final of the European Champions League tournament. The football match is being played in Paris. CRIBBINS owns a mini-bus which is designed to carry 12 passengers and has agreed to drive ten friends to the match free of charge. The vehicle was stopped near the ferry port by police, who found that most of the passengers were completely drunk and CRIBBINS admitted that alcohol had been brought onto the vehicle and had been consumed on the way to the port.

Have any offences been committed under the Sporting Events (Control of Alcohol etc.) Act 1985, in these circumstances?

A Yes, CRIBBINS committed the offence, as well as any people who were either in possession of alcohol or drunk.

B No, offences under this Act do not apply to people attending a designated sporting event in another country.

C No, the vehicle was not a public service vehicle; therefore the offence was not committed.

D Yes, but because the vehicle was not a public service vehicle, only CRIBBINS is guilty of the offence.

Question 12.8

Constable AFRIDI was working at a Premier League football match when the officer was approached by a steward who claimed to have seen a fan in possession of a distress flare, who had passed the object on to another fan. The steward was able to provide the approximate seat number where the fans were sitting and physical descriptions of the suspects. Constable AFRIDI attended the location and spoke to PARSONS, who the steward believed to have had the flare originally and CONNORS, who was believed to be in possession of it now.

What powers does Constable AFRIDI have to deal with the incident, under s. 7 of the Sporting Events (Control of Alcohol etc.) Act 1985 (alcohol at sports grounds)?

A Constable AFRIDI may search CONNORS, who is reasonably suspected to be in possession of a flare.

B Constable AFRIDI may arrest and search PARSONS, who *was* reasonably suspected to be in possession of the flare and arrest and search CONNORS, who *is* reasonably suspected to be in possession of a flare.

C Constable AFRIDI may arrest PARSONS, who *was* reasonably suspected to be in possession of the flare and arrest and search CONNORS, who *is* reasonably suspected to be in possession of a flare.

D Constable AFRIDI may search PARSONS and CONNORS and arrest any person who is in possession of the flare.

Question 12.9

WINGROVE supports a football team which is a member of the English Football League, which has qualified for the Champions League. WINGROVE has managed to buy 50 tickets for an away game in Germany and has advertised them for sale on a website. WINGROVE intends making a profit by selling the tickets at more than their market value.

Does WINGROVE commit an offence under s. 166 of the Criminal Justice and Public Order Act 1994, in these circumstances?

A No, the offence does not apply to football matches abroad.

B No, the offence will only be committed when WINGROVE actually sells a ticket.

C No, the offence only applies to international football matches abroad.

D Yes, provided WINGROVE is not authorised by the organisers of the match.

ANSWERS

Answer 12.1

Answer **B** — Under s. 3(1) of the Football (Offences) Act 1991, it is an offence for a person to engage or take part in chanting of an indecent or racialist nature *at a designated football match*. Since the incident took place away from the ground, answers A, C and D will be incorrect whatever the other circumstances.

For clarity, s. 1(2) of the 1991 Act provides that references to things done at a 'designated football match' include anything done at the ground:

- within the period beginning two hours before the start of the match or (if earlier) two hours before the time at which it is advertised to start and ending one hour after the end of the match;
- where the match is advertised to start at a particular time on a particular day but does not take place, within the period beginning two hours before and ending one hour after the advertised starting time.

Had the incident taken place at the football ground, s. 3(1) would have been applicable, as the chanting took place within two hours of the kick off (and answers A and D would have also been incorrect for this reason).

General Police Duties, para. 4.12.2.1

Answer 12.2

Answer **A** — Under s. 14A of the Football Spectators Act 1989, the court may make a banning order against a person who is convicted of a relevant offence. The relevant offences are set out in sch. 1 and include offences relating to drunkenness, violence or threats of violence, or public order offences committed at or in connection with a football match *or when travelling to or from a football match* (whether or not the match was actually attended by the offender). Answer C is therefore incorrect.

The order may be made if the court is satisfied that there are reasonable grounds to believe that the order would help prevent violence or disorder at/in connection with a 'regulated football match'. Violence here includes violence towards property and disorder includes stirring up racial hatred (s. 14C of the 1989 Act). Answer B is therefore incorrect.

However, in *R* v *Elliott* [2007] EWCA Crim 1002, banning orders were quashed where it was found that violence involving a group of men in a public house was unrelated to the match. See also *DPP* v *Beaumont* [2008] EWHC 523 (Admin). There-fore, even though REYNOLDS was on his way to a football match when he commit-ted the offences, it *could* be argued that the incident was unconnected to the match itself (and the court may decide not to consider a banning order). Answer A is correct for this reason, and answer D is incorrect.

General Police Duties, para. 4.12.3

Answer 12.3

Answer **B** — The Football Spectators Act 1989 contains the powers to impose ban-ning orders that exclude offenders from attendance at regulated football matches. There are two ways in which a banning order can be made, first where a person is convicted of a relevant offence (s. 14A) and, secondly, by way of complaint by the relevant chief officer, or the DPP (s. 14B(1)).

The relevant offences are set out in sch. 1 to the 1989 Act and include offences relating to drunkenness, violence or threats of violence, or public order offences (*including s. 5*) committed at or in connection with a football match or when travel-ling to or from a football match. Answer A is incorrect as the schedule includes offences outside the scope of drunkenness or violent conduct.

Rather than simply having the power to make such orders, courts are under a statu-tory duty to pass them; however, this duty applies only if the court is satisfied that there are reasonable grounds to believe that the order would help prevent violence or disorder at or in connection with a 'regulated football match'. If the court is satisfied that KELLY is unlikely to engage in such behaviour at a football match again, they are not bound to give an order in these circumstances and therefore answer C is incorrect.

A banning order may only be made in addition to a sentence imposed by the court but can be passed even if the originating offence is dealt with by way of a conditional or absolute discharge, therefore answer D is incorrect.

General Police Duties, para. 4.12.3

Answer 12.4

Answer **A** — Banning orders may be made under s. 14A or s. 14B of the Football Spec-tators Act 1989. Under s. 14A, the court may make a banning order against a person who is convicted of a relevant offence. The relevant offences are set out in sch. 1 and include offences relating to drunkenness, violence or threats of violence, or public order offences. Under s. 14B, the Chief Officer of police or the Director of Public

Prosecutions may submit a request to the court, by way of complaint, to make such an order, even when the person has not been convicted of a relevant offence. Answer B is therefore incorrect.

On application to the court under s. 14B, the magistrates may make an order if the person has at any time *caused or contributed to* any violence or disorder in the United Kingdom or elsewhere. Therefore, since the police are able to produce evidence that CORTEZ caused or contributed to violence abroad, answer D is incorrect.

Finally, if the court imposes a banning order in connection with regulated football matches outside the United Kingdom, it *must* require the surrender of the person's passport and/or identity card (s. 14E(3)). Answer C is therefore incorrect.

General Police Duties, para. 4.12.3

Answer 12.5

Answer **A** — Under s. 21A of the Football Spectators Act 1989, if a constable in uniform

(a) has reasonable grounds for suspecting that the condition in s. 14B(2) is met in the case of a person present before him, and
(b) has reasonable grounds to believe that making a banning order in his case would help to prevent violence or disorder at or in connection with any regulated football matches,

the constable may detain the person in his custody (whether there or elsewhere) until he has decided whether or not to issue a notice under s. 21B, and shall give the person his reasons for detaining him in writing. (The condition under s. 14B(2) referred to is that the person has at any time caused or contributed to any violence or disorder in the United Kingdom or elsewhere.)

Answer C is incorrect as there is no requirement to serve a notice on a person *before* detaining them under s. 21A(2). The actual purpose of the power is to detain a person in order to decide whether or not to serve a notice of a banning order on him/her.

A person may not be detained under subs. (2) for more than four hours or, with the authority of an officer of at least the rank of inspector, six hours (s. 21A(3)). Therefore, the *maximum* period of detention while deciding whether or not to serve the notice is six hours and therefore answer D is incorrect.

Finally, both answers B and D are also incorrect because the power under s. 21A(2) is only applicable during any control period in relation to a regulated football match outside the United Kingdom or an external tournament. 'Control period' means, in relation to a regulated football match outside England and Wales, the period:

(a) beginning five days before the day of the match, and

(b) ending when the match is finished or cancelled.

This means there is no power to detain JENSEN at this time; however, the opportunity to do so will come before the next game for the club, in the five-day period leading up to the second leg.

General Police Duties, para. 4.12.3.2

Answer 12.6

Answer **D** — Section 1 of the Sporting Events (Control of Alcohol etc.) Act 1985 applies to people who are being conveyed in public service vehicles or railway passenger vehicles, which are being used for the principal purpose of carrying passengers to *or from* designated sporting events (s. 1(1)). Answer A is therefore incorrect.

Under s. 1(2), a person who knowingly causes or permits alcohol to be carried on a vehicle to which the section applies is guilty of an offence (which makes HUNTER guilty of the offence). Other offences are committed by any person who has alcohol in his/her possession while on a vehicle to which this section applies (s. 1(3)), or to a person who is drunk on such a vehicle (s. 1(3)). Since the offence applies to both classes of people, answer C is incorrect.

Section 1 does not actually mention people who are *drinking* alcohol whilst in a vehicle to which this section applies (although by implication, such people are likely to be in possession of alcohol). Since the wording is incorrect (and the offence applies both to people who have alcohol in their possession *and* who are drunk), answer B is incorrect.

General Police Duties, para. 4.12.4

Answer 12.7

Answer **A** — Section 1 of the Sporting Events (Control of Alcohol etc.) Act 1985 creates offences which may be committed by people who are either in possession of alcohol or drunk, whilst being conveyed in public service vehicles or railway passenger vehicles, which are being used for the principal purpose of carrying passengers to or from designated sporting events.

However, s. 1A(1) of the Sporting Events (Control of Alcohol etc.) Act 1985 applies to a motor vehicle which is *not* a public service vehicle but is adapted to carry more than eight passengers, and is being used for the purpose described previously.

Section 1A(2)(a) states that a person who knowingly causes or permits alcohol to be carried on a motor vehicle to which this section applies is guilty of an offence if he or she is its driver (or its keeper or the keeper's servant or agent, or the servant or agent of a person to whom it is so made available). Therefore, even though the vehicle was not a public service vehicle, CRIBBINS is still guilty of the offence. Answer C is therefore incorrect.

Further offences are committed under s. 1A(3) and (4), by a person who has alcohol in his/her possession or who is drunk, while on a motor vehicle to which this section applies. Answer D is therefore incorrect.

Finally, offences under s. 1 and s. 1A apply to 'designated' or 'regulated' football matches, *outside the United Kingdom*, including any match involving a club whose national football association is a member of FIFA, where the match is part of a competition or tournament organised by or under the authority of FIFA or UEFA, and where the competition or tournament is one in which a club from the Football League, the Football Association Premier League, the Football Conference or the League of Wales is eligible to participate or has participated. Answer B is therefore incorrect.

General Police Duties, para. 4.12.4

Answer 12.8

Answer **B** — Under s. 2A(1) of the Sporting Events (Control of Alcohol etc.) Act 1985, a person commits an offence if he/she is in possession of an article or substance to which the section applies. Section 2A(3) lists several flare-type articles which are prohibited from designated sporting events at designated sports grounds—a distress flare is included in the list.

A constable may, at any time during the period of a designated sporting event at any designated sports ground, enter any part of the ground for the purpose of enforcing the provisions of this Act (s. 7(1)).

Section 7(2) states that the constable may search a person he or she has reasonable grounds to suspect is committing or has committed an offence under this Act, and may arrest such a person. Therefore, both PARSONS and CONNORS may be searched and both may be arrested, even though PARSONS is no longer believed to be in possession of the flare (answers A and C are therefore incorrect).

There is no requirement to delay either of these powers until the item is found and therefore answer D is incorrect.

General Police Duties, paras 4.12.4.3, 4.12.4.4

Answer 12.9

Answer **D** — It is an offence under s. 166(1) of the Criminal Justice and Public Order Act 1994 for an unauthorised person to sell a ticket for a designated football match, or otherwise to dispose of such a ticket to another person. A person is 'unauthorised' unless he or she is authorised in writing to sell or otherwise dispose of tickets for the match by the organisers of the match (s. 166(2)(a)).

Section 166(2)(aa) outlines the criteria for 'selling' a ticket, which includes offering to sell a ticket, exposing a ticket for sale and advertising that a ticket is available for purchase. Answer B is therefore incorrect.

For the purposes of s. 166(2)(c) a 'designated football match' is described in art. 2(2) of the Ticket Touting (Designation of Football Matches) Order 2007 (SI 2007/790) as an association football match in England and Wales; whereas art. 2(3) designates association football matches *outside* England and Wales involving a national team (of England or Wales), or a team representing a club which is a member of the Football League, the Football Association Premier League, the Football Conference or League of Wales, or matches in competitions or tournaments organised by or under the authority of FIFA or UEFA, in which any of such English or Welsh domestic or national teams is eligible to participate or has participated. Answers A and C are therefore incorrect.

General Police Duties, para. 4.12.5

13 | Weapons

QUESTIONS

Question 13.1

O'CALLAGHAN had recently started watching Kung Fu movies on the Internet and fancied getting a set of 'nunchucks'. O'CALLAGHAN knew that his friend SHELLY had a set and made arrangements to go there occasionally to practise using them, while considering ordering a set himself. On several occasions, O'CALLAGHAN went to SHELLY's house and practised with the weapons in the garden. O'CALLAGHAN did not take the weapons away from the premises at any time.

Given that the nunchucks are weapons made for use for causing injury to a person, could O'CALLAGHAN be guilty of an offence under s. 1(1) of the Prevention of Crime Act 1953?

A Yes, when in possession of the nunchucks at SHELLY's house.
B Yes, when he has the nunchucks with him, when not at his place of abode.
C No; he did not have the nunchucks with him in a public place.
D No; he was not in possession of the nunchucks in a public place.

Question 13.2

AITKEN had recently split up from SPENCER as a result of suffering serious domestic abuse. She had moved into sheltered accommodation and was living anonymously in a different city. She had managed to secure a job in a bar, which meant she finished work late at night. AITKEN had received a phone call from a friend who told her that SPENCER had found out the area she was living in and to be careful. AITKEN believed that SPENCER was resourceful enough to find her and started carrying a knife in her bag for her own protection and would have used it for self-defence, fearing an imminent attack by her ex-partner.

With these circumstances in mind, which of the following statements is correct, in relation to having a reasonable excuse for having an offensive weapon in a public place?

A Carrying a knife for your own protection will not amount to a reasonable excuse; AITKEN would commit this offence in these circumstances.
B Carrying a knife for your protection may amount to a reasonable excuse provided the person believed he or she was at risk of an imminent attack, and the belief was reasonable.

C Having an offensive weapon with you for self-defence may amount to a reasonable excuse, provided you have armed yourself instantaneously, e.g. immediately prior to an attack.

D Carrying a knife as a general precaution that you may be attacked may amount to a reasonable excuse provided the person believed he or she was at risk of an attack at some time in the future.

Question 13.3

FAWCETT was driving home from work when he caused another car, being driven by GRANT, to brake sharply. GRANT followed him, shouting obscenities and sounding his horn. When FAWCETT stopped at traffic lights, GRANT got out of his car and ran towards him. FAWCETT got out of his own car and picked up a steering wheel lock, and threw it at GRANT, intending to injure him.

Is the steering wheel lock an 'offensive weapon' in these circumstances?

A No, FAWCETT formed the intention to use the article after it came into his possession.

B Yes, as soon as FAWCETT formed the intention to use the article.

C Yes, because FAWCETT used the article, intending to injure GRANT.

D Yes, as soon as FAWCETT picked the article up with the intention to use it.

Question 13.4

Constable BAKER was on patrol when she stopped a vehicle owned and being driven by CLEMENT. HARVEY was in the front passenger seat. Constable BAKER made a search of the vehicle and discovered a flick-knife in the glove compartment.

Could HARVEY and CLEMENT be guilty of an offence under the Prevention of Crime Act 1953?

A No, only CLEMENT may commit the offence, being the owner of the car.

B Yes, the offence is complete against both; no further proof is required.

C No, it is not possible for two people to have the same weapon with them.

D Yes, provided they both knew that the other person had it with him at the time.

Question 13.5

PENFOLD was stopped and searched on his way to a football match while he was walking in High Street. The searching officer, Constable MARRIOTT, discovered in PENFOLD's pocket a number of 50 pence pieces that had been sharpened around the edges. Believing that they were offensive weapons, the officer lawfully arrested PENFOLD.

In order to prove that PENFOLD was guilty of possessing an offensive weapon would Constable MARRIOTT need to prove intent by PENFOLD to use the coins to cause injury?

A No, provided it can be shown that the coins have been made to cause injury.
B Yes, because there is no apparent victim in these circumstances.
C Yes, because the coins are not offensive weapons *per se*.
D No, provided it can be shown the coins have been adapted to cause injury.

Question 13.6

BOSWORTH had gone through a relationship break-up with KINGSTON. BOSWORTH was very upset when he discovered that KINGSTON had started seeing BELL. BOSWORTH found out where BELL worked and drove there one day, carrying a Samurai sword in the car. He waited in the car and as BELL came out of the building, got out carrying the sword. BOSWORTH's intention was to cause BELL serious injury with the sword and he began waving it above his head; however, BELL saw him and ran back into the building, fearing immediate physical harm. BOSWORTH realised the police were likely to be called and got back in the car and drove off.

Considering the offence under s. 1A of the Prevention of Crime Act 1953 (threatening with offensive weapon in public), has BOSWORTH committed this offence?

A Yes, because he intends causing BELL serious physical harm with the sword.
B No, he did not use the weapon in such a way that there was an immediate risk of serious physical harm to BELL.
C Yes, he has unlawfully and intentionally threatened BELL with serious physical harm.
D Yes, BELL was put in fear that he would suffer serious physical harm.

Question 13.7

BARRY was stopped and searched in the street by Constable ROCH. The officer found a pocket-knife in BARRY's pocket which had a 4-inch blade. BARRY admitted that he was on his way to a football match and intended to use the knife in a fight with rival fans.

Is this weapon an offensive weapon under the Prevention of Crime Act 1953?

A   Yes, as the blade is more than 3 inches long.

B   Yes, a folding pocket-knife with a blade of more than 3 inches will always be an offensive weapon.

C   Yes, it is an offensive weapon regardless of the length of the blade.

D   No, a folding pocket-knife will not be an offensive weapon regardless of the length of the blade.

Question 13.8

BROOKER was stopped and searched by the police, whilst on the way to a football match. At the time, BROOKER was carrying a butter knife, which was not sharpened, and which had a blade of at least 3.5 inches in length.

Could BROOKER commit an offence under s. 139 of the Criminal Justice Act 1988 in these circumstances?

A   No, because the blade was not sharp.

B   Yes, because the knife was a bladed instrument.

C   Yes, because the knife was a bladed instrument more than 3 inches long.

D   No, because it is unlikely that the blade was capable of causing injury.

Question 13.9

Constable WARREN was on duty on a Sunday evening when he stopped MOHAM-MED, who was driving a car on the road. Constable WARREN conducted a search of the vehicle and found a meat cleaver under the seat. MOHAMMED stated that he worked as a chef in a restaurant and that he used the meat cleaver as part of his work. He further stated that he had put it in his car the previous night, intending to take it to be sharpened on Monday morning.

Would MOHAMMED have a defence to a charge under s. 139 of the Criminal Justice Act 1988 (having a bladed or sharply pointed article) in these circumstances?

A   Yes, the statutory defence of 'good reason'.

B   Yes, because he had it for use in his work.

C   No, the offence is complete in these circumstances.

D   Yes, the statutory defence of 'lawful authority'.

Question 13.10

Constable LLOYD stopped GREGSON, who was driving a motor vehicle on a road, and conducted a search under s. 1 of the Police and Criminal Evidence Act 1984. The officer discovered a Stanley knife underneath GREGSON's seat. Constable LLOYD was of the opinion that GREGSON had concealed the knife in this location and consequently arrested him for having an offensive weapon, contrary to s. 1(1) of the Prevention of Crime Act 1953. GREGSON was later charged with the offence, but pleaded not guilty, stating that he had a 'good reason' for having the weapon: that he undertook casual work at a relative's factory and used the knife for opening boxes. He claimed that he had forgotten that the knife was under the seat, because he had not worked at the factory for a couple of weeks.

Which of the following statements is correct, in relation to GREGSON's claim of 'good reason'?

A Forgetfulness could amount to a 'good reason' for having it; GREGSON must show beyond reasonable doubt that he had a reasonable excuse for having it.

B The prosecution must show beyond reasonable doubt that GREGSON did not have a 'good reason' for having the weapon.

C Forgetfulness would not amount to a 'good reason' for having it; GREGSON has no defence to this charge.

D Forgetfulness could amount to a 'good reason' for having it; GREGSON must show on the balance of probabilities that he had a reasonable excuse for having it.

Question 13.11

A report was received by the police of a disturbance in a high school. The first person to arrive was Constable SANCHEZ, who was in plain clothes. He was told that two pupils had threatened a teacher and that one of them had a knife. After a search, Constable SANCHEZ found the two youths in the street outside.

What powers would Constable SANCHEZ have under the Criminal Justice Act 1988 in these circumstances?

A He has no powers under the 1988 Act and must use his powers under the Police and Criminal Evidence Act 1984.

B He has a power under the 1988 Act to search the youths for an offensive weapon.

C He has no powers under the 1988 Act as the pupils were not trespassing.

D He has no powers under the 1988 Act as he is not in uniform.

Question 13.12

PIETERSEN, a head teacher of a high school in England, was contacted by a member of staff stating that CHAVEZ, a pupil at the school, had been seen carrying a knife on school premises. The teacher kept CHAVEZ under observation until PIETERSEN arrived. Utilising powers under s. 550ZA of the Education Act 1996, PIETERSEN searched CHAVEZ but did not find the knife. CHAVEZ was carrying a bag and the member of staff suggested that CHAVEZ may have hidden the knife inside it.

What authority would PIETERSEN have to search CHAVEZ's possessions under this legislation?

A None, possessions may not be searched under this legislation, only a pupil may be searched.

B A pupil's possessions may be searched, but only in the pupil's presence and in the presence of another member of staff.

C A pupil's possessions may be searched, but only in the presence of another member of staff and with the pupil's permission.

D A pupil's possessions may be searched, but only in the presence of another member of staff.

Question 13.13

MEARS was a pupil of a high school in England on a field trip. The teacher in charge, SMITH, was told by another pupil that MEARS had taken a flick-knife on the trip and had hidden it in a coat pocket. SMITH told MEARS to hand over the weapon; however, MEARS denied being in possession of a knife.

What powers, if any, would SMITH have to search for the weapon, under s. 550ZA of the Education Act 1996?

A SMITH may have searched MEARS, using force if necessary.

B None, as they were not on school premises.

C None, only a head teacher may search a pupil under this legislation.

D SMITH may have searched MEARS, but not by the use of force.

Question 13.14

FLANNAGAN is the head teacher of a high school in England and was informed that a 15-year-old pupil, HEATLEY, had been seen in the classroom with a knife by the teacher, BOYD. FLANNAGAN made his way to the class and spoke to BOYD, who stated he had seen HEATLEY hide the knife down the front of his trousers. FLANNAGAN has entered the room; however, HEATLEY has denied being in possession of a knife and told FLANNAGAN he would have to find the knife himself.

What action is FLANNAGAN entitled to take in order to search for the knife?

A FLANNAGAN may search HEATLEY, provided BOYD is present.

B FLANNAGAN may search HEATLEY, provided BOYD is present and the search is conducted in private.

C As the head teacher, FLANNAGAN has the power to search HEATLEY whether BOYD is present or not.

D FLANNAGAN has no power to search HEATLEY in these circumstances, and will have to call the police if he wishes to recover the knife.

Question 13.15

CRUZ was employed as a computer software programmer, but was sacked for selling material to a rival company. CRUZ returned to the company offices one night, entering the gated compound using an electronic pass that had not been confiscated. CRUZ's intention was to sabotage the company software, by loading a virus onto the server. CRUZ was in possession of a knife, intending to use it to threaten the night security guard if necessary. However, CRUZ was unable to get into the main company building as the electronic pass did not work. CRUZ was disturbed by the security guard and ran off.

Has CRUZ committed an offence contrary to s. 8(1) of the Criminal Law Act 1977 (trespassing with a weapon of offence)?

A No, CRUZ has not entered a dwelling with a weapon of offence.

B Yes, CRUZ has entered premises with a weapon of offence.

C No, CRUZ has not entered a building with a weapon of offence.

D No, CRUZ has not entered a dwelling, or land adjacent to a dwelling with a weapon of offence.

Question 13.16

ANDREWS owned a house which was being renovated. One day he visited it and found HARVEY squatting inside. ANDREWS asked HARVEY to leave. However, HARVEY was carrying a knife and threatened ANDREWS with it. The police were called and Constable RAMAN arrived, and was considering how to deal with HARVEY.

Which of the following is the definition of a weapon of offence under s. 8 of the Criminal Law Act 1977?

A Any article made or adapted for use for causing injury to or incapacitating a person, or intended by the person having it with him or her for that use.

B Any article made or adapted for use for causing injury to or intended by the person having it with him or her for that use.

C Any article intended by the person having it with him or her for the purpose of causing injury.

D Any article made or adapted for use for causing injury to or incapacitating a person.

Question 13.17

STONE owns a shop which sells second-hand goods and has a reputation for being able to supply unusual weapons. COLLINS entered the shop looking for some weapons for himself and his friends for a football match the following week. STONE indicated that he could get his hands on some knuckle dusters, which he could sell at a good price. COLLINS agreed to return three days later to buy them.

At what point, if any, would STONE commit an offence under the Criminal Justice Act 1988?

A Not until he actually sells the weapons to COLLINS.

B Not until he is in possession of the weapons with intent to sell them.

C When he offered to sell the weapons to COLLINS.

D Not until he has the weapons with him with intent to sell them.

Question 13.18

FAHEY is aged 18 and works in a hardware shop. McKAY, aged 17, came into the shop one day and selected a pocket-knife from the display, intending to buy it. The pocket-knife had a blade with a cutting edge of 3.5 inches.

Considering offences under s. 141A of the Criminal Justice Act 1988, could FAHEY lawfully sell this pocket-knife to McKAY?

A Yes, because FAHEY is over 18.

B Yes, because McKAY is over 16.

C No, because McKAY is under 18.

D Yes, this offence does not apply to folding pocket-knives.

Question 13.19

Constable SHAPIRO received a complaint of persons dangerously firing a crossbow in the back garden of a dwelling. On arrival, neighbours showed the officer some bolts from the crossbow, which had penetrated the hedge separating their gardens. Constable SHAPIRO could see BARRYMORE alone in the garden, but there was no sign of a crossbow. BARRYMORE appeared to be about 14 years of age.

Does Constable SHAPIRO have the power to enter BARRYMORE's garden to search for the crossbow in these circumstances?

A Yes, there is a power to enter any land other than a dwelling house in order to conduct such a search.

B No, there is no power to enter land, which forms part of a dwelling under this legislation.

C Yes, there is a power to enter any premises or vehicle in order to conduct such a search.

D No, a constable only has the power to search a person or a vehicle under this legislation.

ANSWERS

Answer 13.1

Answer **C** — Section 1(1) of the Prevention of Crime Act 1953 states:

Any person who without lawful authority or reasonable excuse, the proof whereof shall lie on him, has with him in any public place any offensive weapon shall be guilty of an offence.

First, it must be proved that the defendant has an offensive weapon 'with him', as opposed to being 'in possession' of it. This expression shows that the offence is designed to prevent the carrying of weapons (as opposed to being in possession of them remotely). Answers A and D are therefore incorrect.

Secondly, the offence can only be committed in a public place; answers A and B are incorrect for this reason also.

General Police Duties, para. 4.13.2

Answer 13.2

Answer **B** — To prove an offence contrary to s. 1(1) of the Prevention of Crime Act 1953, the prosecution must first show, beyond reasonable doubt, that the defendant had an offensive weapon with him or her. The burden of proof then shifts to the defendant to show that he or she had a 'reasonable excuse' for having the weapon.

There are several overlapping cases that deal with the issue of carrying an offensive weapon, or a bladed or sharply pointed article in a public place in self-defence or to prevent an attack. The common themes with these cases are

- the defendant's own belief that he or she may be attacked;
- how reasonable that belief was;
- how imminent the attack is likely to be.

The *reasonableness* of the belief was examined in *N* v *DPP* [2011] EWHC 1807 (Admin). The court found that the defence of reasonable excuse was *not* made out where a person picked up a metal bar for protection having been threatened five minutes earlier by a group of young men in a car who were found to have no weapons. Even if the defendant did believe that he was at risk of an imminent attack, the court held that his belief was not a reasonable one in the circumstances.

Also, it is *not* reasonable to have a weapon with you as a general precaution in case you are attacked (*Evans* v *Hughes* [1972] 1 WLR 1452) and the court is more likely to uphold an appeal if the fear is reasonable that an attack is imminent, rather than an imprecise attack sometime in the future (*R* v *McAuley* [2009] EWCA Crim 2130). Answer D is therefore incorrect.

On the other hand, it *may* be reasonable to have a weapon if you have good grounds to anticipate an unprovoked or unlawful attack, for example for a person guarding cash transits (*Malnik* v *DPP* [1989] Crim LR 451), or if you could show on the balance of probabilities that you were in fear of an imminent attack (see *McAuley* noted previously). This approach was confirmed by the Court of Appeal in *R* v *Emmanuel* [1998] Crim LR 347, where it was accepted that 'good reason' could include self-defence. Answer A is therefore incorrect.

None of these cases suggest that this defence is *only* applicable if you have armed yourself instantaneously, for example immediately prior to an attack, and therefore answer C is incorrect.

General Police Duties, paras 4.13.2, 4.13.3.1

Answer 13.3

Answer **A** — The expression 'has with him' will not in most cases include circumstances where a person has an 'innocent' article, which he or she uses offensively. The purpose of the Prevention of Crime Act 1953 is to prevent people from arming themselves for some future event, and the intention of the Act is to deal with preventative issues.

The case of *Ohlson* v *Hylton* [1975] 1 WLR 724 demonstrates this. The defendant had a bag of tools with him in the course of his trade. He produced a hammer from the bag and used it to hit someone. The court held that, as he had formed the intention to use the hammer *after* it came into his possession, the offence was not made out (answers B and C are therefore incorrect). This decision was followed by several other similar cases (*Bates* v *Bulman* [1979] 1 WLR 1190, *R* v *Dayle* [1974] 1 WLR 181 and *R* v *Humphreys* [1977] Crim LR 225).

This is not to say that 'innocent' articles may never become offensive weapons, such as people carrying screwdrivers to defend themselves: it depends on the immediacy of the conversion from one to another, and therefore answer D is incorrect.

General Police Duties, para. 4.13.2

Answer 13.4

Answer **D** — It is possible for more than one person to have the same weapon 'with them' (*R* v *Edmonds* [1963] 2 QB 142), and therefore answers A and C are incorrect. It would be necessary to prove that they knew of the existence of the weapon in the hands of the other.

In this case it was decided that both parties knew of the existence of the weapon and that they knew the other party had it 'with him' at the time of the offence. Answer B is incorrect as the offence is not complete until this is proved.

General Police Duties, para. 4.13.2

Answer 13.5

Answer **D** — The prosecution would have to show that the coins have been adapted to cause injury in order to show that they are offensive weapons. However, once the prosecution have proved this, there is no need to show an intention to use them to cause injury (*Davis* v *Alexander* (1970) 54 Cr App R 398).

Answer A is incorrect because the coins have not been 'made' to cause injury; they are not offensive weapons *per se*. However, the fact that they are not offensive weapons *per se* still does not place a burden upon the prosecution to prove intent to use them (*Davis* v *Alexander*), which is why answer C is incorrect.

Answer B is incorrect because it is the adaptation of the article that is relevant, not the intention of the person carrying it (*Bryan* v *Mott* (1976) 62 Cr App R 71).

If PENFOLD were charged under the third leg of the definition, where the weapon is intended to cause injury, the prosecution would have to prove an intention to cause injury by PENFOLD. This would obviously be a harder case to prove than adaptation in these circumstances.

General Police Duties, para. 4.13.2

Answer 13.6

Answer **B** — Under s. 1A(1) of the Prevention of Crime Act 1953, a person is guilty of an offence if that person—

- (a) has an offensive weapon with him or her in a public place,
- (b) unlawfully and intentionally threatens another person with the weapon, and
- (c) does so in such a way that there is an immediate risk of serious physical harm to that other person.

This offence is meant to bridge the gap between someone who is simply carrying an offensive weapon and someone who actually commits an assault with one. The essence of this offence, therefore, is that a person (A) must have an offensive weapon with him or her and intentionally *uses* the weapon to threaten another (B) creating an immediate risk of serious physical harm to B. While there is no doubt that BOSWORTH had with him an offensive weapon and intended to use it, it would be difficult to argue that BELL was in *immediate* risk of serious physical harm—had he not seen BOSWORTH and run away, matters may have been different. Answers A and C are therefore incorrect.

The fear of the 'victim' that he or she may suffer serious physical harm is not essential to proving the offence (although the evidence may be useful in any trial). It is the intention of the defendant that counts and for that reason answer D is incorrect.

General Police Duties, para. 4.13.2.1

Answer 13.7

Answer **C** — Under the Prevention of Crime Act 1953, an offensive weapon is an article which is made, intended or adapted for causing injury. The weapon in question will be an offensive weapon because BARRY intends that it will be used to cause injury.

Under the 1953 Act, it is irrelevant what length the blade happens to be. However, under s. 139 of the Criminal Justice Act 1988, a person commits an offence if he or she has a bladed or sharply pointed instrument in a public place—unless the instrument is a folding pocket-knife with a blade of less than 3 inches. Do not mix the two Acts.

Answers A and B are incorrect as they refer to the length of the blade as being relevant. Answer D is incorrect because a folding pocket-knife may be an offensive weapon, depending on the circumstances.

General Police Duties, para. 4.13.2

Answer 13.8

Answer **B** — Under s. 139 of the Criminal Justice Act 1988, a person commits an offence if he or she has a bladed or sharply pointed instrument in a public place. The Act provides for a person either carrying a sharply pointed instrument or a bladed instrument. There is no requirement for a bladed instrument to be sharp and in *Brooker* v *DPP* [2005] EWHC 1132 (Admin), it was held that a blunt butter knife fell within s. 139. Answer A is therefore incorrect.

(Note that in a similar case, *R (On the application of the Royal Borough of Windsor and Maidenhead)* v *East Berkshire Justices* [2010] EWHC 3020 (Admin), it was held that a grapefruit knife is not just a gadget but a knife within the meaning of s. 141A(2)(a) of the Criminal Justice Act 1988.)

Under the Act, a folding pocket-knife is excluded, provided the cutting edge of the blade is less than 3 inches long. This does not apply to all bladed instruments and the length of the blade of any other bladed instrument is irrelevant, which is why answer C is incorrect.

There is no requirement under the Act to prove that the instrument was capable of causing injury, and therefore answer D is incorrect.

General Police Duties, paras 4.13.3, 4.13.7.1

Answer 13.9

Answer **C** — A defendant charged with an offence under s. 139(1) of the Act may claim either that he or she had a 'good reason' for having the weapon with him or her, or that he or she had 'lawful authority'. Further, the defendant may also claim that he or she had the weapon for use at work.

The circumstances in the question mirror those in the case of *Mohammed* v *Chief Constable of South Yorkshire* [2002] EWHC 406 (Admin). The defendant appealed against his conviction for an offence under s. 139(1), claiming that he had the meat cleaver with him for a 'good reason' (*per* s. 139(4)), or alternatively that he had it with him for use in his work (*per* s. 139(5)). The appeal failed in the Administrative Court, which held that the defendant had not shown that he had a 'good reason' for having the weapon, as the 'ultimate lawful purpose' claimed was too far distant from the time when the defendant was caught with the article. Answer A is therefore incorrect.

The court also held that the defendant did not have the cleaver for use at work; he had it for the purposes of *rendering it possible* to use at work. The court held that he could have taken the cleaver directly from work on the Monday morning to be sharpened. Answer B is therefore incorrect.

'Lawful authority' means those occasions where people are required to carry weapons as a matter of duty, such as police officers or members of the armed forces (*Bryan* v *Mott* (1976) 62 Cr App R 71). In these circumstances, MOHAMMED could not claim this defence and therefore answer D is incorrect.

General Police Duties, para. 4.13.3.1

Answer 13.10

Answer **D** — To prove an offence contrary to s. 1(1) of the Prevention of Crime Act 1953, the prosecution must first show, beyond reasonable doubt, that the defendant had an offensive weapon with him. The burden of proof then shifts to the defendant to show that he or she had 'good reason' or a reasonable excuse for having the weapon. Answer B is incorrect, as the prosecution bears no further burden once it can be shown that the person has an offensive weapon with him or her.

The burden of proof on the defendant will be judged on the balance of probabilities, and not beyond reasonable doubt; therefore, answer A is incorrect.

Forgetting that you have the article with you is not a general defence (see *DPP* v *Gregson* (1993) 96 Cr App R 240 and *R (On the application of Hilton)* v *Canterbury Crown Court* [2009] EWHC 2867 (Admin)). However, the courts and commentators have debated the issue of forgetfulness in this context and the relevance of 'forgetting' you have a knife or other article with you. The issues were summarised by the Court of Appeal in *R* v *Jolie* [2003] EWCA Crim 1543:

> While it is clear that forgetfulness alone cannot be a 'good reason', from a policing perspective the main thing is to gather any evidence that the defendant had the article with him/her in a public place and to record any explanation given. Whether the defendant had a 'good reason' (which might include forgetfulness combined with other circumstances) is then a matter for the court.

The issue was further examined in *R* v *Chahal* [2010] EWHC 439 (Admin), where the court quashed a conviction under this section. The court held that relevant consideration should have been given where the defendant, who undertook casual work at a relative's factory, forgot about a knife he was carrying. Therefore, the court *could* take this defence into account, and for that reason answer C is incorrect.

General Police Duties, para. 4.13.3.1

Answer 13.11

Answer **A** — Under the Criminal Justice Act 1988, an offence is committed when a person has an offensive weapon with him or her on school premises.

Under the Act, a constable may enter school premises and search those premises and any person for an offensive weapon. Note that the power under the Act only enables a constable to enter and search premises and search people on the premises. The power is not extended to searching people off school premises. The officer may, of course, use his power under s. 1 of the Police and Criminal Evidence Act 1984 to search the youths. This is why answer A is correct and answer B is incorrect.

There is no requirement for the constable to be in uniform, and therefore answer D is incorrect.

A person may commit an offence under this Act whether he or she is on the premises lawfully or not, and therefore answer C is incorrect.

General Police Duties, para. 4.13.4.2

Answer 13.12

Answer **B** — Section 550ZA(1) of the Education Act 1996 states that when a member of staff of a school in England has reasonable grounds for suspecting that a pupil at the school may have a prohibited item with him or her, or in his or her possessions, the member of staff may search that pupil. According to s. 550ZA(3), a prohibited item is:

(a) an article to which section 139 of the Criminal Justice Act 1988 applies (knives and blades etc.), or
(b) an offensive weapon (within the meaning of the Prevention of Crime Act 1953)

A member of staff for these purposes is any teacher who works at the school and any other person who, with the authority of the head teacher, has lawful control or charge of pupils for whom education is being provided at the school (s. 550ZA(5)). Answer A is incorrect because possessions may be searched as well as the pupil themselves.

A pupil's possessions may not be searched under this section except in their presence and in the presence of another member of the staff (s. 550ZB(7)). Since the pupil needs to be present, answer D is incorrect. However, the search may take place without the pupil's permission—indeed, as much force as is reasonable may be used in exercising this power (see s. 550ZB(5)). Answer C is therefore incorrect.

The person carrying out a search may only require the removal of outer clothing; they must be of the same sex and carry out the search in the presence of another member of staff also of the same sex as the pupil if it is reasonably practicable (s. 550ZB(6)).

Note that the provisions of this section are only in force in schools in England at this time.

General Police Duties, para. 4.13.4.3

Answer 13.13

Answer **A** — Section 550ZA(1) of the Education Act 1996 states that when a member of staff of a school in England has reasonable grounds for suspecting that a pupil at the school may have a prohibited item with him or her, or in his or her possessions, the member of staff may search that pupil. According to s. 550ZA(3) , a prohibited item is:

(a) an article to which section 139 of the Criminal Justice Act 1988 applies (knives and blades etc.), or
(b) an offensive weapon (within the meaning of the Prevention of Crime Act 1953)

Under s. 550ZB(4), a search may be carried out only where the member of staff and the pupil are on school premises; or they are elsewhere and the member of staff has lawful control or charge of the pupil. Answer B is therefore incorrect.

A person may carry out a search under this section only if he or she is the head teacher of the school; or he or she has been authorised by the head teacher to carry out the search (see s. 550ZB(1)). Answer C is therefore incorrect.

Finally, such a search may take place without the pupil's permission—indeed, as much force as is reasonable may be used in exercising this power (see s. 550ZB(5)). Answer D is therefore incorrect.

Note that the provisions of this section are only in force in schools in England at this time.

General Police Duties, para. 4.13.4.3

Answer 13.14

Answer **D** — Section 550ZA(1) of the Education Act 1996 states that a member of staff of a school in England who has reasonable grounds for suspecting that a pupil at the school may have a prohibited item with him or her or in his or her possessions, i.e. (according to s. 550ZA(3))

(a) an article to which section 139 of the Criminal Justice Act 1988 applies (knives and blades etc.), or
(b) an offensive weapon (within the meaning of the Prevention of Crime Act 1953),

the member of staff may search that pupil or his or her possessions for that item.

A search under this section may only be conducted by a head teacher, or a person authorised by the head teacher. The Act places certain restrictions on the conduct of the search. The person carrying out the search must be of the same sex and *must* carry out the search in the presence of another member of staff of the same sex (s. 550ZB(6)). Answer C is therefore incorrect.

A further restriction is that any search of the pupil may only require the removal of outer clothing. Therefore, if the pupil has hidden the weapon somewhere more private, the staff at the school will have no power to search for the weapon, whether the search is conducted in private or not. Unless the pupil gives up the weapon voluntarily, the only option available to the head teacher would be to call a constable to conduct the search utilising their powers under the Criminal Justice Act 1988. Answers A, B and C are incorrect for this reason.

Note that the provisions of this section are only in force in schools in England at this time.

General Police Duties, para. 4.13.4.3

Answer 13.15

Answer **B** — Under s. 8(1) of the Criminal Law Act 1977, a person who is on any premises as a trespasser, after having entered as such, is guilty of an offence if, without lawful authority or reasonable excuse, he/she has with him/her on the premises any weapon of offence.

'Premises' for this purpose means

(1) any building; or
(2) any part of a building under separate occupation;
(3) *any land adjacent to and used/intended for use in connection with a building;*
(4) the site comprising any building(s) together with ancillary land;
(5) any fixed structure;
(6) any movable structure, vehicle or vessel designed or adapted for residential purposes.

(Section 12 of the 1977 Act.)

Any building, or land adjacent to a building (not just a dwelling), is covered by s. 8(1), therefore CRUZ has committed the offence and for that reason answers A, C and D are incorrect.

General Police Duties, para. 4.13.5

Answer 13.16

Answer **A** — For an offence contrary to s. 8 of the Criminal Law Act 1977 the definition of 'weapon of offence' is the same as that for aggravated burglary, namely any article made or adapted for use for causing injury to or incapacitating a person, or intended by the person having it with him or her for that use (s. 8(2)). This is answer A; therefore, answers B, C and D are incorrect.

General Police Duties, para. 4.13.5

Answer 13.17

Answer **C** — Section 141 of the Criminal Justice Act 1988 makes it an offence to manufacture, sell, hire, offer for sale or hire, expose, have in possession for the purpose of sale or hire, or lend or give to another person, any weapon listed in the schedule to the Act (knuckle dusters are included).

The offence may be committed by making an offer—the Act makes no mention of being in possession of the article when the offer is made, which is why answer C is correct (this is similar to a case of offering to supply drugs under the Misuse of Drugs Act 1971).

Although offences would be made out in answers A and B, the offence has already been committed.

Answer D would be an incorrect answer in any circumstances, as unlike the original 1953 Act, which requires a person to have the weapon with him, this offence deals with possession for the purpose of sale or hire.

General Police Duties, para. 4.13.6

Answer 13.18

Answer **C** — Under s. 141A of the Criminal Justice Act 1988, it is an offence for any person to sell to a person under 18 a knife, blade, razor blade, axe, or any article which has a blade or sharp point and is made or adapted for causing injury.

Previously, a person would have committed an offence by selling such an article to a person under the age of 16 (and no offence would have been committed in these circumstances). However, the Violent Crime Reduction Act 2006 increased the age limit, so that a sale to any person under the age of 18 is an offence and therefore answer B is incorrect.

The offence does not apply to a razor blade in a cartridge, where not more than 2 mm of the blade is exposed or to a folding pocket-knife with a blade of less than 3 inches. Since the blade in this question was 3.5 inches, it is covered by s. 141A and therefore answer D is incorrect.

The age of the person making the sale is not relevant (which is why answer A is incorrect).

General Police Duties, para. 4.13.7.1

Answer 13.19

Answer **A** — Under s. 3 of the Crossbows Act 1987, a person under the age of 18 who has with him a crossbow which is capable of discharging a missile, or parts of a crossbow which together (and without any other parts) can be assembled to form a crossbow capable of discharging a missile, is guilty of an offence, unless he is under the supervision of a person who is 21 years of age or older.

Under s. 4(1), if a constable reasonably suspects a person is committing or has committed an offence under s. 3, they may search the suspected person or their vehicle for the crossbow (or part of a crossbow). Under s. 4(4), for the purposes of exercising the powers under s. 4(4), a constable may also enter any land other than a dwelling house in order to conduct the search.

In contrast to searches conducted under s. 1 of PACE (where a person cannot be searched in their own garden), the term 'dwelling house' under the Crossbows Act 1987 appears to mean just that—a house. Therefore, while there is no power to enter a person's dwelling house to conduct a search under this section (answer C is therefore incorrect), there is a power to enter other land which is not a dwelling house (such as a garden) in order to do so. Answer B is therefore incorrect.

Lastly, the powers of search under this legislation are not restricted to a search of a person or their vehicle. Answer D is therefore incorrect.

General Police Duties, para. 4.13.8

14 | Civil Disputes

STUDY PREPARATION

After the wealth of detail covered by the previous few chapters, this one may come as something of a relief.

Although the title would tend to suggest that the police have little interest or involvement, civil disputes are nevertheless a significant feature of police patrol work.

The area of domestic violence has received a great deal of political and legislative attention over the years and this chapter covers the powers created by the Crime and Security Act 2010 to secure the immediate protection of victims of domestic violence through Domestic Violence Protection Notices (DVPNs), Domestic Violence Protection Orders (DVPOs) and the Domestic Violence Disclosure Scheme, which is being piloted in some police areas to create further protection for victims of domestic abuse.

In addition to the various statutory measures in place to govern civil disputes, it is in this area that some of the most difficult 'balancing acts' in relation to human rights issues take place. These issues should be borne in mind when addressing questions in this chapter.

QUESTIONS

Question 14.1

Constable GRANT is under investigation for an alleged assault against his wife. Initially, the officer's wife gave a statement outlining a history of domestic abuse that she had suffered and he was charged with assault; however, as the court case neared, she withdrew her complaint and refused to give evidence in court. The Crown Prosecution Service (CPS) was left with no option but to offer no evidence in the case. A misconduct investigation, supervised by the Independent Police Complaints Commission (IPCC), was on hold pending the outcome of the criminal case. The IPCC has now given the appropriate authority a direction to hold a Special Case Hearing and treat the matter as gross misconduct.

Which of the following statements is correct, in relation to the Association of Chief Police Officers (ACPO) guidelines on dealing with police officers accused of domestic abuse?

A If the panel finds, on the balance of probabilities, that Constable GRANT is guilty, he should be dismissed.

B Because Constable GRANT has not been convicted of an offence, he should be given a final written warning.

C If the panel finds, on the balance of probabilities, that Constable GRANT is guilty, he must be dismissed.

D Constable GRANT could be dismissed, but only if the panel hears evidence of the abuse from his wife.

Question 14.2

VIVIERS recently ended a five-year relationship with SIMMS because of SIMMS's alcoholism. SIMMS has a 14-year-old daughter, CLAIRE, from a previous relationship; CLAIRE has no contact with her father. VIVIERS assumed parenting responsibility for CLAIRE while he lived with her, although he did not formally adopt her. CLAIRE is still in regular contact with VIVIERS and has recently disclosed that SIMMS is regularly violent towards her, but she does not wish to contact the police. VIVIERS has contacted a solicitor in relation to taking out a non-molestation order against SIMMS, on CLAIRE's behalf.

Under the Family Law Act 1996, can VIVIERS apply for a non-molestation order in these circumstances?

A No, because he is not CLAIRE's natural or adopted parent.

B No, because he does not have current parental responsibility for CLAIRE.

C Yes, because he had previous parental responsibility for CLAIRE.

D Yes, but only if the court agrees that VIVIERS should have parental responsibility for the child and he is applying for such.

Question 14.3

DANIELS and EVERSHAM used to share a house as friends, but not as cohabitants. Over a period of time, DANIELS became fixated with EVERSHAM. The behaviour caused EVERSHAM considerable distress and she eventually moved out. DANIELS then began following EVERSHAM home from work and she genuinely feared for her safety. EVERSHAM visited a solicitor with a view to obtaining a non-molestation order against DANIELS.

Would EVERSHAM be likely to succeed in obtaining such an order, under s. 42 of the Family Law Act 1996?

A No, DANIELS has not been made subject to a court order under this Act.

B Yes, an application may be made in these circumstances.

C No, DANIELS and EVERSHAM were not cohabitants, or spouses or related to each other.

D No, such an order may only be made to prevent the molestation of a child.

Question 14.4

HANSEN has been made subject to a non-molestation order under the Family Law Act 1996. The family court made the order ex parte, in HANSEN's absence, following evidence from the petitioner, BAIG. The terms of the order state that HANSEN must not contact BAIG in any way. HANSEN has breached the order by telephoning BAIG.

What action could be taken, in respect of HANSEN's breach of the non-molestation order?

A HANSEN could be arrested for a criminal offence, but a lack of knowledge of the order may provide a defence.

B HANSEN can be arrested for a criminal offence; lack of knowledge is no defence—this is an absolute offence.

C No action can be taken, as HANSEN was not in court when the order was made.

D BAIG must return to the family court and request that a power of arrest is attached to the order before HANSEN can be arrested.

Question 14.5

HARRIS and WILLIS are both aged 30 and have lived together for three years in a police area which is piloting Domestic Violence Protection Notices (DVPNs) and Domestic Violence Protection Orders. WILLIS has made numerous complaints to the police after being assaulted by HARRIS; however, each allegation was withdrawn before the courts were able to hear the case. HARRIS is now in police detention for committing another serious assault on WILLIS. The officer in the case is considering whether it would be appropriate for a DVPN to be issued against HARRIS, in order to protect WILLIS from further violence.

Section 24 of the Crime and Security Act 2010 outlines the procedures for issuing such a notice. In relation to this power, which of the following statements is correct?

A The application for a DVPN must be made to a magistrate, provided HARRIS is charged with the assault on WILLIS.

B The application for a DVPN must be made to a magistrate, but this is not dependent on HARRIS being charged with the assault on WILLIS.

C The DVPN may be issued by a senior police officer, but this is not dependent on HARRIS being charged with the assault on WILLIS.

D The DVPN may be issued by a senior police officer, following consultation at a Multi-Agency Risk Assessment Conference (MARAC), but this is not dependent on HARRIS being charged with the assault on WILLIS.

Question 14.6

An emergency Multi-Agency Risk Assessment Conference (MARAC) is meeting in a police area which is piloting Domestic Violence Protection Notices (DVPNs) and Domestic Violence Protection Orders. Members of the meeting are discussing NEW-MAN, the victim of serious domestic abuse. In the last 24 hours, NEWMAN has supported a prosecution against WILSON for assault, and the defendant is currently in police custody waiting to go to court, having been charged with assault. However, NEWMAN has indicated an intention to withdraw the allegation at WILSON's court appearance tomorrow. The various agencies at the MARAC have discussed whether or not a DVPN should be issued against WILSON; however, the meeting has been informed that NEWMAN would be hostile to such a notice being issued.

Which of the following statements is correct in respect of whether a DVPN may be issued against NEWMAN's wishes, under s. 24 of the Crime and Security Act 2010?

A Section 24(3)(b) provides that the opinion of the victim be sought, before a DVPN is issued; it may not, therefore, be issued without NEWMAN's consent.

B A DVPN may be issued without NEWMAN's consent, provided either the victim or some other member of the household is under 18.

C A DVPN may not be issued without NEWMAN's consent; only a Domestic Violence Protection Order (DVPO) may be issued in these circumstances.

D The authorising authority may issue a DVPN in these circumstances, even if NEW-MAN does not consent to it.

Question 14.7

Constable PENGELLI works in the Public Protection Department in a police area piloting the Domestic Violence Disclosure Scheme (DVDS). The officer has just read an intelligence log concerning ARMAND, whom the officer knew to be a previous victim of domestic abuse. ARMAND's ex-partner, KIFF, was convicted 12 months previously for assault relating to the abuse and is currently in prison; however, the intelligence log Constable PENGELLI has read indicates that ARMAND has moved in with a new partner, whose convictions for domestic abuse are worse than KIFF's.

Given that Constable PENGELLI's force is a pilot area for the DVDS, what action should the officer take?

A None, this scheme relates to requests for information from members of the public, who are concerned about people they are in a relationship with.

B Constable PENGELLI should make appropriate police checks and consult with statutory partners, and a decision should be made by the appropriate police officer as to whether disclosure should be made to ARMAND.

C None, intelligence logs are not accurate enough documents to commence an investigation to decide whether to make a disclosure about a person's criminal convictions.

D Constable PENGELLI should make appropriate police checks and pass the matter to statutory partners, who should make a decision as to whether disclosure should be made to ARMAND.

Question 14.8

ASHTON has been sacked from his job at an aeronautical factory. He complains to his union, which takes four weeks to decide his case. The union eventually decides to authorise industrial action and to picket the aeronautical factory. In the intervening period, however, the firm has moved premises and no longer occupies the premises where ASHTON worked. A considerable amount of land at the new factory is private.

In relation to picketing, which of the following is true?

A The pickets cannot enter the private land to picket.

B The pickets could picket the new premises as they are still technically ASHTON's place of work.

C There would be a maximum of six pickets allowed at any one time.
D The right to picket outside the factory is an absolute right and cannot be over-ridden.

Question 14.9

Employees of a company are currently on strike; however, a few have remained at work. One employee, HIGGINS, who is still working, is followed home by two of the strikers; they call him a 'scab' and a 'strike breaker'. They also whistle and jeer at him. HIGGINS is very distressed by this behaviour. Consider the offence of intimidation or annoyance by violence or otherwise contrary to s. 241 of the Trade Union and Labour Relations (Consolidation) Act 1992.

Has this offence been committed?
A No, because there needs to be more than two people following HIGGINS.
B No, because they are not threatening or intimidating HIGGINS or using violence.
C Yes, provided the strikers intended to compel HIGGINS to join the strike.
D Yes, provided the strikers intended to cause the distress that HIGGINS suffered.

ANSWERS

Answer 14.1

Answer **A** — The Association of Chief Police Officers (ACPO) has issued a policy document setting out the approach to be adopted where police officers are personally involved in domestic violence; ACPO advocates a 'presumption towards dismissal' where an officer is convicted of a domestic violence-related offence.

In addition, any officer whose conduct is found to have fallen below the required standard in respect of domestic violence/abuse can expect to be dismissed or required to resign despite not having attracted a criminal conviction. Answer B is therefore incorrect.

While the expectation is that the officer will have to leave the service, the ACPO policy does not make dismissal mandatory and answer C is therefore incorrect.

The standard of proof required in misconduct meetings/hearings is that which applies to civil cases, that is, the balance of probabilities. Conduct will be proved on the balance of probabilities if the persons conducting the meeting/hearing are satisfied by the evidence *that it is more likely than not that the conduct occurred*. Taking everything into account, the panel in Constable GRANT's case *could* dismiss him, even without direct evidence from his wife. Answer D is therefore incorrect.

General Police Duties, paras 4.14.2, 4.2.6.8

Answer 14.2

Answer **C** — Section 42 of the Family Law Act 1996 provides for 'non-molestation' orders. Under s. 42(1), a 'non-molestation order' means an order containing either or both of the following provisions—

(a) provision prohibiting a person ('the respondent') from molesting another person who is associated with the respondent;
(b) provision prohibiting the respondent from molesting a relevant child.

Section 62(3) of the Act describes 'associated' persons who may either be the petitioner or respondent for a non-molestation order. A non-molestation order may be applied for by anyone who is 'associated' with the respondent, including former cohabitants.

Under s. 62(4), a person will be 'associated' with a child if—

(a) he is a parent of the child; or

(b) he has or has had parental responsibility for the child.

Therefore, the fact that VIVIERS does not currently have parental responsibility for CLAIRE, or is not her natural or adopted parent is irrelevant and he may apply for an order. Answers A and B are therefore incorrect.

There is no mention in s. 42 or s. 62 of the petitioner having to apply for a formal parental role in relation to children before an order can be made—this is about preventing an individual from molesting another and therefore answer D is incorrect.

General Police Duties, para. 4.14.2.2

Answer 14.3

Answer **B** — Under s. 42(1) of the Family Law Act 1996, a 'non-molestation order' means an order containing a provision prohibiting a person ('the respondent') from molesting another person who is associated with the respondent or from molesting a relevant child. Since the provisions do not only apply to children, answer D is incorrect.

Under s. 42(2)(a), the court may make a non-molestation order when an application has been made by a person who is associated with the respondent whether or not any other family proceedings have been instituted. Answer A is therefore incorrect.

Section 62 contains a long list of people who are 'associated' with the respondent, including relatives, children, spouses, cohabitants and civil partners (and people who formerly enjoyed such a status). Under s. 62(3)(c), they also include people who live, or have lived, in the same household, otherwise than merely by reason of one of them being the other's employee, tenant, lodger or boarder. Answer C is therefore incorrect.

General Police Duties, para. 4.14.2.2

Answer 14.4

Answer **A** — Section 42A of the Family Law Act 1996 was introduced by the Domestic Violence, Crime and Victims Act 2004 and states—

(1) A person who without reasonable excuse does anything that he is prohibited from doing by a non-molestation order is guilty of an offence.

(2) In the case of a non-molestation order made by virtue of s. 45(1), a person can be guilty of an offence under this section only in respect of conduct engaged in at a time when he was aware of the existence of the order.

Consequently, this provides a power of arrest for the breach of a non-molestation order under the provisions of s. 24(1) of the Police and Criminal Evidence Act 1984. Answer D is incorrect as there is no longer a requirement to attach a power of arrest to an order before a person can be arrested.

In relation to subs. (2), non-molestation orders made by virtue of s. 45(1) are ex parte orders where the respondent has not been present at the proceedings when the order was made. This section makes it clear that if the defendant was not in court *and* he or she was not aware of its existence, he or she cannot be found guilty of the offence—but this does not mean that the person cannot be arrested until the facts have been established. Answers B and C are therefore incorrect.

General Police Duties, para. 4.14.2.3

Answer 14.5

Answer **C** — Section 24 of the Crime and Security Act 2010 creates a power for a Domestic Violence Protection Notice (DVPN) to secure the immediate protection of a victim of domestic violence from future violence or a threat of violence from a suspected perpetrator. The DVPN is intended to prohibit the perpetrator from molesting the victim of domestic abuse and, where they cohabit, may require the perpetrator to leave those premises.

The purpose of a DVPN is to provide an interim solution to protect a vulnerable victim of domestic abuse, pending an application to the magistrates' court for a Domestic Violence Protection Order (DVPO). A DVPN must be issued by a police officer, of at least the rank of superintendent (s. 24(1)). Answers A and B are therefore incorrect.

By its nature, the DVPN is meant to provide a short-term respite, outside the criminal justice system, for the victim, while seeking a longer-term solution through the courts. It is not dependent on the perpetrator being charged with an offence and therefore answer A is incorrect. That said, Home Office guidance suggests that the success of the process will be reliant on the partnership work with other agencies and organisations including those that contribute to Multi-Agency Risk Assessment Conferences (MARACs) and service providers for Independent Domestic Violence Advocates (IDVAs).

Note that ss. 24 to 30 of the 2010 Act were brought into force on 30 June 2012 in pilot areas (Greater Manchester, Wiltshire and West Mercia), for the purpose of assessing the effectiveness of the provisions.

General Police Duties, para. 4.14.2.4

Answer 14.6

Answer **D** — Section 24 of the Crime and Security Act 2010 creates a power for a Domestic Violence Protection Notice (DVPN) to be issued to secure the immediate protection of a victim of domestic violence from future violence or a threat of violence from a suspected perpetrator. The DVPN is intended to prohibit the perpetrator from molesting the victim of domestic abuse and, where they cohabit, may require the perpetrator to leave those premises. The purpose of a DVPN is to provide an interim solution to protect a vulnerable victim of domestic abuse, pending an application to the magistrates' court for a Domestic Violence Protection Order (DVPO).

Section 24(3)(b) *does* provide that the opinion of the victim should be sought, before a DVPN is issued. The authorising officer should also seek to establish whether the *suspect* wishes to make any representations (s. 24(3)(c)), or any other associated person who lives at the premises who may be affected by the DVPN (s. 24(3)(d)). However, s. 24(5) states that the *authorising officer may issue a DVPN in circumstances where the person for whose protection it is issued does not consent to the issuing of the DVPN.* Answers A and C are therefore incorrect.

Finally, before issuing a DVPN, the authorising officer must, in particular, consider the welfare of any person under the age of 18 whose interests the officer considers relevant to the issuing of the DVPN (whether or not that person is an associated person) (s. 24(3)(a)). However, this does not mean that a DVPN may *only* be issued without consent when the victim or some other member of the household is under 18. Answer B is therefore incorrect.

Note that ss. 24 to 30 of the 2010 Act were brought into force on 30 June 2012 in pilot areas (Greater Manchester, Wiltshire and West Mercia), for the purpose of assessing the effectiveness of the provisions.

General Police Duties, para. 4.14.2.4

Answer 14.7

Answer **B** — Pilots of the Domestic Violence Disclosure Scheme are taking place in the Gwent, Wiltshire, Nottinghamshire and Greater Manchester police areas and will run until September 2013.

The principal aim of the scheme is to introduce recognised and consistent procedures for disclosing information which will enable a partner (A) of a previously violent individual (B) to make informed choices about whether and how A takes forward that relationship with B.

There are two distinct entry routes that may lead to a disclosure being made. The first entry route—'right to ask'—is modelled closely on the existing Child Sex Offender Disclosure Scheme, and is triggered when a person makes a direct application to the police for information about B. The second entry route—'right to know'— is triggered when the police receive indirect information or intelligence about the safety of A and where, after appropriate checks are made, the police judge that a disclosure should be made to safeguard A (answer A is therefore incorrect). An intelligence log *could* trigger an investigation under the scheme (although more checks would be required) and therefore answer C is incorrect.

The decision-makers are definitely the police (although it is expected that statutory partners should be consulted unless the matter is urgent). Answer D is incorrect for that reason.

General Police Duties, para. 4.14.2.5

Answer 14.8

Answer **A** — Although picketing is lawful under s. 220 of the Trade Union and Labour Relations (Consolidation) Act 1992, there are some restrictions. It is lawful to picket your former place of work if the action is as a result of the termination of your employment. However, a person's place of work does not include new premises of an employer who has moved since dismissing the people picketing (*News Group Newspapers Ltd* v *SOGAT '82 (No. 2)* [1987] ICR 181), and therefore answer B is incorrect. The 1992 Act does not place restrictions on the number of pickets; the number six is from the agreed Code of Practice on picketing, which has no legal force, and therefore answer C is incorrect.

Note, however, that if numbers are large enough, there might be a presumption that the pickets intend to intimidate others, which would make it unlawful (*Broome* v *DPP* [1974] AC 587). If there is a real danger of any offence (e.g. public disorder) being committed, the pickets have no right to attend at the factory to picket under s. 220 (*Piddlington* v *Bates* [1960] 1 WLR 162), and therefore answer D is incorrect. Section 220 does not authorise pickets to enter onto private land (*British Airports Authority* v *Ashton* [1983] 1 WLR 1079).

General Police Duties, para. 4.14.3.1

Answer 14.9

Answer **C** — This is an offence of 'specific intent', and as such there has to be an element of intention to bring about a specific outcome. It is committed by someone who follows the victim with 'two or more other persons' (therefore answer A is incorrect), where they follow the victim 'in a disorderly manner in or through any street or road'. There does not have to be a threat or use of violence; disorder would be sufficient, and therefore answer B is incorrect. Their intention must be to compel HIGGINS to join the strike, and not simply to cause distress, and therefore answer D is incorrect. (Note that if the circumstances were reversed and HIGGINS was on strike, the offence would still be committed by compelling him to return to work.)

General Police Duties, para. 4.14.3.3

15 Offences Relating to Land and Premises

STUDY PREPARATION

The Criminal Justice and Public Order Act 1994 created several offences which have the effect of allowing the criminal courts to deal with offences of trespass. This chapter deals with offences such as trespassing with intent to disrupt lawful activities, trespassing with intent to reside on land, raves and residing in vehicles on land, all of which are very topical. Each offence has several elements to it, but there are common themes throughout, such as authorising officers, offences of failing to leave land when directed to do so and returning within three months of a direction being given.

The Criminal Law Act 1977 makes up the bulk of the second part of the chapter. Offences under s. 6 and s. 7 of the Act are rarely used, but remain useful pieces of legislation, especially that of using violence for securing entry to premises.

Lastly, do not ignore the offences of being found on enclosed premises and causing a nuisance on educational premises; both are useful offences to remember.

QUESTIONS

Question 15.1

A new football stadium is being built on the outskirts of a town. Vehicles belonging to the building company have been parked in an enclosed warehouse situated adjacent to the building site, which is due to be demolished after the stadium is completed. Environmental protestors have been attempting to stop the building work. The builders arrived for work one morning and as they opened the doors to the warehouse, a number of protestors stormed in and chained themselves to the vehicles. Building work was disrupted for several hours as the police were called to remove them. It was a peaceful protest; no property was damaged and no one was threatened.

Have the protesters committed an offence under s. 68 of the Criminal Justice and Public Order Act 1994 (aggravated trespass), in these circumstances?

A No, as the protestors were not on land in the open air.

B Yes, the offence is complete in these circumstances.

C No, as the protestors were not on land where the building work was due to take place.

D No, as the protestors did not threaten or intimidate the builders, or cause damage.

Question 15.2

OSMAND and NERO entered a building site as trespassers; they were protesting against the construction of a new shopping centre. They had with them a large concrete tube, which they placed on the ground in the middle of the site. OSMAND and NERO then connected their arms through the tube with a padlocked chain. Inspector CORP was the senior officer to arrive and concluded that they had committed an offence contrary to s. 68 of the Criminal Justice and Public Order Act 1994 (aggravated trespass) and directed them to leave. OSMAND and NERO stated that they were unable to leave because they had no key to the padlock. Eventually a locksmith was called to the scene and when they were released, OSMAND and NERO were arrested for failing to leave when directed, under s. 69 of the Act. They were charged with the offence under s. 69 and later in court, claimed they had a reasonable excuse for failing to leave as soon as practicable—that they were unable to do so until they were released.

Could OSMAND and NERO's defence succeed in these circumstances?

A No, they did not leave the site as soon as practicable.

B Yes, they left the site as soon as practicable after they were released.

C No, their intention was to frustrate the police utilising their powers under this Act and they succeeded.

D No, their intention when they chained themselves to the tube is irrelevant; they succeeded in disrupting lawful activities on the site.

Question 15.3

PARSONS, a farmer, agreed to allow a family of travellers to stay on his land for a week. Between them, the travellers had two caravans and two cars. After two weeks, they were still on the land and PARSONS asked them to leave. When they refused, he contacted the police.

Would the officers have the power, under s. 61 of the Criminal Justice and Public Order Act 1994, to direct the family to leave the land?

A No, because the family did not have more than 12 vehicles between them.

B Yes, they could direct the family to leave the land, with their vehicles.

C No, because the family were originally given permission to stay by the land-owner.

D No, because the family have not caused damage or used threatening/insulting behaviour.

Question 15.4

Constable ZIGICH was called to a field owned by STAINES, who was complaining about a caravan that was parked on his land. There was no one with the caravan, but STAINES stated that it belonged to MUIR, who had been one of a number of people that had been forced to leave the land a month previously, following a direction that had been given under s. 61 of the Criminal Justice and Public Order Act 1994 (trespassing for purpose of residence). STAINES was concerned that the presence of the caravan indicated that MUIR and other people intended returning to occupy the land and asked Constable ZIGICH to remove it.

Would Constable ZIGICH have the power to remove the caravan, as requested by STAINES?

A No, the power to remove a vehicle under this Act applies only where a person fails to remove it, when a direction is initially given.

B Yes, the vehicle may be removed under this Act in these circumstances.

C No, MUIR has not returned to the land as a trespasser with two or more vehicles.

D No, a vehicle may only be removed under this Act if the owner is present with it.

Question 15.5

Following numerous complaints from residents, Sergeant BISLAND attended a gathering of people in the early hours of the morning with several constables. On their arrival, the officers saw that approximately 100 people were dancing to loud music. The people had entered land which belonged to the local authority that was adjacent to a beach. Sergeant BISLAND believed the people were trespassing on the land and that the gathering amounted to a rave. The sergeant has contacted Inspector MORGAN for advice as to how to remove the people from the area, and how this decision should be communicated to those present.

Which of the following statements is correct, in relation to the decisions that may be made, under s. 63 of the Criminal Justice and Public Order Act 1994?

A Inspector MORGAN may declare that the gathering is a rave, but any of the officers may communicate this decision to those present.

B Only a superintendent may declare that the gathering is a rave and any of the officers may communicate this decision to those present.

C As the senior officer at the scene, Sergeant BISLAND may declare the gathering is a rave; any of the officers may communicate this decision to those present.

D Only a superintendent may declare the gathering is a rave and only Sergeant BISLAND may communicate this decision to those present, as the senior officer at the scene.

Question 15.6

On a Saturday morning, the police received complaints from residents about a group of people gathered on a beach. The group had arrived the previous evening and were partying all night. The police attended and saw 20 people listening to loud, amplified music. The group stated they intended staying until the Monday as it was a bank holiday weekend and that the music would carry on that night and on the Sunday.

Would a senior officer have sufficient evidence at this stage to reasonably believe that a 'gathering' is taking place, as defined in s. 63(1) of the Criminal Justice and Public Order Act 1994?

A Yes, there were at least ten people gathering at the site of a rave.

B No, the people gathering were not trespassing on land.

C Yes, there is sufficient evidence at this time to define this as a 'gathering'.

D No, s. 63(1) does not apply in the daylight hours, the senior officer would have to wait until night-time to make this decision.

Question 15.7

Detective Constable WU was in plain clothes one evening, when he responded to an assistance call from a uniformed officer, Constable HOLMES. When he arrived, Constable HOLMES informed Detective Constable WU that a gathering was taking place three miles away, which had been declared as a 'rave'. Constable HOLMES had stopped 20 vehicles and was attempting to get them to turn around. Until further assistance arrived, Constable HOLMES continued to stop vehicles, while Detective Constable WU spoke to the drivers suspected of attending the rave and directed them not to proceed.

Were the directions given by Detective Constable WU lawful in the circumstances?

A Yes, he has acted correctly in these circumstances.

B No, he was outside the required radius from the rave to be able to give the directions.

C No, he was inside the required radius from the rave to be able to give the directions.

D No, he should have been in uniform when giving the directions.

Question 15.8

ASHLEY was 17 years of age and lived with his parents and younger brother and sister. ASHLEY's parents were becoming increasingly concerned about his drinking habits because he was disturbing his younger siblings when coming home in the early hours of the morning. ASHLEY had not returned home by 1.00 am after going out and his father sent him a text asking him to find somewhere else to stay that night if he was drunk. ASHLEY read the text at 3.00 am when he was on his way home. He ignored his father's request and arrived at the front door, finding that it was bolted and he couldn't get in the house. ASHLEY lost his temper and began kicking the door and shouting. His father was standing on the other side of the door pleading with him to go and stay somewhere else. ASHLEY ignored him and continued trying to get into the house. A neighbour heard the disturbance and called the police.

Would ASHLEY be guilty of an offence under s. 6 of the Criminal Law Act 1977 (using violence for securing entry)?

A No, ASHLEY could claim to be a displaced residential occupier.

B Yes, ASHLEY is using violence to secure entry to the premises.

C No, neither ASHLEY nor his parents are trespassers.

D Yes, if ASHLEY intends using violence against his parents.

Question 15.9

TILLEY owned a printing business, which was located in a shop premises. TILLEY owned the building, and lived in a flat above the shop. Business was slow and TILLEY had to lay off his assistant, CARNE. CARNE kept his keys to the premises and while TILLEY was away on business the following week, CARNE moved into his flat. When TILLEY returned, CARNE refused to leave the flat, stating that he was homeless as a result of losing his job. TILLEY contacted the police, claiming to be a displaced residential occupier. When the police arrived, CARNE refused to leave.

Given that the flat in question is situated in business premises, what defence is available to CARNE under s. 7 of the Criminal Law Act 1977 (person failing to leave premises)?

A None, failing to leave premises when requested in these circumstances is an absolute offence.

B None, but the prosecution must show that this part of the premises was used mainly for residential purposes.

C CARNE has a defence, unless the prosecution can show that this part of the premises was used mainly for non-residential purposes.

D CARNE has a defence if he can show that this part of the premises was used mainly for non-residential purposes.

Question 15.10

LEHMAN is living in rental property and has been in a long-standing dispute with the owner, CAHIL, over a failure to conduct adequate repairs to the property. LEHMAN's Tenancy Agreement has ended; however, she is refusing to leave because CAHIL has refused to return a bond of £250. CAHIL, on the other hand, is refusing to hand over the bond until LEHMAN allows access to the property for inspection. CAHIL has discovered that LEHMAN's friend MENCE has also moved into the property—MENCE has never been on the Tenancy Agreement. CAHIL has persuaded a court to issue an Eviction Notice in respect of LEHMAN and MENCE and the Notice outlines that if they fail to leave, they will be regarded as trespassers.

Who, if either, of LEHMAN and MENCE would be guilty of an offence under s. 144 of the Legal Aid, Sentencing and Punishment of Offenders Act 2012 (squatting in a residential building), in these circumstances?

A Neither, as long as MENCE is there with LEHMAN's permission.

B Only MENCE; LEHMAN does not commit this offence, provided she does not leave the premises and re-enter.

C Both persons commit the offence as they are now trespassing.

D Only MENCE; LEHMAN does not commit this offence, whether or not she leaves the property and re-enters.

Question 15.11

The police attended an alarm at an office building in a city centre. They made a search of the premises and found PECK, who was hiding in one of the offices. The officers recognised PECK as a homeless person with whom police regularly had dealings. Following questioning, the officers decided that there was insufficient evidence to arrest PECK for burglary. PECK was then arrested for being found on enclosed premises.

Would the premises that PECK was found on amount to an 'enclosed premises', for the purposes of offences under s. 4 of the Vagrancy Act 1824?

A No, 'enclosed premises' will only include outhouses and land ancillary to buildings.

B No, if the person is found in a building, that building must be a dwelling for the purposes of this offence.

C Yes, providing the person is found in a building, or outhouse or land ancillary to a building; it doesn't matter what type of building.

D No, a room within an office building will not amount to an enclosed area for the purposes of this offence.

Question 15.12

BRENT lived in a property owned by Western Housing Association. BRENT owned several abandoned cars which were in a dangerous condition and were parked in a communal parking area at the rear of the property, owned by the association. The association served a notice to remove the cars; however, BRENT refused to do so and attended the company's offices, threatening to tow the cars across the entrance of the parking area to barricade them in. The association was concerned that this action might cause distress to other residents.

Would BRENT's threats be sufficient to merit an application by the association for an anti-social behaviour injunction, under s. 153A of the Housing Act 1996?

A No, the conduct was not directed at a person living in the vicinity of the house.

B Yes, provided the company named the people likely to be affected in the injunction.

C No, as the conduct occurred in the association's offices and not in the vicinity of the house.

D Yes, regardless of where the conduct occurred, or whether the company can name the people likely to be affected in the injunction.

Question 15.13

EASTWOOD is a caretaker at a school maintained by a local authority. He received a call from teachers that some youths from a different school were on the playing fields shouting and swearing at them. EASTWOOD telephoned the police and made his way to the field. He arrived before the police to find several youths sitting next to a classroom quietly.

Which statement will be correct in relation to the youths causing a nuisance on educational premises?

A They may be removed from the premises by either EASTWOOD or the police.

B EASTWOOD has no powers to deal with the youths; he must wait for the police to arrive.

C EASTWOOD has no powers to deal with the youths, as the disturbance has ceased.

D EASTWOOD has a power to detain the youths until the police arrive at the school.

ANSWERS

Answer 15.1

Answer **B** — Under s. 68(1) of the Criminal Justice and Public Order Act 1994, a person commits the offence of aggravated trespass if he/she trespasses on land and, in relation to any lawful activity which persons are engaging in or are about to engage in on that or adjoining land, does there anything which is intended by him to have the effect—

(a) of intimidating those persons or any of them so as to deter them or any of them from engaging in that activity,

(b) of obstructing that activity, or

(c) of disrupting that activity.

Therefore, even though the protestors did not threaten or intimidate the builders, or cause damage, their actions were sufficient to obstruct and disrupt the activity. Answer D is therefore incorrect.

The offence is committed when a person trespasses on land where the activity is due to take place or on *adjoining* land (which makes answer C incorrect).

Section 68 originally included the phrase 'in the open air' but it was removed by the Anti-social Behaviour Act 2003. In *DPP* v *Chivers* [2010] EWHC 1814 (Admin) it was held that the purpose and effect of this amendment was quite plainly to include buildings. Answer A is therefore incorrect.

Note that in order to establish the offence of aggravated trespass under s. 68, you must prove that the defendant had committed the act(s) complained of in the physical presence of a person engaged or about to engage in the lawful activity with which the defendant wished to interfere (*DPP* v *Tilly* [2001] EWHC 821 (Admin)).

General Police Duties, para. 4.15.3

Answer 15.2

Answer **B** — Section 68(1) of the Criminal Justice and Public Order Act 1994 states that a person commits the offence of aggravated trespass if he trespasses on land and, in relation to any lawful activity which persons are engaging in or are about to engage in on that or adjoining land, does there anything which is intended by him to have the effect—

(a) of intimidating those persons or any of them so as to deter them or any of them from engaging in that activity,

(b) of obstructing that activity, or

(c) of disrupting that activity.

The intent of the defendant *is* relevant—if they have not committed the offence of aggravated trespass, then the order under s. 69 directing them to leave is invalid; answer D is therefore incorrect.

It is a defence for the accused to show that they were not trespassing on the land, or had a reasonable excuse for failing to leave the land as soon as practicable or for again entering the land as a trespasser (s. 69(4)).

In circumstances similar to this question, the court quashed the appellants' convictions for failing to leave a shop premises as soon as practicable when so directed by the police, because they were physically unable to move until they had been unchained, and had left as soon as this was done. Answer A is therefore incorrect.

The court also held that what they did was designed to disrupt the shop's trade, not to frustrate the operation of s. 69; the fact that they had voluntarily (and deliberately) placed themselves in a situation in which they could not leave when directed was held to be irrelevant (see *Nero* v *DPP* [2012] EWHC 1238 (Admin) and *Richardson* v *DPP* [2012] EWHC 1238 (Admin)). Answer C is therefore incorrect.

General Police Duties, paras 4.15.3, 4.15.3.1, 4.15.3.2

Answer 15.3

Answer **C** — To prove the offence under s. 61 of the Criminal Justice and Public Order Act 1994, you need to show that at least two people are trespassing on land with a common purpose of residing there and reasonable steps have been taken to ask them to leave.

If these conditions are apparent, you must then show that:

- they have damaged land; *or*
- they have used threatening etc. behaviour; *or*
- they have between them *six* or more vehicles.

As none of these apply, answers B and D are incorrect. Under s. 61(2), if the people had been given permission to stay on the land but had subsequently become trespassers, the officers would have to satisfy themselves that one of the conditions in s. 61(1) had occurred after they had become trespassers.

The original 1994 Act specified 12 vehicles, but this has been amended to six and therefore answer A is incorrect.

(It should be noted that the Home Office has issued guidance to the police on the use of the powers under s. 61. It advises that the police must be able to demonstrate that all eviction and enforcement decisions are 'proportionate' in weighing individual harm against the wider public interest.)

General Police Duties, para. 4.15.4

Answer 15.4

Answer **B** — If a direction has been given under s. 61 of the Criminal Justice and Public Order Act 1994 and a police officer reasonably suspects that any person to whom it applies has, without reasonable excuse:

- failed to remove any vehicle on the land which appears to the officer to belong to him/her or to be in his/her possession or under his/her control; or
- entered the land as a trespasser with a vehicle within the period of three months beginning with the day when the direction was given,

the officer may seize and remove the vehicle (s. 62).

Answer A is incorrect as a vehicle may be removed *either* when the initial direction has been given under s. 61 (and the person failed to remove it), *or* where a person has entered the land as a trespasser with a vehicle within the period of three months beginning with the day when the direction was given.

It does not state in s. 62 that the owner must return to the land as a trespasser with two or more vehicles before it can be removed under this section, nor does it state that the owner of the vehicle must be present before it can be seized and removed. Answers C and D are therefore incorrect.

General Police Duties, para. 4.15.4.1

Answer 15.5

Answer **B** — The elements of a 'gathering' for a rave are found in s. 63(1) of the Criminal Justice and Public Order Act 1994. The senior officer (a superintendent) would have to be satisfied that these elements are present before giving a direction for people to leave under this section. Those elements are that:

- the gathering is on land in the open air;
- the gathering is likely to be attended by 20 or more persons (whether or not they are trespassers);

- amplified music is played during the night (with or without intermissions), which by reason of its loudness and duration and the time at which it is played, is likely to cause serious distress to the inhabitants of the locality.

Under s. 63(2) of the Act, when these elements are present, a direction may be given for the people gathered there to leave the land and take any vehicles or property with them. Such a direction may only be made by an officer of at least the rank of *superintendent*. Answers A and C are therefore incorrect.

Section 63(3) states that if the direction under s. 63(2) is not communicated to the people at the scene by the officer making the direction, it may be communicated to them by *any constable at the scene*. Answer D is therefore incorrect.

General Police Duties, paras 4.15.6, 4.15.6.1

Answer 15.6

Answer **C** — The elements of a 'gathering' for a rave are found in s. 63(1) of the Criminal Justice and Public Order Act 1994. The senior officer (a superintendent) would have to be satisfied that these elements are present before giving a direction for people to leave under this section. Those elements are that:

- the gathering is on land in the open air;
- the gathering is likely to be attended by 20 or more persons (whether or not they are trespassers);
- amplified music is played during the night (with or without intermissions), which by reason of its loudness and duration and the time at which it is played, is likely to cause serious distress to the inhabitants of the locality.

Taking matters in order, the superintendent must first believe that a gathering of 20 people is likely to take place—not ten. This is the figure described in s. 63(2)(b), which is the preventative element of this section, where officers can tell people to leave to prevent the rave from taking place. Answer A is therefore incorrect.

It is irrelevant whether the gathering is trespassing and answer B is incorrect. (Note that s. 63(1A) of the Act deals specifically with gatherings where people are trespassing.)

Generally, the amplified music must be played during the night; however, there will be occasions where raves take place over several days. This is provided for in s. 63(1)(a), which states that this section applies when:

such a gathering continues during intermissions in the music and, where the gathering extends over several days, throughout the period during which amplified music is played at night (with or without intermissions).

Therefore, as the officers attending the scene (and their superintendent) had reason to believe that a rave would take place the same evening, they would not have to wait until the evening before taking action. Answer D is therefore incorrect.

General Police Duties, para. 4.15.6.1

Answer 15.7

Answer **D** — Under s. 65 of the Criminal Justice and Public Order Act 1994, where a constable in uniform reasonably believes a person is on his or her way to a gathering to which s. 63(2) applies (direction to leave land in respect of a rave), the officer may stop the person and direct him or her not to proceed in the direction of the gathering. Unlike other directions under this Act, a direction under s. 65 must be given by a constable in uniform, and therefore answer A is incorrect.

The power may be exercised within *five* miles of the boundary of the site of the gathering. Answers B and C are incorrect, as the officers were inside this radius; and had Detective Constable WU been in uniform, the directions not to proceed would have been lawful.

General Police Duties, para. 4.15.6.4

Answer 15.8

Answer **B** — A person is guilty of an offence under s. 6(1) of the Criminal Law Act 1977 if he or she uses or threatens violence for the purpose of securing entry to premises, provided there is someone on the premises who is opposed to the entry and the person using/threatening the violence knows that this is the case. Clearly, in this question ASHLEY knows that his father is opposed to his entry into the premises.

The person would have a defence if he or she could show that he or she was either a displaced residential occupier (DRO) or a protected intended occupier (PIO). ASHLEY is not a PIO as per the definition and to be a DRO, a person would have to show that he or she was occupying premises immediately before being excluded by a person who entered those premises as a trespasser. As his parents are not trespassers (and it is irrelevant whether ASHLEY is a trespasser), ASHLEY could not be a DRO and would have no defence. Answers A and C are therefore incorrect.

It is immaterial whether the violence used/threatened is against a person or property, or whether the purpose of the entry is to gain possession of the premises or any other purpose (s. 6(4)). Whether or not ASHLEY intended using violence against his parents is irrelevant and therefore answer D is incorrect.

General Police Duties, paras 4.15.8.2, 4.15.8.3

Answer 15.9

Answer **D** — The offence of failing to leave premises when requested is covered by s. 7(1) of the Criminal Law Act 1977. The offence is complete, because CARNE entered the premises as a trespasser and refused to leave when requested by a displaced residential occupier (TILLEY).

A defence is provided under s. 7(3)(a) of the Act (and answer A is therefore incorrect); it is for the accused to prove that the premises are or formed part of premises used mainly for non-residential purposes. Answers B and C are therefore incorrect. (Whether CARNE would be able successfully to claim this defence is doubtful, as the flat is clearly residential premises.)

General Police Duties, para. 4.15.8.4

Answer 15.10

Answer **D** — Section 144 of the Legal Aid, Sentencing and Punishment of Offenders Act 2012 states:

(1) A person commits an offence if—
    (a) the person is in a residential building as a trespasser having entered it as a trespasser,
    (b) the person knows or ought to know that he or she is a trespasser, and
    (c) the person is living in the building or intends to live there for any period.

However, the offence is not committed by a person holding over after the end of a lease or licence *even if the person leaves and re-enters the building* (s. 144(2)) and therefore answers B and C are incorrect.

For the purposes of this section the fact that a person derives title from a trespasser, or has the permission of a trespasser, does not prevent the person from being a trespasser (s. 144(4)). In other words, even though MENCE is on the premises with LEHMAN's permission, she is a trespasser and could commit this offence. Answer A is therefore incorrect.

General Police Duties, para. 4.15.8.5

Answer 15.11

Answer **D** — It is a summary offence under s. 4(1) of the Vagrancy Act 1824 for any person to be found in or upon any dwelling house, warehouse, coach house, stable or outhouse or in any enclosed yard, garden or area for *any unlawful purpose*. This ancient offence was created to prevent vagrancy and the original definition gives a clue as to the type of premises that might be considered enclosed—

(i) every person wandering abroad and lodging in any barn or outhouse, or in any deserted or unoccupied building, or in the open air, or under a tent, or in any cart or waggon, and not giving a good account of himself or herself;

(ii) every person being found in or upon any dwelling house, warehouse, coach-house, stable, or outhouse, or in any enclosed yard, garden, or area, for any unlawful purpose;

commits an offence.

Answers A and B are incorrect as the Act covers many buildings that are not merely dwellings or outhouses and land ancillary to buildings.

However, a room within an office building has been held *not* to amount to an enclosed area for the purposes of this offence (*Talbot* v *Oxford City Justices* [2000] 1 WLR 1102). Answer C is therefore incorrect.

General Police Duties, para. 4.15.8.6

Answer 15.12

Answer **D** — Under s. 153A(3) of the Housing Act 1996, a court may, on the application of a relevant landlord, grant an anti-social behaviour injunction if:

the person against whom the injunction is sought is engaging, has engaged or threatens to engage in housing-related conduct capable of causing a nuisance or annoyance to:

(a) a person with a right (of whatever description) to reside in or occupy housing accommodation owned or managed by a relevant landlord,

(b) a person with a right (of whatever description) to reside in or occupy other housing accommodation in the neighbourhood of housing accommodation mentioned in paragraph (a),

(c) a person engaged in lawful activity in, or in the neighbourhood of, housing accommodation mentioned in paragraph (a), or

(d) a person employed (whether or not by a relevant landlord) in connection with the exercise of a relevant landlord's housing management functions.

Therefore, as the conduct can be directed at a person employed by the company, answer A is incorrect. Further, it is immaterial where conduct to which this section applies occurs (answer C is therefore incorrect).

Finally, an injunction may be granted without a particular individual being named as someone adversely affected by the conduct referred to in the injunction, and in respect of conduct that is not described by reference to any person or persons at all. If conduct is described in an injunction by reference to a person or persons, these may be persons generally, or persons of a particular description, or a specified person. Answer B is therefore incorrect.

General Police Duties, para. 4.15.8.7

Answer 15.13

Answer **A** — Where a person has caused a nuisance, disturbance or annoyance on educational premises, a police constable, or a person authorised by the local authority, may remove that person from the premises (s. 547(3) of the Education Act 1996). The power is to remove, not to detain, which is why answers B and D are incorrect.

Answer C is incorrect because the power to remove a person may be used even when the disturbance has ended.

General Police Duties, para. 4.15.8.8

16 Licensing and Offences Relating to Alcohol

STUDY PREPARATION

The Licensing Act 2003 brought licensing and licensed premises into line with the Government's effort to place crime and disorder matters at the top of the policing agenda. Licensing matters are dealt with by licensing authorities (made up of local authority members).

Operating schedules place the emphasis firmly on the holders of personal licences to run orderly premises, taking into account such matters as crime and disorder, public safety and protection of children. Knowledge of the different types of licences and the new system of objecting to them is critical. You should also learn the powers to enter premises and, once inside, how to deal with offences and/or drunkenness.

Ages are important, and most of the original offences of under-age drinking under the 1964 Act have remained.

The Confiscation of Alcohol (Young Persons) Act 1997 first introduced the concept of confiscating alcohol from young people in public places. The Criminal Justice and Police Act 2001 introduced a similar power to confiscate alcohol from people in designated public places.

Further powers of enforcement are provided, allowing the courts and the police to make an order requiring licensed premises to be closed.

The Gambling Act 2005 reformed the laws relating to gambling and introduced a licensing system to regulate operating licences, personal licences, premises licences and temporary use of premises notices. The responsibility for granting licences is shared between the Gambling Commission and local licensing authorities.

QUESTIONS

Question 16.1

CALE is the chair of a residents' association on a housing estate. The public house on the estate, the Anchor, has caused considerable concern recently due to the number of public order incidents that have occurred in the vicinity of the premises on weekends. CALE and other residents have raised the issue several times in PACT meetings; however, their perception is that the police and the local authority are reluctant to take action against the licensee.

In which circumstances could CALE and the residents' association apply to the licensing authority for a review of the premises licence, under s. 51 of the Licensing Act 2003?

A The residents' association may apply for a review of the premises licence if there have been incidents of serious crime or serious disorder or both.

B There is no facility for the residents' association to request a review of the premises licence; they would have to rely on the police or the local authority licensing department to act on their behalf.

C The residents' association may apply for a review of the premises licence, or the application may be made by the police or the local authority licensing department if necessary.

D The residents' association may apply for a review of the premises licence, if they are asked to do so following an investigation by the police or the local authority licensing department.

Question 16.2

A request has been made by the local police for an accelerated review of the conditions of the licence of the Horse and Jockey public house, because of the number of serious disorder incidents that have occurred there recently.

Within what period of time must such an application be considered?

A Within 24 hours.

B Within 36 hours.

C Within 48 hours.

D Within seven days.

Question 16.3

In the last four weeks, the police have been called to numerous violent incidents at the Railway public house, which reopened two months ago after refurbishment, with a new personal licence holder and extended opening times. During this period, two people have been stabbed and this weekend another person received serious facial injuries after being hit with a beer glass. The police are considering making a request for an accelerated review of the conditions of the licence because of the serious disorder.

How must an application be pursued under the terms of s. 53A of the Licensing Act 2003?

A A senior police officer or a senior representative of the local authority must present the application to the licensing authority.

B A senior police officer must present the application to the licensing authority.

C A senior police officer must present the application to the magistrates' court.

D A senior representative from any responsible authority must present the application to the licensing authority.

Question 16.4

Section 97 of the Licensing Act 2003 provides a power of entry for a constable to enter and search any premises which hold a club premises certificate.

What restrictions are placed on this power of entry and search?

A Entry is allowed to detect licensing offences or to prevent a breach of the peace only.

B Entry is allowed to prevent a breach of the peace only.

C Entry is allowed to detect licensing offences, to search for offences relating to the supply of drugs, or to prevent a breach of the peace.

D Entry is allowed to search for offences relating to the supply of drugs, or to prevent a breach of the peace only.

Question 16.5

The West End Social Club has been closed for some time because, due to financial hardships experienced by members, the club was not making enough money to survive. A group of local residents is seeking to reopen the premises as a qualifying club, with a view to forming a committee and applying for a club premises certificate. Their intention is to seek a licence to serve alcohol on the weekends only, with the proceeds being invested back into the club. The committee is concerned about the number of members it will attract.

Which of the following statements is correct, in relation to the committee's concerns?

A There must be at least 20 members for the club to qualify as a qualifying club.

B There must be at least 25 members for the club to qualify as a qualifying club.

C There must be at least 50 members for the club to qualify as a qualifying club.

D There must be at least 100 members for the club to qualify as a qualifying club.

Question 16.6

COURTNEY is the holder of a personal licence and is the manager of the Railway public house, a premises situated in a small village. Residents of the village wish to start a commercial venture by renting out their village hall to wedding parties. The hall is situated in a picturesque location, next to the church and a river. The intention is to rent the hall out during the summer months on Saturdays only and the committee has approached COURTNEY to manage a bar for the weddings.

Which of the following statements is correct, in relation to COURTNEY being able to apply for a temporary event notice (TEN), to be able to assist?

A As a personal licence holder, COURTNEY could apply for 50 TENs in a calendar year; however, the premises are limited to 12 TENs in a calendar year.

B As a personal licence holder, COURTNEY could only apply for 12 TENs in a calendar year; there are no limits to the number of TENs that can be applied for in respect of a premises.

C As a personal licence holder, COURTNEY could apply for five TENs in a calendar year; however, the premises are limited to 12 TENs in a calendar year.

D As a personal licence holder, COURTNEY could apply for 50 TENs in a calendar year; however, the premises are limited to 21 TENs in a calendar year.

Question 16.7

Constable KHAN was on duty as part of a plain-clothes team of police officers, working with LEWIS, a licensing officer from the local authority and a person authorised under the Licensing Act 2003. The team was tasked with visiting public houses in the locality to identify licensing offences. They arrived at the Royal Oak public house at 10.50 pm and identified themselves to GEORGE, the door supervisor, and asked to enter the premises. GEORGE refused, stating the premises were about to close. The operating schedule stated that the premises should close at 11 pm.

Does either Constable KHAN or LEWIS have the power to enter the premises using reasonable force under the Licensing Act 2003?

A No, the power to enter by reasonable force is restricted to uniformed officers only.

B Constable KHAN only; LEWIS does not have a power to enter by force in these circumstances.

C Yes, both have the power to enter using reasonable force in these circumstances.

D Yes, but only if they have reason to believe that offences are being committed.

Question 16.8

RICHARDS entered the Horse and Groom public house in an intoxicated condition and was served a pint of beer by HOPKINS. RICHARDS walked away from the bar and began abusing other customers. RICHARDS was ejected from the premises before drinking any of the beer. HOPKINS is a bar worker and is neither the holder of a premises licence nor the designated premises supervisor.

Has HOPKINS committed an offence by selling alcohol to a person who is drunk, under s. 141 of the Licensing Act 2003?

A Yes, HOPKINS would commit the offence in these circumstances.

B No, the offence will only be committed by the holder of a premises licence and the designated premises supervisor.

C No, as RICHARDS did not consume the drink.

D No, the offence will only be committed by the holder of a premises licence.

Question 16.9

HORAN is a committee member of the East Side Social Club, premises which have had problems recently with the licensing authority. The premises are covered by a club premises certificate, however, the licensing authority recently withdrew its author-isation to provide entertainment in the form of live acts due to numerous complaints from residents. HORAN has been under pressure from members to reintroduce the live acts, many of whom have stated they will drink elsewhere if the entertainment is not resumed. HORAN has agreed to do so and has arranged for ZANE to provide entertainment this evening.

If ZANE were to perform at the club tonight, would any offences be committed under s. 136 of the Licensing Act 2003?

A Yes, by HORAN, for allowing a licensable activity to take place.

B Yes, by HORAN, for allowing a licensable activity to take place and by ZANE for actually carrying on a licensable activity.

C No, this offence does not cover activities on premises with a club premises certificate.

D No, this is not a licensable activity, as it does not involve the sale of alcohol.

Question 16.10

HOULIE was in the Glendale public house one evening and was asked to leave by GREEN, the holder of the premises licence. HOULIE was drunk and abusive towards the bar staff. HOULIE left the premises voluntarily. However, once outside, he began banging on the door trying to get back into the pub. GREEN ignored HOULIE and contacted the police and when they arrived, HOULIE was walking away from the premises.

Has HOULIE committed an offence under s. 143 of the Licensing Act 2003 in these circumstances?

A No, because HOULIE has not actually re-entered the premises after being asked to leave.

B No, as no one has requested that he not re-enter the pub.

C Yes, as he was trying to regain entry to the pub in which he was drunk and disorderly.

D Yes, as it is an offence to be or have been drunk and disorderly on licensed premises.

Question 16.11

Constable TERRY was called to the garden of a house in the early hours of the morning. On arrival, Constable TERRY found COYLE drunk and asleep in a flowerbed. COYLE woke up as a result of being prodded by the officer. COYLE stood up, but was clearly unsteady and out of concern for his safety, Constable TERRY took hold of COYLE by the arm and led him out of the garden. Once they reached the street, COYLE became violent and disorderly towards Constable TERRY. The officer then decided to arrest COYLE for being drunk and disorderly.

Would COYLE's behaviour amount to an offence of drunk and disorderly, under s. 91(1) of the Criminal Justice Act 1967?

A No, the original incident took place in a private place, where the offence cannot be committed.

B Yes, COYLE's disorderly behaviour occurred before being arrested by Constable TERRY.

C No, COYLE's disorderly behaviour occurred after being taken hold of by the officer, which amounts to an arrest.

D Yes, it is irrelevant where Constable TERRY took hold of COYLE, this offence may be committed in a private place, as well as a public place.

Question 16.12

JENKINS is a heavy drinker, and is well known for being able to handle his liquor. One night he is out drinking with his friends and as a prank one of them drops amphetamine powder into JENKINS's pint of lager. Two hours later, in the street outside the pub, JENKINS begins to shout and swear at people. JENKINS is drunk, having consumed ten pints of lager. Police officers approach him and he shouts and physically threatens the officers. They arrest JENKINS for being drunk and disorderly. At court, it is argued that his disorderly behaviour was due entirely to the drug, of which he had no knowledge, and that he is not guilty.

In relation to this offence, which of the following statements is correct?
A He may be guilty, as alcohol is a partial cause of his intoxication.
B He is guilty, as it is immaterial what caused the intoxication.
C He is not guilty, as this offence is not made out where there are several causes of the incapacitated state.
D He is not guilty, as the cause of his intoxication was not self-induced.

Question 16.13

APPLEBY is 16 years old and in a public house which is open for the purposes of supplying alcohol for consumption on those premises. She is passing through the main area to go to the toilet as there is no other way to get into there. She is not accompanied by anyone as her parents are outside in the beer garden.

Has an offence been committed contrary to the Licensing Act 2003?
A Yes; as she is 16 and unaccompanied, the licensee commits an offence of allowing her to be in there.
B Yes; as she is 16 and unaccompanied, both APPLEBY and the licensee commit an offence.
C No; because she is 16, neither APPLEBY nor the licensee commits the offence.
D No, because she is only passing through the premises, there being no other way to get to the toilet.

Question 16.14

JABLONOWSKI is working in the Masons Arms public house. She serves TINNEY who is aged 16 and, generally speaking, looks his age. JABLONOWSKI believes TINNEY is 18 years of age, but asks for identification to impress her boss and TINNEY produces a student ID card stating he is 18; the card, however, is a very poor fake and should have been easily perceived as such. JABLONOWSKI, however, serves TINNEY alcohol.

Which of the following is true in relation to selling alcohol to someone under 18?

A JABLONOWSKI has a defence in that she honestly believed that TINNEY was over 18.

B JABLONOWSKI has a defence in that she asked for evidence of his age and it was produced.

C JABLONOWSKI has a defence in that she believed TINNEY was over 18 *and* she asked for evidence of his age.

D JABLONOWSKI has no defence as TINNEY produced fake evidence and it should have been obvious to her it was fake.

Question 16.15

In the Horse and Jockey public house, GILES, aged 18, went to the bar and ordered a pint of beer for himself, and another for his friend HARRISON, whom he knew was aged 17; both were consuming table meals. PARRY, who was serving at the time, provided the beer, but was not aware one of them was for HARRISON whom she knew was aged 17. HARRISON drinks his beer.

In relation to offences under the Licensing Act 2003, who of those listed, if any, have committed offences?

A No offences have been committed, as HARRISON was consuming a table meal and can drink beer in such circumstances.

B Only GILES, of buying alcohol on behalf of an individual aged under 18.

C GILES, of buying alcohol on behalf of an individual aged under 18, and PARRY for serving it.

D All three; GILES for buying, PARRY for selling and HARRISON for consuming the drink, which was not cider or wine.

Question 16.16

During the summer months, DENNIS organised a series of Twenty 20 cricket matches. DENNIS was granted temporary event notices to sell alcohol at each of the matches. After the first week, the police received information that alcohol was being sold to young people. They conducted test purchase operations over the next two weeks and, on two occasions, alcohol was sold to different young people under the age of 18. DENNIS was responsible for both sales.

Would DENNIS be guilty of an offence under s. 147A of the Licensing Act 2003 (persistently selling alcohol to children) in these circumstances?

A No, the alcohol was sold to different individuals.

B Yes, regardless of the fact that alcohol was sold to different individuals.

C No, there is only evidence that alcohol was sold to individuals on two occasions.

D No, this section does not apply to premises authorised to be used for permitted temporary activities.

Question 16.17

GREEN owns an off-licence which is being monitored by the local Neighbourhood Policing Team, because of complaints that alcohol is being sold to young people on a regular basis. During an operation in March, the police caught GREEN selling alcohol to ZENDEN, aged 16. In April, the police again detected GREEN selling alcohol to ZENDEN on one other occasion.

Would GREEN's behaviour amount to an offence under s. 147A of the Licensing Act 2003 (persistently selling alcohol to children under the age of 18)?

A Yes, GREEN has sold alcohol to a person under 18, on two or more occasions, in two consecutive months.

B No, GREEN has not sold alcohol to a person under 18, on three or more occasions, in three consecutive months.

C No, GREEN has not sold alcohol to a person under 18, on two or more occasions in three consecutive months.

D No, GREEN has not sold alcohol to a person under 18, on four or more occasions, in three consecutive months.

Question 16.18

FABIEN, aged 21, was entering an off-licence one evening when a group of young people were standing outside. One of the group asked FABIEN to buy four cans of lager for them. FABIEN suspected that the young people were under age, but agreed to buy the cans. However, the conversation was overheard by the owner of the off-licence, who refused to sell the lager to FABIEN.

Does FABIEN commit an offence under s. 149 of the Licensing Act 2003, in these circumstances?

A No, because the shop owner refused to sell the alcohol to FABIEN.

B No, the alcohol was not intended for consumption on relevant premises.

C No, both because the shop owner refused to sell the alcohol to FABIEN *and* it was not intended for consumption on relevant premises.

D Yes, regardless of whether the shop owner refused to sell the alcohol to FABIEN, or where it was to be consumed.

Question 16.19

GARDINER is 17 years old and works for ASDA as a temporary worker. His supervisor is YANCEY. Whilst on the tills GARDINER checks through a four-pack of Fosters Ice bottles. YANCEY is at the till next to GARDINER but does not notice that the sale of alcohol has happened and she did not tell GARDINER he was not allowed to sell alcohol.

In relation to the sale of alcohol by GARDINER, which of the following statements is correct?

A YANCEY has committed an offence as she failed to supervise the sale of alcohol properly.

B YANCEY has committed an offence as she failed to train GARDINER in the sale of alcohol.

C GARDINER has committed an offence of selling alcohol whilst under 18 years of age.

D Neither has committed an offence in these circumstances.

Question 16.20

Constable PERRY was walking through the Anchor public house one evening. The officer saw FLETCHER sitting at a table with a group of people, drinking a pint of beer. On two occasions in the past six months, Constable PERRY had confiscated alcohol from FLETCHER in a public place, and was aware that the person was under 18 years of age.

Has FLETCHER committed an offence under s. 30(1) of the Policing and Crime Act 2009 (persistently possessing alcohol in a relevant place) in these circumstances?

A No, a public house is not a relevant place for the purposes of this section.

B Yes, FLETCHER has been in possession of alcohol in a relevant place on two or more occasions in six consecutive months.

C Yes, FLETCHER has been in possession of alcohol in a relevant place on three or more occasions in 12 consecutive months.

D Yes, FLETCHER has been in possession of alcohol in a relevant place on three or more occasions in six consecutive months.

Question 16.21

Whilst on patrol in a housing estate, Constable CAMPBELL came across HICKS, who was in possession of four unopened cans of lager. HICKS admitted being aged 13, but stated she was taking the drink home to her father. HICKS did not appear to be drunk at the time; however, the officer took the decision to confiscate the lager.

Did Constable CAMPBELL have an additional power to remove HICKS to a place of safety, or take her home?

A No, because HICKS was not drunk at the time.

B Yes, provided Constable CAMPBELL reasonably suspected HICKS was going to drink from the cans.

C Yes, because HICKS was under 14 years of age.

D Yes, because HICKS was under 16 years of age.

Question 16.22

Constable SINGH was walking through a park when he came across two young people, who were intoxicated. He discovered they were 15 years old and that they had been given drink by HAWKINS. Constable SINGH intercepted HAWKINS, who was walking away from the park, and saw that he was in possession of a can of lager from which he was drinking. HAWKINS is over 18 years old.

What are Constable SINGH's powers to deal with HAWKINS in these circumstances?

A He has the power to confiscate the alcohol from HAWKINS and demand his name and address.

B He has no powers, as HAWKINS did not intend to supply the alcohol to a person under 18.

C He has no powers, as HAWKINS is not under 18.
D He has no powers, as HAWKINS is not in the company of a person under 18 to whom he intends to supply the alcohol.

Question 16.23

The police have conducted a series of test purchase operations over a period of a month at the Railway public house, due to suspected under-age drinking. The officers conducting the exercise have reported that GREEN, the premises licence holder, served alcohol to five under-age drinkers during this period. The duty inspector considers that an offence has been committed under s. 147A of the Licensing Act 2003, and a closure notice should be served on GREEN, to prevent further sales to young people.

Which of the following statements is correct, in relation to such a notice, under s. 169A of the Act?

A The inspector may authorise a closure notice, provided GREEN accepts responsibility for the offence under s. 147A.
B The inspector may authorise a closure notice in these circumstances alone.
C A superintendent may authorise a closure, provided GREEN accepts responsibility for the offence under s. 147A.
D A superintendent may authorise a closure, provided there is a realistic prospect of prosecuting GREEN for an offence under s. 147A.

Question 16.24

The Swan public house is situated on a housing estate and there have been complaints by residents that on weekends customers are allowed to drink in the car park at the premises long after the pub closes and that their rowdy behaviour causes a disturbance until the early hours of the morning. The licensee, PROSSER has been visited by licensing officers and has been instructed to put an action plan in place to address the issue. However, residents say that the problem is still ongoing and a licensing review is due to take place. One suggestion being put forward is to 'designate' the car park and the surrounding area under s. 13 of the Criminal Justice and Police Act 2001, to give police officers more power to require people not to consume alcohol late at night.

Which of the following statements is correct, in relation to the suggestion to designate the car park under this Act?

A This power only applies to public places, and premises in respect of which a premises licence is in place may not be designated.

B This power only applies to public places; however, the car park of premises in respect of which a premises licence is in place may be designated, but not the premises itself.

C This power only applies to public places, and premises in respect of which a licence under the Act is in place may not be designated, unless a temporary event notice is in force.

D This power only applies to public places; however, this only applies when alcohol is actually being lawfully sold or supplied and for another 30 minutes thereafter.

Question 16.25

Constable PARIS was on patrol in a public park, which the local authority has designated as an area where alcohol may not be consumed. Constable PARIS saw BELL sitting on a park bench with four unopened cans of lager. BELL was intoxicated, but did not consume alcohol from the cans in the officer's presence.

What power was available to Constable PARIS to deal with BELL under the Criminal Justice and Police Act 2001 (alcohol consumption in designated places)?

A Constable PARIS had a power to direct BELL not to drink from the cans.

B None, Constable PARIS did not see BELL drinking from the cans.

C None, as the cans were unopened.

D Constable PARIS had a power to confiscate the cans, but not to dispose of them.

Question 16.26

Over several weekends, young people have been congregating in a local park, where they have been drinking. Residents have experienced anti-social behaviour by the group, and minor damage and graffiti has been caused to a play area in the park. Whilst on patrol in the park, Constable THAME, the local neighbourhood police officer has come across a group of ten young people, all of whom are drunk.

What powers, if any, does Constable THAME have to direct the individuals to leave the locality to prevent crime and disorder, under s. 27 of the Violent Crime Reduction Act 2006?

A None, the young people have not been responsible for serious crime or disorder.

B Constable THAME may give written notice, directing the individuals to leave the locality.

C Constable THAME may give oral directions for individuals to leave the locality, which must be confirmed in writing as soon as possible by an inspector.

D Constable THAME may give oral directions for individuals to leave the locality, which must be confirmed in writing as soon as possible by any constable.

Question 16.27

A direction has been given to a large group of individuals to leave a locality, because local residents have been experiencing serious alcohol-related disorder.

To which members of the group would such a direction apply, according to s. 27(1) of the Violent Crime Reduction Act 2006?

A To any individual over the age of 10.

B To any individual over the age of 16.

C To any individual under the age of 16.

D To any individual under the age of 18.

Question 16.28

A licensing authority is considering imposing a Late Night Levy on all licensed premises in a city centre in its area, to raise revenue in relation to the costs of policing and the reduction and prevention of crime and disorder during the night.

Which of the following statements is correct, in relation to the time parameters for such a levy, under s. 125 of the Police Reform and Social Responsibility Act 2011?

A It may be applied for any period of time between midnight and 6 am, but the time parameters must be the same every day.

B It may be applied for any period of time between midnight and 6 am and the time parameters may vary, depending on the specific requirements of the area.

C It may be applied for any period of time between 2 am and 6 am, but the time parameters must be the same every day.

D It may be applied for any period of time between 10 pm and 6 am and the time parameters may vary, depending on the specific requirements of the area.

Question 16.29

COURTNEY lives in a local justice area which is trialling drinking banning orders, under the Violent Crime Reduction Act 2006. COURTNEY has been made subject to such an order.

Which of the following statements is correct, in relation to the conditions that can be imposed on COURTNEY under a drinking banning order?

A COURTNEY may be excluded from specified licensed premises in a defined area.

B COURTNEY may only be excluded from the licensed premises connected with an offence.

C COURTNEY must be excluded from all licensed premises in a defined area.

D COURTNEY must be excluded from consuming alcohol in specified licensed premises in a defined area.

Question 16.30

The Albion public house is situated in the middle of a residential estate. The premises have live bands playing on weekend evenings. One Saturday afternoon, Constable TELFORD was called to speak to several residents in the area, who were complaining about the noise that had come from the live band the night before. They all stated that there was another live band booked for that evening, and that the excessive noise was causing a serious disturbance in the area. As a result of speaking to the neighbours, Constable TELFORD contacted her inspector, who attended the scene. The inspector was considering whether or not to type out a closure order to serve on the licensee.

In the circumstances, would the inspector be able to implement a closure order under s. 161(1)(b) of the Licensing Act 2003?

A No, because the disturbance was not ongoing at the time.

B Yes, provided the noise was actually coming from the premises themselves.

C No, closure orders are designed for disorder at licensed premises, not noise complaints.

D Yes, provided the noise was coming either from the premises, or from the vicinity of the premises.

Question 16.31

Inspector CARROLL was working a late shift when she received information that several disturbances had taken place in the Admiral public house during the evening. Inspector CARROLL was aware that the police had dealt with a number of public order situations at the Admiral in the previous week and that the owner, HALL, had a reputation of being unable to control his customers. The inspector typed out a closure order for the premises, which she intended serving on HALL; however, she was called away to deal with a firearms incident in another area before she could serve the notice.

Could Inspector CARROLL delegate the serving of the notice to another officer?
A No, the order must be served by the inspector making it.
B Yes, the order may be served by any other inspector.
C Yes, the order may be served by any other officer.
D Yes, the order may be served by the senior officer on duty in the area.

Question 16.32

Inspector CLINTON was working late shifts on a Sunday. During the weekend, he had dealings with PARKS, the licensee of the Ship public house. The police were called to the premises several times on Friday evening because of fighting and persons were arrested. Intelligence suggested on the Saturday evening that further trouble was likely, and Inspector CLINTON served a closure order on PARKS at 8 pm. There was no court on the Sunday and Inspector CLINTON visited the Ship again at 5 pm that evening. PARKS said that he was going to open the pub again that night, because it was costing him too much money to stay closed.

What powers would be available to Inspector CLINTON, if he reasonably believed there was likely to be further disorder at the premises on the Sunday evening?
A None, the closure order has expired; he must wait until Monday to report the matter to the court.
B He may extend the closure order by serving a notice on PARKS when the existing one expires at 8 pm.
C He may extend the closure order, provided he serves a notice on PARKS before 8 pm.
D He must serve a new closure order on PARKS, and attend court on Monday to report the matter.

Question 16.33

Constable WARREN works as a Licensing Officer based in a co-located office with the local authority Licensing Department. Constable WARREN has attended premises in High Street with CANTEBURRY, a local authority Licensing Officer. They have received intelligence that NEWMAN is using the premises for the unlicensed sale of alcohol. Their intention is to gather evidence and, if necessary, close the premises down.

Section 19 of the Criminal Justice and Police Act 2001 allows for a closure notice to be served in respect of unlicensed premises. In respect of this power, which of the following statements is correct?

A A closure notice may be served by Constable WARREN only, provided this is done in consultation with the local authority (which would include consulting with CANTEBURRY).

B Either Constable WARREN or CANTEBURRY could serve a closure notice in these circumstances.

C A closure notice may only be served by an inspector; neither Constable WARREN nor CANTEBURRY has the authority to do so in these circumstances.

D A closure notice may only be authorised by a magistrate; either Constable WARREN or CANTEBURRY would have to apply to the court for such a notice.

ANSWERS

Answer 16.1

Answer **C** — Section 51 of the Licensing Act 2003 allows for an application for a review of a premises licence by a responsible authority *or any other person*. Answer B is therefore incorrect.

It is not necessary to wait for an investigation to take place by the police or the local authority licensing department—the whole point of the 2003 Act is that processes must be transparent and communities are encouraged to contribute to matters that affect them and their families and neighbours. Similarly, there is no need for a member of the public to wait for an incident of serious crime or serious disorder to occur before challenging the activities of a licensed premises. The *licensee* is required to demonstrate through the licensing objectives how he or she is going to contribute to the prevention of crime and disorder—the onus is on him or her to resolve this issue, not the community. Answers A and D are therefore incorrect.

General Police Duties, para. 4.16.4.2

Answer 16.2

Answer **C** — Section 53A of the Licensing Act 2003 provides for an accelerated review of licensed premises by a licensing authority, and the attaching of temporary conditions to a premises licence pending a full review of the licence.

The procedure provides for a senior police officer (of or above the rank of superintendent) to certify to a licensing authority, that he or she considers licensed premises to be associated with serious crime and/or serious disorder.

On receiving the application the licensing authority will be obliged to consider *within 48 hours* whether it is necessary to take interim steps pending a full review of the licence, which must take place within 28 days. Answers A, B and D are therefore incorrect.

General Police Duties, para. 4.16.4.2

Answer 16.3

Answer **B** — There is a general provision under s. 51 of the Licensing Act 2003 for an interested party or responsible authority to apply to a relevant licensing authority for a review of the premises licence. For example, a local resident may consider that the measures taken by the licensee to prevent public nuisance are insufficient and request that they be reviewed. Similarly, the police may consider that the measures put in place to prevent crime and disorder are not being effective and need to be reviewed.

However, s. 53A of the Act provides for an accelerated review of licensed premises by *a licensing authority*, and the attaching of temporary conditions to a premises licence pending a full review of the licence. Answer C is therefore incorrect.

The procedure involves a senior police officer—of or above the rank of super-intendent—certifying to a licensing authority that he/she considers licensed prem-ises to be associated with serious crime and/or serious disorder. Answers A and D are therefore incorrect.

General Police Duties, para. 4.16.4.2

Answer 16.4

Answer **D** — Under s. 97 of the Licensing Act 2003, where a club premises certificate has effect in respect of any premises, a constable may enter and search the premises if he/she has reasonable cause to believe:

(a) that an offence under section 4(3)(a), (b) or (c) of the Misuse of Drugs Act 1971 (sup-plying or offering to supply, or being concerned in supplying or making an offer to supply, a controlled drug) has been, is being, or is about to be, committed there, or
(b) that there is likely to be a breach of the peace there.

This section does not allow a constable to enter the premises to detect licensing of-fences; therefore, answers A and C are incorrect. Entry is allowed (using reasonable force if necessary) in order to detect offences under the Misuse of Drugs Act 1971, or if a breach of the peace is likely to occur in the premises. Answers A and B are in-correct for this reason.

General Police Duties, para. 4.16.4.4

Answer 16.5

Answer **B** — Under s. 60 of the Licensing Act 2003, a club premises certificate may be granted by a licensing authority certifying that the premises may be used by the club for one or more qualifying club activities specified in the certificate, and that the club is a qualifying club in relation to each of those activities (s. 60). One of the general conditions that applies for a club to qualify as a qualifying club under s. 62 is that *the club has at least 25 members.*

Answers A, C and D are therefore incorrect.

General Police Duties, para. 4.16.4.4

Answer 16.6

Answer **A** — A Temporary Event Notice (TEN), issued by the licensing authority, is required where a person (the premises user) intends to carry out a licensable activity on unlicensed premises or wishes to operate outside the terms of their existing premises licence or club premises licence (s. 100 of the 2003 Act).

A 'licensable activity' is the sale or supply of alcohol, regulated entertainment (e.g. music, singing or dancing), or provisions of late night refreshment (hot food or drink between the hours of 2300 and 0500). Such activities might include a publican engaged to run a temporary bar for a wedding at a venue not licensed for the sale of alcohol, or a person not being the holder of a personal licence who may wish to run a bar and provide a band at a party to celebrate a significant anniversary.

A personal licence holder is permitted *50* TENs per calendar year and an individual who is not the holder of a personal licence is permitted five TENs a year. Answers B and C are incorrect for this reason.

However, while a personal licence holder is permitted 50 TENs, all *premises* are limited to *12* TENs in a calendar year. Answers B and C are incorrect for this reason. (Note that a TEN can last up to 168 hours but in total the 12 TENs cannot exceed 21 days in a calendar year, i.e. the TEN may last for more than a 24-hour period, for example an event lasting over the weekend).

General Police Duties, para. 4.16.4.5

Answer 16.7

Answer **C** — Under s. 179 of the Licensing Act 2003, where a constable or an authorised person has reason to believe that any premises are being, or are about to be, used for a licensable activity, they may enter the premises with a view to seeing whether the activity is being, or is to be, carried on under and in accordance with an authorisation (s. 179(1)). A person exercising the power conferred by this section may, if necessary, use reasonable force (s. 179(3)). Since the power under this section is not restricted to police officers, answer B is incorrect. Also, there is no requirement for a police officer to be in uniform, therefore answer A is incorrect.

There is a separate power, under s. 180 of the Act, for a constable to enter premises in order to investigate offences. A constable may enter by reasonable force under this section. However, s. 179 shows that a constable or authorised person may enter premises using reasonable force simply to make sure that licensing activities are being carried out within the law. Answer D is therefore incorrect.

(Note that an authorised person exercising the powers conferred on them must, if so requested, produce evidence of their authority to exercise the power.)

General Police Duties, para. 4.16.5

Answer 16.8

Answer **B** — The Licensing Act 2003, s. 141 states:

(1) A person to whom subsection (2) applies commits an offence if, on relevant premises, he knowingly—
 (a) sells or attempts to sell alcohol to a person who is drunk, or
 (b) allows alcohol to be sold to such a person.

This subsection applies:

(2) (a) to any person who works at the premises in a capacity, whether paid or unpaid, which gives him authority to sell the alcohol concerned,
  (b) in the case of licensed premises, to—
   (i) the holder of a premises licence in respect of the premises, and
   (ii) the designated premises supervisor (if any) under such a licence.

Under s. 141(2)(a), the offence may be committed by any person who works on the premises, whatever their capacity. However, on licensed premises (which is the case in this question) the offence is covered by s. 141(2)(b), which restricts liability to the holder of a premises licence and/or the designated premises supervisor. Answers A and D are therefore incorrect. It is irrelevant that RICHARDS did not consume the drink—the offence is complete when the alcohol is sold to a person who is intoxicated. Answer C is therefore incorrect.

General Police Duties, para. 4.16.7.5

Answer 16.9

Answer **A** — Section 136(1) of the Licensing Act 2003 states that a person commits an offence if—

(a) he carries on or attempts to carry on a licensable activity on or from any premises otherwise than under and in accordance with an authorisation, or

(b) he knowingly allows a licensable activity to be so carried on.

This offence requires that the person carried on (or attempted to carry on) the licensable activity *either* in a manner not authorised by or in accordance with an appropriate authorisation, or *knowingly* allowed the activity to be carried on in that way. Therefore, the offence could be committed by both persons.

However, where the licensable activity in question is the provision of regulated entertainment, a person will generally *not* commit an offence under this section if his/her only involvement in the provision of the entertainment is that he/she played the music, performed the dance, etc. (see s. 136(2)). Answer B is therefore incorrect.

'Licensing activity' includes any activity mentioned on the licence which is covered by the licence; it could include serving alcohol, but could equally include providing live entertainment. Answer D is therefore incorrect.

'Authorisation' here means activities at premises with a premises licence, a club premises certificate or a temporary event notice in respect of which the relevant conditions have been met. While some offences apply only to 'relevant premises', s. 136(1) is wider than that and applies to any premises. Answer C is therefore incorrect.

General Police Duties, para. 4.16.7.1

Answer 16.10

Answer **B** — Under s. 143(1)(a) of the Licensing Act 2003, a person who is drunk or disorderly commits an offence if, without reasonable excuse, he or she fails to leave relevant premises when requested to do so by a constable or by a person to whom subs. (2) applies (the holder of a premises licence in respect of the premises, and/or the designated premises supervisor). Since HOULIE left when requested by GREEN, no offence was committed under this subsection; answer D is therefore incorrect.

Under s. 143(1)(b) of the Act, a further offence is committed if a person enters or attempts (answer A is therefore incorrect) to enter relevant premises after a constable or a person to whom subs. (2) applies has requested him or her not to enter. GREEN was not so requested and therefore would also not commit this offence; answer C is therefore incorrect.

General Police Duties, para. 4.16.7.7

Answer 16.11

Answer **B** — Under s. 91(1) of the Criminal Justice Act 1967, a person commits an offence if, in a public place, he or she is guilty, while drunk, of disorderly conduct. Since the offence may only be committed in a public place, answer D is incorrect.

The offence will not be committed when a person does not commit a disorderly act until after their arrest (*H* v *DPP* (2006) 170 JP 4). However, in *McMillan* v *Crown Prosecution Service* [2008] EWHC 1457 (Admin), it was held that where a police officer took hold of a drunken person by the arm to steady them for their own safety it was not an arrest. The circumstances in this case entailed the officer leading the drunken person from a private garden to a public place. It was then legitimate for the officer to arrest for this offence where the accused then displayed disorderly behaviour. The circumstances in *McMillan* mirror those in this question—it is irrelevant where the original incident commenced, the disorderly behaviour occurred in a public place, *before* the officer decided to make an arrest. Answers A and C are therefore incorrect.

General Police Duties, para. 4.16.7.8

Answer 16.12

Answer **A** — For this offence the drunkenness must be caused by excessive amounts of alcohol; where this is not the case and his state is caused by some other intoxicant, e.g. a drug, the offence is not made out (*Neale* v *RMJE (a minor)* (1985) 80 Cr App R 20) and therefore answer B is incorrect. In *Neale*, Goff LJ held that 'drunkenness' means taking intoxicating liquor to an extent that affects steady self-control. However, where there are several causes of a person's intoxicated state, one of which is alcohol, a court can find the person was in fact drunk even though some other intoxicant had an effect on this 'steady self-control' and therefore answer C is incorrect. Answer D is a defence from the Public Order Act 1986 and has no impact on this offence and is incorrect.

General Police Duties, para. 4.16.7.8

Answer 16.13

Answer **C** — Section 145 of the Licensing Act 2003 states that it is an offence for a person holding roles in public houses that would allow them to take appropriate action to prevent the presence of children in the way prohibited to allow unaccompanied children on those premises. This applies to licensees, staff working in the pub, etc.; the children themselves commit no offence by just being in there. Answer B is therefore incorrect.

No offence is committed if the unaccompanied child is on the premises solely for the purpose of passing to or from some other place to or from which there is no other convenient means of access or egress (s. 145(5)).

However, by virtue of s. 145(2)(a), 'child' means an individual aged under 16, and APPLEBY is 16. No offence is committed as she is not an 'unaccompanied child' as defined by the Act and not because she is passing through: that exception to the legislation applies only to unaccompanied children. Answers A and D are therefore incorrect.

General Police Duties, para. 4.16.8.1

Answer 16.14

Answer **D** — It is an absolute offence to sell alcohol to someone who is under 18, but there are some defences available.

To begin with, the person selling the alcohol must believe the person is aged 18 or over; lack of this belief loses the defence immediately. However, this belief must then be supported by either of the following circumstances:

- nobody could reasonably have suspected from the individual's appearance that he or she was aged under 18; *or*
- all reasonable steps to establish the individual's age had been taken.

JABLONOWSKI's belief is not enough on its own; answer A is therefore incorrect.

In the scenario TINNEY did not look over 18, so JABLONOWSKI would have to follow the reasonable steps route to establish identity.

The Licensing Act 2003 further defines what 'reasonable steps' are in relation to establishing identification. They are:

- the individual was asked for evidence of his or her age; *and*
- the evidence produced would have convinced a reasonable person.

Producing identification does not negate the offence if such identification is obviously fake (as it was in the scenario). Answers B and C are therefore incorrect.

In summary then, for the defence to succeed, the person selling must believe the individual buying to be 18 or over. If it is not obvious to everyone else that this individual, by appearance, is over 18 then proof of age is required; such proof has to be convincing.

General Police Duties, para. 4.16.8.4

Answer 16.15

Answer **A** — The offences referred to in this question relate to various sections of the Licensing Act 2003:

- s. 146, the sale of alcohol to children;
- s. 149, purchase of alcohol by or on behalf of children;
- s. 150, consumption of alcohol by children.

They all relate to selling and consumption of alcohol by a person aged under 18, and if the person is indeed under 18 then the offences are complete. However, offences under ss. 149 and 150 do not apply where a person is 16 or 17, provided they are accompanied at a table meal by someone aged 18 or over. In these circumstances they can have bought for them and consume beer, wine and cider (although hopefully not all in the same glass!).

In the scenario the buying and consumption of the beer was lawful and in consequence the selling was also lawful and no one commits an offence. Answers B, C and D are therefore incorrect.

General Police Duties, paras 4.16.8.3, 4.16.8.9, 4.16.8.10

Answer 16.16

Answer **B** — Under s. 147A(1) of the Licensing Act 2003, a person is guilty of an offence if:

(a) on 2 or more different occasions within a period of 3 consecutive months alcohol is unlawfully sold on the same premises to an individual aged under 18;
(b) at the time of each sale the premises were either licensed premises or premises authorised to be used for a permitted temporary activity; and
(c) that person was a responsible person in relation to the premises at each such time.

Under s. 147A(5), the individual aged under 18, to whom the sale is made, can be the same person or different people and therefore answer A is incorrect.

The Policing and Crime Act 2009, s. 28, amended s. 147A(1)(a) so that the offence is committed if alcohol is sold on 'two or more different occasions', whereas it was previously 'three or more different occasions'. Answer C is therefore incorrect.

No, this section *does* apply to premises authorised to be used for permitted temporary activities and for that reason answer D is incorrect.

General Police Duties, para. 4.16.8.6

Answer 16.17

Answer **A** — Under s. 147A(1) of the Licensing Act 2003, a person is guilty of an offence if:

(a) on 2 or more different occasions within a period of 3 consecutive months alcohol is unlawfully sold on the same premises to an individual aged under 18.

The Policing and Crime Act 2009, s. 28, amended s. 147A(1)(a) so that the offence is committed if alcohol is sold on 'two or more different occasions', whereas it was previously 'three or more different occasions'.

Answers B, C and D are therefore incorrect.

General Police Duties, para. 4.16.8.6

Answer 16.18

Answer **D** — Under s. 149(3)(a) of the Licensing Act 2003, a person commits an offence if he or she buys or attempts to buy alcohol on behalf of an individual aged under 18. The offence is complete when the person attempts to purchase the alcohol; therefore, answers A and C are incorrect.

There is a separate offence under s. 149(4) of the Act, of a person buying or attempting to buy alcohol for consumption by a person under 18, for consumption on relevant premises—however, since the offence may be committed in either of the circumstances described, answers B and C are incorrect.

General Police Duties, para. 4.16.8.9

Answer 16.19

Answer **D** — Clearly, selling alcohol in premises like ASDA has to be controlled and there is an offence under s. 153(4) of the Licensing Act 2003 of unsupervised sales by children (those under 18). The offence is committed by 'a responsible person' allowing an individual aged under 18 to make on the premises any sale of alcohol; a responsible person being defined as:

- the holder of a premises licence in respect of the premises;
- the designated premises supervisor (if any) under such a licence; or
- any individual aged 18 or over who is authorised for the purposes of this section by such a holder or supervisor.

(Section 153(4) of the Licensing Act 2003.)

Only the responsible person commits this offence not the person under 18; answer C is therefore incorrect. The offence, however, is perpetrated 'knowingly', and as such there has to be conscious awareness of what was happening. Answer A is incorrect because YANCEY has no such knowledge.

It is not committed by omission or error in training; answer B is therefore incorrect.

General Police Duties, para. 4.16.8.13

Answer 16.20

Answer **A** — Under s. 30(1) of the Policing and Crime Act 2009, a person under the age of 18 is guilty of an offence if, without reasonable excuse, the person is in possession of alcohol in any relevant place on three or more occasions within a period of 12 consecutive months.

Section 30(2) defines a 'relevant place' as:

(a) any public place, other than excluded premises, or
(b) any place, other than a public place, to which the person has unlawfully gained access.

In relation to subs. (2)(a), 'excluded premises' means premises with a premises licence or permitted temporary activity used for the supply of alcohol, and premises with a club premises certificate used for the supply of alcohol to members or guests.

Therefore, while FLETCHER has previously been in possession of alcohol in a relevant place on two occasions in 12 consecutive months, a public house is an 'excluded premises' and the provisions of this section do not apply there. Answers B, C and D are incorrect for this reason.

Answers B and D would also have been incorrect, had FLETCHER been in possession of alcohol in a relevant place, as the time period which triggers this offence is three or more occasions in 12 consecutive months.

General Police Duties, para. 4.16.8.14

Answer 16.21

Answer **D** — Under s. 1(1)(a) of the Confiscation of Alcohol (Young Persons) Act 1997, a constable who reasonably suspects that a person who is in a relevant place is in possession of alcohol, may confiscate the alcohol if the person is under 18.

Under subs. (1AB), a constable who imposes a requirement on a person under subs. (1) may, if the constable reasonably suspects that the person is under the age of

16, remove the person to the person's place of residence or a place of safety. Answer C is therefore incorrect.

Subsection (1AB) does not specifically define a 'place of safety', although this may be with a relative or friend, or where necessary, a police station or social services accommodation. There is no requirement for the officer to reasonably suspect that the person was going to drink from the cans if they are unopened, or that they were drunk at the time. Answers A and B are therefore incorrect.

General Police Duties, para. 4.16.8.15

Answer 16.22

Answer **A** — Under s. 1(1) of the Confiscation of Alcohol (Young Persons) Act 1997, a constable who reasonably suspects that a person who is in a relevant place (public place etc.) is in possession of alcohol, may confiscate the alcohol if:

(a) the person is under 18; *or*

(b) the person intends that any of the alcohol shall be consumed by a person under 18 in a relevant place; *or*

(c) the person is with *or* has recently been with a person under 18 and that person has recently consumed alcohol in the relevant place.

Under para. (c), as HAWKINS has recently been with a person under 18 who has consumed alcohol, regardless of whether he intends to supply more alcohol to the children, the officer will have the power to confiscate the alcohol he is in possession of. Answers B and D are therefore incorrect.

Also, alcohol may be confiscated from a person who is over 18 if he or she has committed an act mentioned under paras (b) and (c)—the power is designed to prevent alcohol either being consumed by, or supplied to, people under 18. Answer C is therefore incorrect.

Note that under subs. (1AA) of the Act (inserted by s. 29 of the Policing and Crime Act 2009), a constable exercising the power under s. 1 *shall* require the person to state their name and address. The previous subsection (now omitted) stated that a constable *may* require the person to give their name and address.

General Police Duties, para. 4.16.8.15

Answer 16.23

Answer **D** — Section 169A of the Licensing Act 2003 provides that a senior police officer (of the rank of superintendent or higher), or an inspector of weights and measures, may give a closure notice where there is evidence that a person has committed the offence of persistently selling alcohol to children at the premises in question. Answers A and B are therefore incorrect.

A further condition exists under s. 169A—the superintendent must consider that the evidence is such that there would be a realistic prospect of conviction if the offender was prosecuted for it. Answer C is therefore incorrect.

General Police Duties, para. 4.16.8.17

Answer 16.24

Answer **D** — A designation under s. 13 of the Criminal Justice and Police Act 2001 is restricted to 'any place to which the public (or a section of the public) has access, on payment or otherwise, as of right or by virtue of any express or implied permission' (s. 16(1)).

Generally, premises in respect of which a premises licence, club premises licence or temporary event notice is in force cannot be designated public places for the purposes of this section. However, this only applies when alcohol is actually being sold or supplied in accordance with the licence or notice and for another 30 minutes thereafter (s. 14). Answer A is therefore incorrect.

This exception applies to both the car park and the premises itself, and applies to all premises in respect of which a licence under the Act is in force. Answers B and C are therefore incorrect.

General Police Duties, para. 4.16.9.1

Answer 16.25

Answer **A** — Under s. 13 of the Criminal Justice and Police Act 2001, local authorities may identify and designate public places within their areas as 'alcohol free zones', provided they are satisfied that nuisance, annoyance or disorder has occurred as a result of consumption of intoxicating liquor in those areas. Section 12 of the Act provides a constable with powers to deal with people who contravene orders, if he or she reasonably believes that a person is or has been consuming, or intends to consume alcohol in that place. Answer B is therefore incorrect.

A constable is provided with three distinct powers:

- to require the person not to consume alcohol;
- to require the person to surrender the alcohol;
- to dispose of anything surrendered in a manner he or she considers appropriate.

Answer D is incorrect, because the officer may exercise any of these powers and dispose of anything surrendered in such a manner as he or she considers appropriate. The fact that the cans were unopened is not relevant and they may be confiscated utilising the powers described previously. Answer C is therefore incorrect.

General Police Duties, para. 4.16.9.2

Answer 16.26

Answer **B** — Section 27(1) of the Violent Crime Reduction Act 2006 states that where an individual aged 10 or over is in a public place, a constable in uniform may give a direction to that individual requiring him or her to leave the locality of that place and prohibiting the individual from returning to that locality for such period (not exceeding 48 hours) from the giving of the direction as the constable may specify.

Under s. 27(2), such a direction may only be given if:

(a) the presence of the individual in that locality is likely, in all the circumstances, to cause or to contribute to the occurrence of alcohol-related crime or disorder in that locality, or to cause or to contribute to a repetition or continuance there of such crime or disorder; and

(b) the giving of a direction under this section to that individual is necessary for the purpose of removing or reducing the likelihood of there being such crime or disorder in that locality during the period for which the direction has effect or of there being a repetition or continuance in that locality during that period of such crime or disorder.

Since there is no mention of *serious* crime or disorder, answer A is incorrect.

A direction under this section must be given in writing (see s. 27(3)). Answers C and D are therefore incorrect.

Note that the Policing and Crime Act 2009, s. 31, amended subs. (1) from 'an individual aged 16 or over' to 'an individual aged 10 or over'.

General Police Duties, para. 4.16.9.3

Answer 16.27

Answer **A** — Section 27(1) of the Violent Crime Reduction Act 2006 states that where *an individual aged 10 or over* is in a public place, a constable in uniform may give a direction to that individual requiring him/her to leave the locality of that place and prohibiting the individual from returning to that locality for such period (not exceeding 48 hours) from the giving of the direction as the constable may specify.

The Policing and Crime Act 2009, s. 31, amended subs. (1) from 'an individual aged 16 or over' to 'an individual aged 10 or over'.

Answers B, C and D are therefore incorrect.

General Police Duties, para. 4.16.9.3

Answer 16.28

Answer **A** — Section 125 of the Police Reform and Social Responsibility Act 2011 introduced provisions for a Late Night Levy on licensed premises. The levy may be applied by a licensing authority in its area if it considers it desirable to raise revenue in relation to the costs of policing and other arrangements for the reduction or prevention of crime and disorder, in connection with the supply of alcohol between midnight and 6 am. Answers B and C are therefore incorrect.

The period can be for any length of time within these parameters *but must be the same every day*. Answers C and D are incorrect for this reason.

The levy is payable by the holders of premises licences or club premises certificates which authorise the supply of alcohol during those hours. The licensing authority is expected to consider the need for a levy with the chief officer of police and Police and Crime Commissioner.

General Police Duties, para. 4.16.9.4

Answer 16.29

Answer **A** — Section 1 of the Violent Crime Reduction Act 2006 provides for a civil order, a drinking banning order, which is designed to protect persons and their property from criminal or disorderly conduct by an individual while he/she is under the influence of alcohol.

Orders may be made on the application (by way of complaint) of the police or local authority to a magistrates' court that an individual, aged 16 or over, has engaged in criminal or disorderly conduct while under the influence of alcohol, and that such an order is necessary to protect other persons from further conduct by him/her of that kind while he/she is under the influence of alcohol (s. 3(2)). Such orders must be for not less than two months and not more than two years in duration.

Under s. 1(2), such an order may impose any prohibition on the subject which is necessary for the purpose of protecting other persons from criminal or disorderly conduct by the subject while he/she is under the influence of alcohol.

Under s. 1(3)(a), the order *must* include such prohibition as the court making it considers necessary, on the subject's entering premises in respect of which there is a premises licence authorising the use of the premises for the sale of alcohol by retail; however, the section is not prescriptive as to what those conditions are (answers C and D are therefore incorrect).

On the other hand, the wording of s. 1 means that the court can be flexible in other respects regarding the conditions it sets, such as being able to exclude the person from specified licensed premises in a defined geographic area, depending on what it considers necessary. The power is not restricted to excluding the person from the licensed premises connected with a particular offence committed by an individual and therefore answer B is incorrect.

General Police Duties, para. 4.16.9.5

Answer 16.30

Answer **A** — There are two general powers to serve closure orders under s. 161 of the Licensing Act 2003. First, when a senior police officer (an officer of at least the rank of inspector) has reason to believe that there is disorder on, or in the vicinity of and related to the premises, or there is likely to be disorder on, or in the vicinity of and related to the premises, and in either case he or she reasonably believes that the order is necessary in the interests of public safety (s. 161(1)(a)).

Secondly, a closure notice may be served when it is reasonably believed that a disturbance is being caused to the public by excessive noise emitted from the premises and a closure order is necessary to prevent the disturbance. Since a closure order may be served in relation to noise only (s. 161(1)(b)), answer C is incorrect.

However, this power is restricted to ongoing incidents and may be used only where a disturbance is occurring, which means that answers B and D are incorrect. Lastly, the senior police officer must be satisfied that the excessive noise is actually being emitted from the premises (unlike the power to deal with disorder, which may occur in the vicinity of the premises). Answer D is also incorrect for this reason.

General Police Duties, para. 4.16.10.2

Answer 16.31

Answer **C** — Under s. 161 of the Licensing Act 2003, a senior police officer (an inspector) may make an order requiring the relevant licensed premises to be closed if it is necessary in the interests of public safety, where disorder is occurring or where it is likely to occur, either on the premises or in the vicinity. Past conduct of the licensee may be taken into consideration.

The closure order must be a written notice and comes into effect when a constable serves notice on the holder of the premises licence or the designated premises supervisor in respect of licensed premises (s. 161(5)). Because another police officer of any rank may actually serve the written notice on the relevant person, the senior police officer making the order need not be present on the premises when the order is served. Answers A, B and D are therefore incorrect.

Note that the power to order the closure cannot be delegated to a person below the rank of inspector.

General Police Duties, para. 4.16.10.2

Answer 16.32

Answer **C** — Under s. 164(1) of the Licensing Act 2003, where a closure order has been made, the responsible officer must apply to the relevant justices for them to consider the order as soon as reasonably practicable after the order was made, so that the court may consider the order and any extension to it. The responsible officer must also notify the relevant licensing authority.

However, a closure order will expire 24 hours after the notice was served on the relevant person. The legislators have allowed for the fact that most areas do not have a court sitting on a Sunday by allowing the senior police officer to extend the existing closure order by serving a new written notice on the relevant person (s. 162). This extension will last for another 24 hours, allowing the responsible officer to attend court on the Monday. Answers A and D are therefore incorrect.

The original closure order in the question expired at 8 pm on the Sunday. The further extended period of 24 hours commences when the previous order expires; however, the written notice must be served on the relevant person before the existing closure order expires (see s. 162(3) and (4)). Answer B is therefore incorrect.

Note that in order to extend a closure order the senior police officer would still reasonably have to believe that it is necessary in the interests of public safety or to prevent excessive noise. Therefore, if the inspector in the question had no reason to suspect that there would have been further problems on the Sunday, he could not have closed the premises down. He would still have to attend court on the Monday to report on the facts of the closure order served on the Saturday.

General Police Duties, paras 4.16.10.3, 4.16.10.4

Answer 16.33

Answer **B** — Under s. 19 of the Criminal Justice and Police Act 2001, where a constable is satisfied that any premises (including land or any place whether covered or not):

- are being used or
- have been used within the last 24 hours
- for the unlicensed sale/exposure for sale
- of alcohol
- for consumption on or in the vicinity of the premises

he/she may serve a closure notice.

This power is available to any police officer of any rank, therefore, Constable WARREN does not need to call an inspector or go to court. Answers C and D are therefore incorrect.

In addition, under s. 19, the power to serve a notice is available to any police officer of any rank and *may also be exercised by the relevant local authority*. Answer A is therefore incorrect.

General Police Duties, para. 4.16.10.6

17 Offences and Powers Relating to Information

STUDY PREPARATION

The management—and mismanagement—of information is an area of increasing importance to the police generally and therefore to its supervisors, managers, trainers and examiners.

The key issues here are the statutory restrictions on who can access what type of information and for what purpose. Much accessing of information involves the use of computers and it is therefore necessary to understand the relevant aspects of the Computer Misuse Act 1990.

Also covered are the control measures, which are required to be in place to protect data held on individuals, under the Data Protection Act 1998, and the powers given to the Information Commissioner to regulate the storage of such data.

A large part of this chapter contains the provisions of the Regulation of Investigatory Powers Act 2000 (RIPA), which covers the covert acquisition of information about people, through the use of covert human intelligence sources (CHIS), surveillance and the interception of communications.

QUESTIONS

Question 17.1

BERGMAN is a Dutch national studying for a Ph.D. in Criminology in a university in England and is a temporary resident in the country. BERGMAN is writing a dissertation on the effectiveness of criminal justice interventions in young people's offending and requires statistical information on arrests, methods of disposal and re-offending amongst young people. BERGMAN has written to the Youth Justice Board (YJB) with specific questions relating to these matters, requesting disclosure under the Freedom of Information Act 2000.

Which of the following statements is correct, in relation to BERGMAN's request under the 2000 Act?

A The Act is designed to cover disclosure to organisations as opposed to individuals and the YJB is not obliged to supply this information to BERGMAN.

B Any person or organisation is entitled to request information; however, public authorities are only obliged to supply information to people or organisations who are UK nationals.

C Any person or organisation is entitled to request information, including those who are not UK nationals.

D Any person or organisation is entitled to request information, excluding those who are not UK nationals; however, as a temporary UK resident, BERGMAN is entitled to this information.

Question 17.2

Chief Inspector KEYES works in the Call and Incident Management Department of Eastshire Police and has received an email from the Data Protection Officer. A freedom of information request has been received relating to 101 call-handling statistics. The applicant has requested information on how many of the 101 calls received in the last calendar year were dealt with by the police, and how many of the 101 calls were passed on to the local authority because they related to non-police incidents. Chief Inspector KEYES has replied that the department receives about 10,000 101 calls every month and the Force's command and control system does not allow a search identifying how such calls were dealt with; to comply with the request, the department would have to set aside significant resources to gather accurate information and the chief inspector has refused to do this.

Which of the following statements is correct, in relation to Chief Inspector KEYES's refusal to comply with the request?

A Eastshire Police must provide this information; it may only refuse to do so if disclosing such information is not in the public interest.

B Eastshire Police may decide not to provide this information, if the costs associated with retrieving the information are disproportionate compared to the request.

C Eastshire Police must provide this information; it may only refuse to do so if disclosing such information is prejudicial to law enforcement, national security or legal professional privilege.

D Eastshire Police may decide not to provide this information, but it may only do so if it considers that the application is repeated or vexatious.

Question 17.3

Section 1 of the Computer Misuse Act 1990 makes provision in relation to unauthorised access to computer material.

Where a person is not authorised and they have the required intent and knowledge, at which point would an offence under this section first be committed?

A When the computer is switched on.

B When the 'log on screen' is filled out.

C When they are successfully logged onto the system.

D When the actual program is accessed.

Question 17.4

BIGNELL worked for a large bank and was dating BRADY who, unknown to her, had ties with an organised crime gang. BRADY persuaded BIGNELL to access information from customers' accounts and pass the details to him. BIGNELL was afraid to ask BRADY why he wanted the information and was unaware that he was selling on the data to credit card forgers.

What would have to be proved, in order to convict BIGNELL of an offence contrary to s. 1 of the Computer Misuse Act 1990?

A That she was not authorised to access the data and that she knew this was the case.

B That she was not authorised to access the data and that she knew this was the case, or was reckless as to whether or not this was the case.

C Only that she was not authorised to access the data.

D That she was not authorised to access the data and that she knew what the information was being used for.

Question 17.5

DAVIDSON is a computer programmer who has been asked by JELLIS to assist in a crime. JELLIS wants him to access the computer records of a Ferrari dealership's new customers' accounts and add JELLIS's details as a bona fide customer. This will, he believes, enable him to test drive a Ferrari. He intends not to return the car but take it for a 'joy-ride', amounting to an offence under s. 12(1) of the Theft Act 1968 (taking a motor vehicle or other conveyance without authority etc.). DAVIDSON 'hacks' into the company's computer and makes the changes. However, in reality, JELLIS will not be able to carry out his plan as the company always sends a representative on the test drive.

Has DAVIDSON committed an offence under s. 2 of the Computer Misuse Act 1990 (unauthorised access with intent to commit or facilitate commission of further offences)?

A Yes, even though the commission of the offence intended was impossible.

B Yes, even though he was merely facilitating the crime.

C No, as the intention to commit the crime lay with JELLIS.

D No, as the offence intended is not covered by s. 2.

Question 17.6

LENNON was a computer software engineer who worked for a company which distributed electronic equipment bought by customers online. LENNON was sacked by the company for allegedly stealing. Seeking revenge, LENNON devised a program which sent three million emails to the company's inbox in one day. LENNON hoped that the volume of emails would cause the company's online computer package to crash. However, another software engineer working for the company realised what was happening and implemented a program which intercepted the emails. In the end, no damage was done to the company.

If LENNON were to be prosecuted for an offence under s. 3 of the Computer Misuse Act 1990, which of the following statements would be correct in respect of the 'intent' required for this offence?

A The prosecution would have to show that LENNON intended causing an economic loss to the company.

B The prosecution must show that LENNON intended to impair the operation of the company's software program.

C The prosecution would have to show that LENNON intended to impair the operation of the company's software program, or was reckless as to whether it would be impaired.

D The prosecution would have to show that LENNON intended causing permanent damage to the company's computer program.

Question 17.7

PREEDY is a security guard in a hospital and suspects a colleague, WALL, of stealing from patients' lockers. PREEDY approached Constable HARPER with his concerns. There was insufficient evidence to act on at this stage. Constable HARPER asked PREEDY to keep an eye on WALL and to report any unusual activity. PREEDY decided to take matters a step further and undertook some covert questioning of WALL, trying to get information on the thefts. WALL inadvertently let slip where some of the stolen property was hidden and PREEDY contacted Constable HARPER to pass on the information.

In relation to PREEDY, could he be described as having acted as a covert human intelligence source (CHIS), in these circumstances?

A Yes, when Constable HARPER asked PREEDY to keep an eye on WALL, they established a relationship.

B Yes, when PREEDY undertook covert questioning of WALL, he established a relationship.

C Yes, but only when PREEDY passed on the information to Constable HARPER.

D No, Constable HARPER did not task PREEDY or direct his activities.

Question 17.8

Officers from the Dedicated Source Unit are seeking to recruit CURTIS, aged 17, as a CHIS. CURTIS is known to circulate with local drug dealers and will be in a position to provide valuable source information.

If the authorising officer agrees to CURTIS's recruitment, what restrictions, if any, would there be in relation to authorisation?

A Because CURTIS is under 18, the initial authorisation may only last for 72 hours.

B Because CURTIS is under 18, the initial authorisation may only last for one month.

C Because CURTIS is over 17, the initial authorisation may last for 12 months.

D If the authorisation is non-urgent, it will last for 12 months, regardless of CURTIS's age.

Question 17.9

The police have received information relating to corruption in a local authority. Officers from a Dedicated Source Unit have recruited O'CALLAGHAN, who is able to pass on confidential information about a multimillion pound contract to redevelop a landfill site, which is subject to a tender application by several building companies. O'CALLAGHAN has intimated that officers from the legal and planning departments of the local authority and some councillors have taken 'bungs' from a certain building company, in order to secure the contract. The officers would like to recruit O'CALLAGHAN as a CHIS and have spoken to their detective inspector.

Which of the following statements is correct in relation to the authorisation for the recruitment of O'CALLAGHAN as a CHIS?

A O'CALLAGHAN's recruitment as a CHIS may be authorised by the detective inspector.

B O'CALLAGHAN's recruitment as a CHIS must be authorised by a superintendent.

C O'CALLAGHAN's recruitment as a CHIS must be authorised by an assistant chief constable.

D O'CALLAGHAN's recruitment as a CHIS must be authorised by a chief constable.

Question 17.10

Detective Constable WONG has conducted an intelligence interview with FRATTON, aged 21, who is in the cells; due to be bailed shortly. FRATTON gave information about a large quantity of Class A drugs due to be delivered to a local drug dealer imminently. FRATTON said she knows the dealer well enough to make a direct approach to find out the delivery time. Detective Constable WONG has asked Detective Inspector YOUNG for an urgent authorisation to recruit FRATTON as a CHIS to discover the delivery time.

Does Detective Inspector YOUNG have the authority to authorise CHIS activity in such circumstances?

A Yes, the inspector may give urgent written authorisation for CHIS activity; the authorisation will last for 72 hours unless renewed.

B Yes, the inspector may give urgent oral authorisation, but the authorisation must be confirmed in writing by a superintendent after 24 hours.

C Yes, the inspector may give urgent oral authorisation for CHIS activity; the authorisation will last for 72 hours unless renewed.

D No, only a superintendent may give an urgent authorisation for CHIS activity.

Question 17.11

Officers received information that JOHNSON was dealing drugs while sitting in his car in a car park on the outskirts of town. After some research, the officers discovered that a new closed circuit television (CCTV) camera had been installed in the area, overlooking the car park, which was powerful enough to see inside parked cars. The officers considered using the CCTV office as an observation point, in an operation to catch JOHNSON handing over the drugs and collecting his money inside his vehicle.

Would the use of the CCTV camera to look inside JOHNSON's vehicle amount to intrusive surveillance?

A No, intrusive surveillance applies to residential premises only.

B Yes, this would amount to intrusive surveillance and would require the appropriate authorisation.

C No, this would amount to directed surveillance and would require the appropriate authorisation.

D No, it would be intrusive surveillance only if the vehicle was on residential property.

Question 17.12

DAWSON was arrested for a series of frauds against elderly people, involving the theft of £250,000. The police believed that SHELLEY, a solicitor, had been passing information to DAWSON about clients and their bank accounts in a conspiracy to commit fraud. DAWSON asked for SHELLEY to represent him while he was in custody. The officer in charge, DCI PATTERSON, considered making an application to place covert listening devices in the police station interview room, to listen in on their consultation.

Which of the following statements is correct, in relation to the police being allowed to use such surveillance methods?

A This is not permissible, as it amounts to directed surveillance.

B This is permissible, as it only amounts to directed and not intrusive surveillance.

C This is permissible, even though it amounts to intrusive surveillance.

D This is not permissible; all communications between lawyers and their clients are subject to legal privilege.

Question 17.13

Police officers wish to use surveillance on a newspaper office, with a view to obtaining material of a journalistic nature, which will be used in the investigation of an offence of murder.

Who can grant authorisation for such surveillance?

A An officer of at least the rank of superintendent only.

B An officer of at least the rank of superintendent, or an inspector in cases of urgency.

C The chief officer only.

D Any Association of Chief Police Officers (ACPO)-ranking police officer.

Question 17.14

Undercover police officers have infiltrated a large gang which is organising armed robberies in banks and building societies throughout the country. It is estimated that the gang is responsible for 30 crimes, which have so far yielded over £500,000. The investigating officers believe that the investigation would be assisted by obtaining a warrant to intercept communications between the various members of the gang.

Would the authorising officer be able to agree to such a warrant under s. 5 of the Regulation of Investigatory Powers Act 2000?

A Yes, provided the information would prove valuable to the investigation.

B No, the case is not one which affects the interests of national security.

C No, the case is not one which affects the interests of national security or which would affect the economic well-being of the United Kingdom.

D Yes, provided the information would prove necessary to the investigation.

Question 17.15

PRIESTLEY is employed by the police as an analyst in a police staff role, in a force intelligence bureau. He goes home one evening and, as a matter of conversation, he tells his wife, a serving police officer, that he saw an interception warrant issued in relation to a local company, but does not mention which company it is.

In relation to unauthorised disclosures, contrary to s. 19 of the Regulation of Investigatory Powers Act 2000, which of the following is true?

A PRIESTLEY cannot commit the offence as he is a member of the support staff.

B PRIESTLEY does not commit the offence as he does not name the company.

C PRIESTLEY commits the offence simply by mentioning it to his wife.

D PRIESTLEY commits the offence, but has a defence that he did not disclose it outside the police service.

Question 17.16

Constable FULLER was called to an incident involving a person in a public place, who was suffering from a mental disorder. The incident eventually led to Constable

FULLER conveying the person to the police station, under s. 136 of the Mental Health Act 2007. Constable FULLER spent a considerable time trying to identify the person without success; the person had no identifying papers in his possession and was unable to communicate with the officer to state who he was. The person had a mobile phone with him, but there were no contact numbers on the phone. The mobile had only contacted one number, on several occasions; however, Constable FULLER tried it with no reply. As a last resort, Constable FULLER wondered whether the police could request a telephone subscriber's check, to try to identify the person.

Would Constable FULLER be able to request a telephone subscriber's check in these circumstances?

A No, such a check could only be requested for the purpose of preventing death or serious injury.

B Yes, such a check could be requested where a person is unable to identify themselves because of a mental condition, to assist in identifying them or obtaining information about their next of kin.

C No, such a check could only be requested for the purpose of preventing or detecting crime, preventing disorder, protecting the interests of national security or the economic well-being of the UK.

D No, such a check could only be requested where a person has died, to assist in identifying them or their next of kin.

ANSWERS

Answer 17.1

Answer **C** — Under s. 1 of the Freedom of Information Act 2000, a public authority is under a duty to comply with properly made requests from any 'person' who makes a request for information in writing and to inform that person whether the public authority holds specified information and if it does, communicate that information to the applicant unless one of the exemptions applies.

The requirement to disclose such information is not restricted to 'organisations'— individuals may make legitimate requests for information. Answer A is therefore incorrect.

The requirement to make a disclosure includes communicating information to a representative organisation or a person who is *not* a UK national and it is irrelevant that BERGMAN is a temporary UK resident. Answers B and D are therefore incorrect.

General Police Duties, para. 4.17.1.1

Answer 17.2

Answer **B** — Under s. 1 of the Freedom of Information Act 2000, a public authority is under a duty to comply with properly made requests from any 'person' who makes a request for information in writing and to inform that person whether the public authority holds specified information and if it does, communicate that information to the applicant unless one of the exemptions applies.

There are significant exemptions to the duty of disclosure and assistance. One of these exemptions will be the practicalities arising from the cost of obtaining the information sought. There are internal costs associated with assimilating and disclosing large amounts of information and, if that cost exceeds the appropriate fee payable by the applicant, the public authority will usually be exempt from complying.

There are a number of other exemptions, such as the public interest in withholding the information outweighs that of disclosing it; information which would be prejudicial to law enforcement, national security or defence; information which attracts legal professional privilege or information related to ongoing investigations being conducted by public authorities. The Act also states that the authority must also provide advice and assistance to the person applying *unless* there is an exemption or the application is repeated or vexatious.

However, these exemptions are not stand-alone or exclusive as suggested in the scenario, which means that answers A, C and D are incorrect.

General Police Duties, para. 4.17.1.1

Answer 17.3

Answer **A** — An offence under s. 1 of the Computer Misuse Act 1990 is committed by causing a computer to perform a function, and all the answers would amount to 'functions'. As you were asked at which point an offence would first be committed, answer A is the correct answer. Although answers B, C and D all may fall under the section, they are incorrect, as switching the computer on is the first function that would amount to the offence.

General Police Duties, para. 4.17.2.1

Answer 17.4

Answer **A** — Under s. 1(1) of the Computer Misuse Act 1990, a person is guilty of an offence if—

(a) he causes a computer to perform any function with intent to secure access to any program or data held in any computer;
(b) the access he intends to secure is unauthorised; and
(c) he knows at the time when he causes the computer to perform the function that that is the case.

In order to prove the offence under s. 1, you must also show that the defendant knew the access was unauthorised and that he/she intended to secure access to the program or data. More proof is required than simply showing the defendant was not authorised to access the data and therefore answer C is incorrect.

This is an offence of 'specific intent', therefore lesser forms of *mens rea* such as recklessness will not be sufficient to convict a person. Answer B is therefore incorrect.

The offence is complete when the person knowingly accesses unauthorised data. There is no requirement to show that he/she knew what the information was being used for (albeit, if BIGNELL *did* know what the data was being used for, she could commit an offence under s. 2 of the Act). Answer D is therefore incorrect.

General Police Duties, para. 4.17.2.1

Answer 17.5

Answer **D** — Section 2 of the Computer Misuse Act 1990 requires intent on the part of the defendant; and this is either intention to commit an offence to which s. 2 applies, or the intention to facilitate the commission of such an offence. DAVIDSON has this intention, as he knows the purpose of his actions and is aware that it will facilitate the taking and driving away (TADA), and therefore answer C is incorrect. Section 2 applies to the particular classes of offences set out in s. 2(2) of the 1990 Act. Section 12(1) of the Theft Act 1968 (taking a motor vehicle or other conveyance without authority etc.) is such a summary offence and therefore does not fall within offences outlined in s. 2(2), and therefore answer B is incorrect. As to impossibility, s. 2(4) of the 1990 Act makes clear that a person may be guilty of an offence even though the facts are such that the commission of the further offence is impossible; but as the offence intended is not covered by s. 2 of the 1990 Act this is immaterial. Therefore, answer A is incorrect.

General Police Duties, para. 4.17.2.3

Answer 17.6

Answer **C** — Under s. 3(1) of the Computer Misuse Act 1990, a person is guilty of an offence if he/she does any unauthorised act in relation to a computer and at the time he/she does the act he/she knows that it is unauthorised; and either subs. (2) or subs. (3) applies.

Under subs. (2), the person must *intend* by doing the act:

(a) to impair the operation of any computer;
(b) to prevent or hinder access to any program or data held in any computer; or
(c) to impair the operation of any such program or the reliability of any such data.

This section is designed to ensure that adequate provision is made to criminalise all forms of denial of service attacks in which the attacker denies the victim(s) access to a particular resource, typically by preventing legitimate users of a service accessing that service. An example of this is where a former employee, acting on a grudge, impaired the operation of a company's computer by using a program to generate and send 5 million emails to the company (*DPP* v *Lennon* [2006] EWHC 1201 (Admin)).

Section 3(3) of the Act states that this subsection also applies if the person is *reckless* as to whether the act will do any of the things mentioned in paras (a) to (c) of subs. (2) above. Therefore, the offence can be committed by a person who intends or is reckless as to whether the program is impaired and answer B is incorrect.

There is no requirement to prove an intent to cause an economic loss to the company and therefore answer A is incorrect.

An 'unauthorised act' can include a series of acts, and a reference to impairing, preventing or hindering something includes a reference to doing so temporarily (s. 3(5)) and therefore answer D is incorrect.

General Police Duties, para. 4.17.2.4

Answer 17.7

Answer **B** — A covert human intelligence source is someone who establishes or maintains a relationship with another person for the *covert* purpose of:

- obtaining information,
- providing access to information

or who *covertly* discloses information obtained by the use of such a relationship.

The main purpose of the Regulation of Investigatory Powers Act 2000 is to control the use of surveillance and covert human intelligence sources (CHIS) operations by public authorities and to ensure that any infringement of a person's human rights is lawful.

The definition would not usually apply to members of the public generally supplying information to the police. Similarly, people who have come across information in the ordinary course of their jobs who suspect criminal activity (such as bank staff, local authority employees, etc.) do not have a covert relationship with the police simply by passing on information. However, if the person supplying the information is asked by the police to do something further in order to develop or enhance it, any form of direction or tasking by the police in this way could make the person a CHIS and thereby attract all the statutory provisions and safeguards.

In the circumstances in this question, the officer has simply asked PREEDY to keep an eye on things and this would not actually amount to 'tasking' or 'directing' a person's activities and Constable HARPER has certainly not asked him to develop a relationship with WALL. Answer A is incorrect, as PREEDY was not acting as a CHIS as a result of his conversation with the officer.

Nevertheless, PREEDY went on to act as a CHIS, according to this above definition, when he covertly questioned WALL for information (and thus formed a 'relationship' with him) and later when he covertly disclosed the information to the officer. Answer D is therefore incorrect. The first point that this happened was during the questioning; therefore, answer C is incorrect.

General Police Duties, para. 4.17.4.2

Answer 17.8

Answer **B** — Generally, the authorisation for use and conduct of a CHIS will last for 12 months (unless an urgent authorisation has been made, when it will last for 72 hours unless renewed).

However, stricter controls are in place in respect of a juvenile CHIS (see Regulation of Investigatory Powers (Juveniles) Order 2000). Under the Order, an authorisation for a juvenile CHIS will last for 1 month, even if it is a non-urgent authorisation (answers A and D are therefore incorrect).

A juvenile CHIS is a person under the age of 18; therefore, answer C is incorrect.

General Police Duties, para. 4.17.4.2

Answer 17.9

Answer **D** — Authorisations for CHIS activity under the Regulation of Investigatory Powers Act 2000 must normally be given by officers of the rank of at least superintendent. In cases where an urgent authority is required, it may be given by an inspector, when it is not reasonably practicable to have the application considered by a superintendent.

However, stricter controls are in place in respect of a juvenile CHIS or a situation where a CHIS may obtain confidential information. In the case of a juvenile CHIS, authorisation must be given by an officer of at least the rank of assistant chief constable. In the case of a CHIS who may obtain confidential information, authorisation must be given by an officer of at least the rank of chief constable.

Answers A, B and C are therefore incorrect.

General Police Duties, para. 4.17.4.2

Answer 17.10

Answer **A** — Authorisations for CHIS activity under the Regulation of Investigatory Powers Act 2000 must normally be given by officers of the rank of at least superintendent. However, urgent authorisations *may* be given by an inspector, when it is not reasonably practicable to have the application considered by a superintendent. Answer D is therefore incorrect. However, s. 43 of the Regulation of Investigatory Powers Act 2000 sets out general rules about grant, renewal and duration of authorisations surrounding CHIS activity. This section states:

(1) An authorisation under this Part—
   (a) may be granted or renewed orally in any urgent case in which the entitlement to act of the person granting or renewing it is not confined to urgent cases; and
   (b) in any other case, must be in writing.

This is a rather long-winded way of saying that because inspectors are restricted to granting urgent authorities, they may only give such authorities in writing. Only a person of the rank of superintendent and above may give an urgent, oral authority for CHIS-related activities. Answer C is incorrect for this reason.

The authorisation will cease to have effect 72 hours later, unless it is renewed. Answer B is therefore incorrect.

General Police Duties, para. 4.17.4.2

Answer 17.11

Answer **B** — Normally, the use of CCTV to prevent and detect crime will not amount to covert surveillance. However, if CCTV is used for a planned operation, it may amount to covert surveillance, which will require authorisation. Under s. 26(3) of the Regulation of Investigatory Powers Act 2000, if surveillance is covert and is carried out in relation to anything taking place on any residential premises, or in any private vehicle, and it involves the presence of an individual on the premises or in the vehicle, or is carried out by means of a surveillance device, it will generally be intrusive surveillance. Since the officers in the scenario were seeking to monitor activities inside a private vehicle, the operation would amount to intrusive surveillance, and therefore answers A and D are incorrect.

Note that the use of a surveillance device will be 'intrusive' if that device consistently provides information of the same quality and detail as might be expected from a device that was actually present on the premises or in the vehicle (s. 26(5)). Surveillance will be either 'directed' or 'intrusive', it cannot be both; therefore, answer C is incorrect.

General Police Duties, para. 4.17.4.3

Answer 17.12

Answer **C** — In relation to 'legal privilege' the House of Lords held that the Regulation of Investigatory Powers Act 2000 permits covert surveillance of communications between lawyers and their clients even though these may be covered by legal professional privilege (*Re McE (Northern Ireland)* [2009] UKHL 15). Answers A and D are therefore incorrect.

The Regulation of Investigatory Powers (Extension of Authorisation Provisions: Legal Consultations) Order 2010 (SI 2010/461) provides that directed surveillance carried out in relation to anything taking place on any premises that are being used for the purpose of legal consultations shall be treated as 'intrusive surveillance'. The consultation may be between a professional legal adviser and their client or person representing their client, or with a medical practitioner, where legal proceedings are contemplated and for the purposes of such proceedings.

'Any premises' includes prisons, police stations, legal advisers' business premises and courts. Since the proposal amounts to intrusive surveillance, answers A and B are incorrect.

General Police Duties, para. 4.17.4.3

Answer 17.13

Answer **C** — In general, directed surveillance can be authorised by an officer of at least the rank of superintendent, or an inspector in cases of urgency, making answer A incorrect. However, the Codes of Practice again restrict this practice. For instance, where the material sought by the surveillance is subject to legal privilege, or is confidential personal information or journalistic material, the only person who can authorise it is the chief officer; therefore, answers B and D are incorrect.

General Police Duties, para. 4.17.4.3

Answer 17.14

Answer **D** — Section 5 of the Regulation of Investigatory Powers Act 2000 allows the Secretary of State to issue interception warrants under certain, very stringent, conditions. Section 5(2) says that the Secretary of State must not issue an interception warrant unless he or she believes that the warrant is necessary:

- in the interests of national security;
- for the purpose of preventing or detecting 'serious crime', e.g. offences for which a person aged 18 or over could reasonably expect to be sentenced to at least three years' imprisonment on his or her first offence, or offences resulting in substantial financial gain, involving the use of violence or a large number of people pursuing a common purpose;
- for the purpose of safeguarding the economic well-being of the United Kingdom (where the relevant acts or intentions relate to people outside the United Kingdom);
- for the purpose of 'international mutual assistance'.

Therefore, although a warrant may be issued when it is necessary in the interests of national security or for the purpose of safeguarding the economic well-being of the United Kingdom, one may also be issued where the offence is one in which people commit offences resulting in substantial financial gain and which involve the use of violence or a large number of people pursuing a common purpose. Answers B and C are therefore incorrect.

It is not enough that the Secretary of State 'suspects' that these threats or needs exist, nor that he or she considers that an interception warrant might be useful, valuable or effective. The Secretary of State must believe that the warrant is necessary for one of the purposes set out. Answer A is therefore incorrect.

General Police Duties, para. 4.17.4.8

Answer 17.15

Answer **C** — This offence applies to police officers and police staff alike, and would apply to anyone involved in an investigation (answer A is therefore incorrect). It deals with interception warrants, and requires those to whom it applies to keep secret any knowledge they have in relation to that warrant. The offence would be committed by simply mentioning the warrant's existence, irrespective of whether any individual or company was named (answer B is therefore incorrect). Although there is a defence, it relates to the accused taking steps to prevent the disclosure; in the circumstances of the question this is clearly not the case and PRIESTLEY has no defence (answer D is therefore incorrect).

Note that there are other defences available to s. 19, but they relate to communication with legal advisers and the Interception of Communications Commissioner.

General Police Duties, para. 4.17.4.9

Answer 17.16

Answer **B** — Chapter II of the Regulation of Investigatory Powers Act 2000 deals with the concept of 'communications data'. This is broadly information that relates to the use of the particular communications service but not the *content* of the communication itself. The full definition can be found in s. 21(4). Examples of communications data would include:

- itemised telephone bills;
- telephone subscriber details;
- addresses or other marks on the outside of postal packages and letters.

Section 22 of the Act sets out the circumstances when, and the purposes for which, such communications data may be obtained. In order to obtain communications data the designated person must believe it is necessary to obtain the data:

- for the purpose of preventing or detecting crime or preventing disorder;
- in the interests of national security, public safety or the economic well-being of the United Kingdom;
- for the purposes of protecting health or collecting or assessing any tax, duty, etc.;
- in an emergency, for the purpose of preventing (or mitigating) death, injury or damage to a person's physical or mental health;
- to assist investigations into alleged miscarriages of justice;
- for the purpose of assisting in identifying any person who has died otherwise than as a result of crime, or who is unable to identify him/herself because of a physical or mental condition, other than one resulting from crime, or obtaining information about the next of kin or other connected persons of such a person or about the reason for his/her death or condition;
- for any other purpose specified by an order made by the Secretary of State;

and that to do so is *proportionate* to what is sought to be achieved.

Therefore, while the general reason for accessing a telephone subscriber's check might centre on the prevention and detection of serious crime etc., or preventing death or serious injury, subscriber details *may* be requested where a person is unable to identify themselves because of a mental condition, to assist in identifying them or obtaining information about their next of kin.

Answers A, C and D are therefore incorrect.

General Police Duties, para. 4.17.4.12

18 Equality

STUDY PREPARATION

At last, the final chapter!

Although it would be easy to dismiss this area as merely a bit of political correctness, this chapter contains some of the most relevant and important legislation for supervisors and managers.

This area of legislation has undergone a complete overhaul with the Equality Act 2010 pulling together all strands of diversity and discriminatory behaviour under one umbrella.

It is essential that all employers understand their legal obligations in relation to the equal and/or fair treatment of others. You will need to know what will amount to discrimination, how to distinguish between direct and indirect discrimination, and familiarise yourself with the protected characteristics covered in the Act.

It is also as important to understand the concept of victimisation and to recognise when and where it can arise.

When dealing with this area, it is worth remembering that in some circumstances you have to treat everyone in the same way, while in others treating everyone in the same way is discriminatory—and if you don't understand this point, you need to revise this chapter!

QUESTIONS

Question 18.1

NORTON is a post-operative male–female transsexual and is alleging discrimination by the Chief Constable of Eastshire Police. NORTON applied to become a police officer in the force and openly declared that she had undergone a gender reassignment process. NORTON's application was rejected, on the grounds that she could not lawfully conduct a strip search or an intimate search of female suspects and, because of her appearance as a woman, she could not, in practice, search male suspects. The Chief Constable's opinion was that being a non-transsexual person was a genuine occupational qualification for the job and that NORTON could not fully perform the role of a constable.

Which of the following statements is correct, in respect of the Chief Constable's decision?

A This is direct discrimination; the Chief Constable *must* regard NORTON as a female and has no option but to offer her a post.

B This is not discrimination; gender reassignment does not alter a person's birth gender—NORTON was born a male and remains one.

C This could amount to discrimination; however, the Chief Constable may consider it is not in the public interest to employ NORTON because of her gender reassignment.

D This is not discrimination; employers are not required to consider a person's birth gender when it comes to transsexuals.

Question 18.2

Eastshire Constabulary is the respondent in a case of discrimination brought by Chief Inspector ASHTON, who claims that he has been passed over several times for promotion to superintendent because of his sexual orientation.

Which of the following statements is correct in relation to the burden of proof that the court would have to consider?

A Chief Inspector ASHTON must establish facts that point to a presumption of discrimination; the burden of proof then shifts to Eastshire Constabulary to prove that he was not treated unfairly.

B Eastshire Constabulary must establish the facts in their entirety that Chief Inspector ASHTON was not treated unfairly.

C Chief Inspector ASHTON must establish the facts in their entirety that he was treated unfairly by Eastshire Constabulary.

D Eastshire Constabulary must establish that Chief Inspector ASHTON was not treated unfairly; the burden then rests with him to rebut the facts.

Question 18.3

Constable JOHN is a response officer and is the sole carer of his elderly parent, who is 94 years of age. Constable JOHN has submitted a flexible working request to the senior management team, which would mean working fewer night shifts, but would assist the officer financially due to the cost of carers. The senior management team has rejected the application for operational reasons. Constable JOHN is considering taking action against the force for discrimination, citing that the decision of the senior management team is unreasonable.

Which of the following statements would be correct, in relation to Constable JOHN's potential claim of discrimination?

A Constable JOHN would only have to demonstrate that the senior management team's decision was unreasonable, in order to succeed with the claim.

B Constable JOHN could succeed with the claim, by showing that some other hypothetical person would have been treated more favourably.

C Constable JOHN would have to demonstrate that some other person was treated more favourably, in order to succeed with the claim.

D Constable JOHN would have to demonstrate that there would be a tangible or material loss as a result of the decision.

Question 18.4

CHEUNG, who is of Chinese origin, applied for a job in a Youth Offending Team, but failed the interview. She sought feedback from the panel and was told that her English language skills were not good enough to be considered for the role. CHEUNG felt she had been discriminated against and sought advice from a firm of solicitors. Acting on her behalf, they submitted a request under the Freedom of Information Act 2000 to the local authority, seeking details on how many people of Chinese descent the authority had employed in the previous five years and how many successful women applicants there had been for jobs in the Youth Offending Team in the same period. CHEUNG's solicitor believes she has a strong case against the local authority for direct discrimination on the grounds of a combination of two protected characteristics—those of race and sex—depending on the answer to these questions.

What would the local authority need to show, in order to defeat a claim of direct discrimination on both counts?

A If they could show that they employ Chinese men *and* white women, they could show they are not guilty on both counts.

B If they could show that they employ Chinese men *or* white women, they could show they are not guilty on both counts.

C They would have to show that they had previously employed Chinese men and women to be not guilty on both counts.

D The characteristics are unconnected; therefore, they would have to answer each case independently.

Question 18.5

Constable GERMAIN worked in the force control room and was absent after being diagnosed as suffering from schizophrenia. The Force Medical Officer advised that the officer should not return to work in a capacity that included dealing with members of the public. The officer's Federation Representative met with HR and proposed either moving Constable GERMAIN into a post-trial role in the Criminal Justice Department, or creating a role for the officer in the control room. The first suggestion was dismissed as it would mean moving a fit officer out of another Department and the second suggestion was dismissed as being too costly. Instead, Constable GERMAIN was offered a role in the Firearms Admin Department in another part of the force area, which would involve minimal contact with the public. The officer refused to take this role and remained on the sick. Constable GERMAIN is now considering action against the force, for failing to make reasonable adjustments for his disability.

Could Constable GERMAIN be protected by s. 21 of the Equality Act 2010, in these circumstances?

A Yes, cost should not be a consideration when it comes to making reasonable adjustments; the force should have created a new role for Constable GERMAIN.

B No, it would not be reasonable to move another officer out of a role they were in, simply to accommodate Constable GERMAIN's disability.

C Yes, it would have been reasonable to move another officer out of a role they were in, to accommodate Constable GERMAIN's disability.

D Yes, by offering Constable GERMAIN an admin role, the force is discriminating against the officer because of his disability.

Question 18.6

Constable GILLIS is on the High Potential Development Scheme (HPDS) and works as a staff officer to the ACPO team in her force. The officer is currently on statutory maternity leave, having given birth to her child ten weeks ago. Constable GILLIS had

originally stated that she would return to work after 26 weeks (the ordinary maternity leave period), but has now stated that she wishes to take leave for a further 26
weeks (additional maternity leave period). A decision has been taken to move Constable GILLIS to a different post and replace her, because the ACPO team is unable to
manage her abstraction for the additional 26 weeks. Constable GILLIS has sought
advice from her Federation Representative, believing that she has been treated unfavourably because of her request for additional maternity leave.

Would Constable GILLIS be protected by s. 18 of the Equality Act 2010, in these
circumstances?

A No, s. 18 only applies in the period of 26 weeks after the employee has given birth
(ordinary maternity leave period).

B Yes, this is sex discrimination by the employer; Constable GILLIS has been treated
less favourably because she is female.

C Yes, Constable GILLIS is in the 'protected period', as defined by s. 18, and has been
treated unfavourably.

D No, s. 18 only applies during an employee's pregnancy and two weeks after she
has given birth.

Question 18.7

A force motor cycle section has advertised a vacancy. One selection criterion is that
police officers must be able to pick up a large, heavy motor cycle from being on its
side, and put it on its stand.

Would the selection criterion amount to indirect discrimination?

A Yes, this is not a fair condition and could disadvantage a person with a protected
characteristic.

B No, it is a legitimate expectation of the job and must be able to be performed by
all successful applicants.

C Yes, any condition other than one related to performance of duties is unlawful.

D No, provided the condition is the same for all applicants.

Question 18.8

Constable MELROSE has just started work on a response team in a new area. Officers
are aware that before moving to the team, Constable MELROSE had made a complaint of racial discrimination against colleagues on another team and that the complaint had been unsubstantiated. Some officers on Constable MELROSE's new team

decided to record problems they encountered with the officer, in fear that they may be the subject of a race discrimination claim at some future date.

Would the officers' behaviour amount to victimisation, because of Constable MELROSE's previous complaint?

A Yes, even though the previous complaint was unsubstantiated, this amounts to victimisation.

B No, if a complaint is unsubstantiated, any future complaint of similar actions cannot amount to victimisation.

C No; however, the officers' behaviour could amount to direct discrimination.

D No, the behaviour of the officers concerned would not amount to victimisation in these circumstances.

Question 18.9

Constable THORNE resigned from the service 14 months ago due to her dissatisfaction at the way her sexual harassment complaint was dealt with—the case was taken to a tribunal, which did not find in the officer's favour. At the end of the hearing, the judge was severely critical of THORNE, because of inconsistencies in her account, and the court stated openly that it believed the complaint was malicious. Since leaving, she has applied for, and been offered, a job as a police staff member with her old force. However, prior to starting, the job offer was withdrawn. THORNE has found out that this was because Superintendent CHANG had spoken to the recruitment department and told them that THORNE's integrity was questionable.

Could Constable THORNE take action against the police service for victimisation, under s. 27 of the Equality Act 2010?

A Yes, if it can be demonstrated that the force would have employed another person whose circumstances were similar to THORNE's, who had not made a complaint under the Act.

B Yes, THORNE has suffered victimisation because she had done a protected act, in bringing proceedings against the force.

C No, THORNE's case was unsuccessful, which means she is not protected by s. 27.

D No, a person who makes a malicious complaint is not protected by this section.

Question 18.10

Eastshire Constabulary is being sued by Constable AMIR. The claim relates to a failure by the force to allow Constable AMIR time off to attend a number of religious festivals throughout the year. Constable AMIR's line managers have not been cited, as the officer understands the pressures of delivering operational policing; however, the claim is made against the force for failing to have policies and procedures in place to account for the religious beliefs of its staff.

Which of the following statements is correct, in relation to Eastshire Constabulary's liability under s. 42 of the Equality Act 2010?

A Constable AMIR's line managers and the Chief Constable may be liable; the responsible authority is only liable for discrimination by members of staff towards people outside the force.

B The Chief Constable alone may be liable in these circumstances; the responsible authority has no liability under this Act.

C The Chief Constable and the responsible authority may be liable in these circumstances.

D Constable AMIR's line managers may be liable; the Chief Constable and the responsible authority are only liable for discrimination by members of staff towards people outside the force.

Question 18.11

Detective Inspector FRENCH is in charge of the Public Protection Unit and has a vacancy. The officer is of the opinion that children of female victims seem to respond more positively to female officers, and would like the replacement to be a female officer. Detective Inspector FRENCH wishes to place the following words in the advertisement for the post: 'On this occasion only female officers can apply for this post.'

In relation to these words, which of the following is true?

A This is direct discrimination and is unlawful.

B This is positive action and is lawful.

C This is a case of a genuine occupational requirement and is not unlawful.

D This is indirect discrimination and is unlawful.

Question 18.12

Constable STUBBS is currently suing her employers for discrimination in the workplace. She has cited several instances of inappropriate sexual behaviour towards her by her line managers in work. Constable STUBBS has also included evidence in her statement of inappropriate sexual behaviour towards her by work colleagues while they were at a social Christmas function in a nearby public house.

Would Constable STUBBS be able to rely on *all* of this evidence in her claim of discrimination against her employers?

A Yes, she may be able to rely on this evidence because the function was an extension of the workplace.

B No, but she would have been able to if the behaviour had taken place at an off-duty function at her actual workplace.

C Yes, she may rely on evidence of any inappropriate behaviour, inside or outside the workplace.

D No, her employers cannot be held liable for the behaviour of her colleagues outside the workplace.

ANSWERS

Answer 18.1

Answer **C** — The established legal principle in law is that gender is set at birth—if you are born male you remain male and vice versa (see *Corbett* v *Corbett* [1970] 2 WLR 1306). However, in *A* v *Chief Constable of West Yorkshire and the Secretary of State for Work and Pensions* [2004] UKHL 21 it was held that it was no longer possible in the context of *employment* to regard a 'transsexual' as being his/her birth gender and that principles of *Corbett* should not apply in this context (the *Corbett* case related to marriage). Answers B and D are therefore incorrect.

On the other hand, the court held that public interest considerations in relation to the police service *may* determine that a gender-reassigned applicant is not offered employment (and answer A is therefore incorrect).

General Police Duties, para. 4.18.2.3

Answer 18.2

Answer **A** — Sexual orientation is one of the protected characteristics covered by the Equality Act 2010 and it is unlawful to discriminate against a person due to their sexual orientation.

In proceedings relating to contraventions of the Act the burden of proof initially rests with the complainant. Answers B and D are therefore incorrect.

Once the complainant establishes facts from which it might be presumed that there had been discrimination the burden of proof shifts to the respondent to prove no breach of the principle of equal treatment (s. 136). Answer C is therefore incorrect.

General Police Duties, para. 4.18.3

Answer 18.3

Answer **B** — Section 13(1) of the Equality Act 2010 states:

A person (A) discriminates against another (B) if, because of a protected characteristic, A treats B less favourably than A treats or would treat others.

Less favourable treatment of a person because that person is associated with a protected characteristic, for example because the person has a friend or partner with a particular protected characteristic, or carries out work related to a protected characteristic, is within the scope of this section. This might include carers of disabled people and elderly relatives, who can claim they were treated unfairly because of duties that they had to carry out at home relating to their care work. For example, the non-disabled mother of a disabled child can be discriminated against because of the child's disability (*Coleman* v *Attridge Law* (Case C-303/06) [2008] IRLR 722). This is known as 'associative discrimination'.

To constitute direct discrimination the treatment experienced by B must be different from that of another person. This difference is often referred to as a 'comparator'. The treatment of B must be less favourable than the treatment afforded a comparator. The comparator can be hypothetical where B can establish direct discrimination by showing that if there was another person in similar circumstances, but without B's protected characteristic, that person would be treated more favourably (for an explanation of hypothetical comparators see *Shannon* v *Chief Constable of the Royal Ulster Constabulary* [2003] UKHL 11). This is why answer B is correct, and answer C is incorrect.

Less favourable treatment is a broad concept and any disadvantage to which B has been subject will constitute such treatment. B need not have suffered a tangible or material loss (*Chief Constable of West Yorkshire Police* v *Khan* [2001] UKHL 48) and therefore answer D is incorrect.

However, it is not enough merely to show unreasonable treatment (*Bahl* v *The Law Society* [2004] IRLR 799). Answer A is therefore incorrect.

General Police Duties, para. 4.18.3.1

Answer 18.4

Answer **A** — Section 14(1) of the Equality Act 2010 states that a person (A) discriminates against another (B) if, because of a combination of two relevant protected characteristics, A treats B less favourably than A treats or would treat a person who does not share either of those characteristics. This section applies in the context of employment rights and allows those who have experienced less favourable treatment because of a combination of two relevant protected characteristics to bring a direct discrimination claim, where the single-strand approach may not succeed.

Where an employer fails to employ a black woman because of particular prejudices about black women, but employs black men and white women, it is likely that the employer could defeat both claims of direct sex discrimination and direct race discrimination, by showing they are not 'racist' or 'sexist'. They would need to show that they employed both opposites to defeat both claims (i.e. Chinese men *and* white women); therefore, answers B and C are incorrect.

Answer D is incorrect because the local authority *could* use s. 14 to defeat a claim of direct discrimination on both counts.

General Police Duties, para. 4.18.3.2

Answer 18.5

Answer **C** — The duty to make reasonable adjustments is a key element of a range of measures intended to eliminate barriers to access and participation for disabled people. Section 21 of the Equality Act 2010, provides that a failure to comply with any one of the reasonable adjustment requirements amounts to discrimination against a disabled person to whom the duty is owed. However, the test of reasonableness is an objective one (*Collins* v *Royal National Theatre Board Ltd* [2004] IRLR 395), and will always depend on the particular circumstances in an individual case (*Archibald* v *Fife County Council* [2004] IRLR 651).

For example, in *Chief Constable of South Yorkshire* v *Jelic* [2010] IRLR 744, it was determined that the force had *not* acted 'reasonably' when it failed to allow an officer suffering from chronic anxiety syndrome to swap jobs with another officer. Answer B is incorrect as this was one of the options that could have been considered to accommodate Constable GERMAIN's disability.

Also, in *Hinsley* v *Chief Constable of West Mercia Constabulary* [2010] UKEAT 0200 10 0911, it was decided that there was a breach of duty to make reasonable adjustments where there was a failure to reinstate a probationary police officer who had resigned whilst depressed.

However, where an officer was perceived to have a dangerous mental condition the adjustments made to ensure he did not present a danger to colleagues or to the public were considered reasonable (*Aitken* v *Commissioner of Police of the Metropolis* [2010] UKEAT 0226 09 2106). It *would* have been reasonable to place Constable GERMAIN in an admin role because of his illness and therefore answer D is incorrect.

Cost *can* be considered when making reasonable adjustments. In *Cordell* v *Foreign and Commonwealth Office* (2011) 155(42) SJLB 31, a tribunal dismissed claims of direct discrimination and discrimination by way of failure to make reasonable adjustments where the costs of providing English-speaking lip-speaker support for a deaf employee were about £230,000 a year. Answer A is therefore incorrect.

General Police Duties, para. 4.18.3.4

Answer 18.6

Answer **C** — An employee generally has the right to 26 weeks of ordinary maternity leave and 26 weeks of additional maternity leave making one year in total. The combined 52 weeks is known as Statutory Maternity Leave.

The Equality Act 2010, s. 18 states:

(1) This section has effect for the purposes of the application of Part 5 (work) to the protected characteristic of pregnancy and maternity.

(2) A person (A) discriminates against a woman if, in the protected period in relation to a pregnancy of hers, A treats her unfavourably—

    (a) because of the pregnancy, or

    (b) because of illness suffered by her as a result of it.

(3) A person (A) discriminates against a woman if A treats her unfavourably because she is on compulsory maternity leave.

(4) A person (A) discriminates against a woman if A treats her unfavourably because she is exercising or seeking to exercise, or has exercised or sought to exercise, the right to ordinary or *additional* maternity leave.

The duration of the protected period depends on the statutory maternity leave entitlements as set out in the Employment Rights Act 1996, which defines the right to compulsory, ordinary and additional maternity leave. The protected period starts when a woman becomes pregnant and ends either:

- if she has the right to ordinary and additional maternity leave, at the end of the additional maternity leave period or (if earlier) when she returns to work after the pregnancy; or
- if she does not have that right, at the end of the period of two weeks beginning with the end of the pregnancy.

Answer A is incorrect, because compulsory maternity leave is only one of the areas covered by s. 18.

Answer D is incorrect since the officer has a statutory entitlement to ordinary and additional maternity leave; the protection does not end two weeks after she has given birth, it ends when she returns to work.

Whilst this case may amount to a breach of s. 18, sex discrimination does not apply to treatment of a woman insofar as it is in the protected period, or it is for a reason mentioned in s. 18(3) or (4). Answer B is therefore incorrect.

General Police Duties, paras 4.18.3.6, 4.18.3.7

Answer 18.7

Answer **A** — Indirect discrimination occurs when a policy which applies in the same way for everybody has an effect which particularly disadvantages people with a protected characteristic. Where a particular group is disadvantaged in this way, a person in that group is indirectly discriminated against if he or she is put at a disadvantage, unless the person applying the policy can justify it.

When a policy would put a person at a disadvantage if it were applied, for example, where a person is deterred from applying for a job or taking up an offer of service, because a policy which would have applied would result in his or her disadvantage, this may also amount to indirect discrimination. Examples of indirect discrimination include requiring all employees to work within 'normal office hours' (*Bhudi* v *IMI Refiners* [1994] IRLR 204); requiring all workers to have short hair thereby making it difficult for some groups such as Sikhs to comply (*Mandla* v *Dowell Lee* [1983] 2 AC 548); where 100 per cent of males could comply with a policy relating to rostering duties, but only 95.2 per cent of women were able to do so, the policy discriminated indirectly against females (*London Underground Ltd* v *Edwards (No. 2)* [1998] IRLR 364).

Given the size and weight of the machine in the question, it is likely that fewer women than men could comply with the condition, and it is this that potentially makes the requirement discriminatory and unlawful. Even if only one female officer could not comply with a condition of employment, it could still be indirect discrimination.

There is nothing inherently unlawful about setting legitimate conditions for a job vacancy (e.g. 'must have two A levels'), and therefore answer C is incorrect as it is too broad. However, any criteria must not disadvantage a significant proportion of people from a protected group. Simply setting the same condition for all does not make it lawful (e.g. 'applicants must be able to climb stairs' is the same for all, but would disadvantage wheelchair users) and therefore answer D is incorrect.

As far as answer B is concerned, is it a legitimate requirement of the job? Imposing this requirement on all applicants appears to be far too broad, wholly unreasonable and, in relation to the differences in relative strength of male and female applicants, appears disproportionately to disadvantage the latter, and therefore answer B is incorrect.

General Police Duties, para. 4.18.3.8

Answer 18.8

Answer **D** — Section 27 of the Equality Act 2010 states:

(1) A person (A) victimises another person (B) if A subjects B to a detriment because—
    (a) B does a protected act, or
    (b) A believes that B has done, or may do, a protected act.
(2) Each of the following is a protected act—
    (a) bringing proceedings under this Act;
    (b) giving evidence or information in connection with proceedings under this Act;
    (c) doing any other thing for the purposes of or in connection with this Act;
    (d) making an allegation (whether or not express) that A or another person has contravened this Act.

This would mean that generally, if a person makes a claim, he or she could still be the subject of victimisation at some time in the future, regardless of whether the claim was substantiated. Answer B is therefore incorrect.

However, in *Bayode* v *Chief Constable of Derbyshire* [2008] UKEAT 0499 07 2205, the tribunal held that the complainant, a police constable who was a black African and Nigerian by national origin, had *not* been victimised where his colleagues recorded any problems they encountered with him in their PNBs for fear that he might make a race discrimination claim at some future date. Previous unsubstantiated discrimination claims had been made by the complainant. Answer A is therefore incorrect.

Direct discrimination is an entirely different matter to victimisation, and generally involves employers treating one group of people less favourably than others based on protected grounds, such as their racial origin, marital status, sex, religion or belief or sexual orientation. It is out of context in this scenario, and for that reason answer C is incorrect.

General Police Duties, para. 4.18.3.11

Answer 18.9

Answer **D** — Section 27 of the Equality Act 2010 states:

(1) A person (A) victimises another person (B) if A subjects B to a detriment because—
    (a) B does a protected act, or
    (b) A believes that B has done, or may do, a protected act.
(2) Each of the following is a protected act—
    (a) bringing proceedings under this Act;
    (b) giving evidence or information in connection with proceedings under this Act;

(c) doing any other thing for the purposes of or in connection with this Act;

(d) making an allegation (whether or not express) that A or another person has contravened this Act.

Under the 2010 Act, victimisation is technically no longer treated as a form of discrimination, so there is no longer a need to compare treatment of an alleged victim with that of a person who has not made or supported a complaint under the Act. Answer A is therefore incorrect.

The fact that a person takes action against their employer and fails would not automatically mean that he or she is not protected by s. 27; victimisation where one person treats another badly because he or she in good faith has done a 'protected act', for example taken or supported any action taken for the purpose of the Act, including in relation to any alleged breach of its provisions. Answer C is therefore incorrect.

However, under s. 27(3), a person is not protected from victimisation where he/she maliciously makes or supports an untrue complaint. The judge's comment in the question would certainly give rise to the belief that THORNE's complaint was malicious, which means she is unlikely to be able to use s. 27 to bring a further case against the force (of course, this would not prevent THORNE from bringing a case under one of the other sections, if applicable). Answer B is therefore incorrect.

General Police Duties, para. 4.18.3.11

Answer 18.10

Answer **C** — Section 42 of the Equality Act 2010 states:

(1) For the purposes of this Part, holding the office of constable is to be treated as employment—

(a) by the chief officer, in respect of any act done by the chief officer in relation to a constable or appointment to the office of constable;

(b) by the responsible authority, in respect of any act done by the authority in relation to a constable or appointment to the office of constable.

The Equality Act 2010 makes provisions for chief officers *and* 'responsible' authorities to be liable for acts done by them towards their staff. Answer B is therefore incorrect.

This liability is not limited to discrimination by members of staff towards people outside the force; it can include discrimination by members of staff towards people within the force and therefore answers A and D are incorrect.

The chief officer of police is also vicariously liable for acts of race discrimination by staff under his or her direction and control. The statutory defence that an employer took all reasonable steps to prevent the acts of discrimination complained of is also available to chief officers (s. 109(4)).

Note that s. 42(3) still lists the 'responsible authority' as 'the police authority that maintains the police force to which the appointment relates'. Presumably, with the appointment of Police and Crime Commissioners, this responsibility will pass to them.

General Police Duties, paras 4.18.4, 4.18.6

Answer 18.11

Answer **A** — An attempt to recruit female officers into a specialist department by excluding male applicants has been held to be unlawful (*Jones* v *Chief Constable of Northamptonshire Police* The Times, 1 November 1999). Answer C is incorrect as a genuine occupational requirement is where there is a legitimate reason (such as grounds of decency) to state that only certain groups may apply and not just a hunch by the Detective Inspector!

Answer B is incorrect because positive action refers to measures to alleviate disadvantage experienced by people who share a protected characteristic, reduce their under-representation in relation to particular activities, and meet their particular needs (see s. 158 of the Equality Act 2010). Here the officer's actions go way beyond simple encouragement.

It is direct discrimination because it is treating one group of people less favourably than others based on their sex. Answer D is incorrect because indirect discrimination involves setting the same criteria for a job, but the criteria are such that a significant proportion of people from a protected group are less likely to be able to achieve the criteria because of their membership of that group (e.g. a height restriction, which would affect female and some minority ethnic groups).

General Police Duties, para. 4.18.5

Answer 18.12

Answer **A** — Section 109 of the Equality Act 2010 states:

(1) Anything done by a person (A) in the course of A's employment must be treated as also done by the employer.

(2) ...

(3) It does not matter whether that thing is done with the employer's or principal's knowledge or approval.

Where acts amounting to discrimination take place outside the workplace, the employer and employees may still be caught within the framework of the legislation. So, for instance, where police officers engage in inappropriate sexual behaviour towards a colleague at a work-related social function, a tribunal may be entitled to hold that the function was an extension of the workplace and so hold the chief officer liable for the acts of his/her officers at that function (see *Chief Constable of Lincolnshire* v *Stubbs* [1999] IRLR 81). Answer D is therefore incorrect.

This case deals with a specific example of behaviour where the officers were at a work-related function, which was an 'extension of the workplace'. The decision does not therefore mean that any behaviour can be included in such a claim (although it is worth noting that discrimination and victimisation are included in the Code of Conduct for police officers, which may include the conduct of an off-duty officer). Answer C is therefore incorrect. Lastly, this case did not specify that the location of the function was important, merely that it was an off-duty function and an extension of the workplace. Answer B is therefore incorrect.

General Police Duties, para. 4.18.6

Question Checklist

The following checklist is designed to help you keep track of your progress when answering the multiple-choice questions. If you fill this in after one attempt at each question, you will be able to check how many you have got right and which questions you need to revisit a second time. Also available online: to download visit www.blackstonespolicemanuals.com.

	First attempt Correct (✓)	Second attempt Correct (✓)
1 The Policing Family		
1.1		
1.2		
1.3		
1.4		
1.5		
1.6		
1.7		
1.8		
1.9		
1.10		
1.11		
1.12		
1.13		
1.14		
1.15		
2 Complaints and Misconduct		
2.1		
2.2		
2.3		
2.4		

	First attempt Correct (✓)	Second attempt Correct (✓)
2.5		
2.6		
2.7		
2.8		
2.9		
2.10		
3 Unsatisfactory Performance and Attendance		
3.1		
3.2		
3.3		
3.4		
3.5		
3.6		
3.7		
3.8		
3.9		
3.10		
3.11		
4 Human Rights		
4.1		
4.2		

	First attempt Correct (✔)	Second attempt Correct (✔)
4.3		
4.4		
4.5		
4.6		
4.7		
4.8		
4.9		
4.10		
4.11		
4.12		
4.13		
4.14		

5 Powers of Arrest (including Code G Codes of Practice) and Other Policing Powers

5.1		
5.2		
5.3		
5.4		
5.5		
5.6		
5.7		
5.8		
5.9		
5.10		
5.11		
5.12		
5.13		
5.14		
5.15		

6 Stop and Search

6.1		
6.2		
6.3		
6.4		
6.5		
6.6		
6.7		

	First attempt Correct (✔)	Second attempt Correct (✔)
6.8		
6.9		
6.10		
6.11		

7 Entry, Search and Seizure

7.1		
7.2		
7.3		
7.4		
7.5		
7.6		
7.7		
7.8		
7.9		
7.10		

8 Harassment, Stalking, Hostility and Anti-social Behaviour

8.1		
8.2		
8.3		
8.4		
8.5		
8.6		
8.7		
8.8		
8.9		
8.10		
8.11		
8.12		
8.13		
8.14		
8.15		
8.16		
8.17		
8.18		
8.19		
8.20		
8.21		

	First attempt Correct (✓)	Second attempt Correct (✓)
8.22		
8.23		

9 Offences Involving Communications

	First attempt Correct (✓)	Second attempt Correct (✓)
9.1		
9.2		
9.3		
9.4		
9.5		
9.6		
9.7		
9.8		

10 Terrorism and Associated Offences

	First attempt Correct (✓)	Second attempt Correct (✓)
10.1		
10.2		
10.3		
10.4		
10.5		
10.6		
10.7		
10.8		
10.9		
10.10		
10.11		

11 Public Disorder

	First attempt Correct (✓)	Second attempt Correct (✓)
11.1		
11.2		
11.3		
11.4		
11.5		
11.6		
11.7		
11.8		
11.9		
11.10		
11.11		
11.12		
11.13		
11.14		
11.15		
11.16		
11.17		
11.18		
11.19		
11.20		
11.21		

12 Sporting Events

	First attempt Correct (✓)	Second attempt Correct (✓)
12.1		
12.2		
12.3		
12.4		
12.5		
12.6		
12.7		
12.8		
12.9		

13 Weapons

	First attempt Correct (✓)	Second attempt Correct (✓)
13.1		
13.2		
13.3		
13.4		
13.5		
13.6		
13.7		
13.8		
13.9		
13.10		
13.11		
13.12		
13.13		
13.14		
13.15		
13.16		
13.17		

Question Checklist

	First attempt Correct (✓)	Second attempt Correct (✓)
13.18		
13.19		
14 Civil Disputes		
14.1		
14.2		
14.3		
14.4		
14.5		
14.6		
14.7		
14.8		
14.9		
15 Offences Relating to Land and Premises		
15.1		
15.2		
15.3		
15.4		
15.5		
15.6		
15.7		
15.8		
15.9		
15.10		
15.11		
15.12		
15.13		
16 Licensing and Offences Relating to Alcohol		
16.1		
16.2		
16.3		
16.4		
16.5		
16.6		
16.7		
16.8		

	First attempt Correct (✓)	Second attempt Correct (✓)
16.9		
16.10		
16.11		
16.12		
16.13		
16.14		
16.15		
16.16		
16.17		
16.18		
16.19		
16.20		
16.21		
16.22		
16.23		
16.24		
16.25		
16.26		
16.27		
16.28		
16.29		
16.30		
16.31		
16.32		
16.33		
17 Offences and Powers Relating to Information		
17.1		
17.2		
17.3		
17.4		
17.5		
17.6		
17.7		
17.8		
17.9		
17.10		
17.11		

	First attempt Correct (✓)	Second attempt Correct (✓)
17.12		
17.13		
17.14		
17.15		
17.16		
18 Equality		
18.1		
18.2		
18.3		

	First attempt Correct (✓)	Second attempt Correct (✓)
18.4		
18.5		
18.6		
18.7		
18.8		
18.9		
18.10		
18.11		
18.12		

BLACKSTONE'S POLICE SERGEANTS' & INSPECTORS' MOCK EXAMINATION PAPER 2014

Paul Connor

- Test yourself with a Police Promotion Exam-style examination paper - 150 Type A questions based on the 2014 syllabus

- Refine your exam technique using the 3 hour time limit - don't risk running out of time and losing marks!

- Assess both your strengths and weaknesses - channel your revision into more productive areas

- Includes a separate, sealed Answer Booklet with full explanations and cross-references to the College of Policing-endorsed *Blackstone's Police Manuals 2014*, as well as a helpful marking matrix

OCTOBER 2013 | 132 PAGES
978-0-19-968450-2 | PAPERBACK

OXFORD
UNIVERSITY PRESS

For more information visit
www.oup.com

Blackstone's

Police Q&A

General Police Duties 2014